Psychology

Third Edition

Craig Roberts
Seth Alper
Susan Bantu
Andrew Gilbert-Dunnings

Great Clarendon Street, Oxford, OX2 6DP, United Kingdom

Oxford University Press is a department of the University of Oxford.

It furthers the University's objective of excellence in research, scholarship, and education by publishing worldwide. Oxford is a registered trade mark of Oxford University Press in the UK and in certain other countries

© Oxford University Press 2023

The moral rights of the author have been asserted

First published in 2023

All rights reserved. No part of this publication may be reproduced, stored in a retrieval system, or transmitted, in any form or by any means, without the prior permission in writing of Oxford University Press, or as expressly permitted by law, by licence or under terms agreed with the appropriate reprographics rights organization. Enquiries concerning reproduction outside the scope of the above should be sent to the Rights Department, Oxford University Press, at the address above.

You must not circulate this work in any other form and you must impose this same condition on any acquirer

British Library Cataloguing in Publication Data
Data available

9781382052733

10 9 8 7 6 5 4 3 2 1

The manufacturing process conforms to the environmental regulations of the country of origin.

Printed in the UK by Bell and Bain Ltd, Glasgow

Acknowledgements
This Student Book refers to the Cambridge International AS & AL Psychology syllabus published by Cambridge Assessment International Education.

This work has been developed independently from and is not endorsed by or otherwise connected with Cambridge Assessment International Education.

The publisher would like to thank the following for permissions to use copyright material:

Cover: Nikada/Getty Images.

Artwork by Aptara and Q2A Media.

Every effort has been made to contact copyright holders of material reproduced in this book. Any omissions will be rectified in subsequent printings if notice is given to the publisher.

IGCSE® is the registered trademark of Cambridge Assessment International Education

Contents

Introduction ... iv

1 Approaches, Issues, and Debates ... 2

2 Research Methods ... 40

3 Specialist Options: Approaches, Issues, and Debates ... 68

4 Specialist Options: Application and Research Methods ... 120

Index ... 160

AS Level

AL Level

Introduction

The Exam Success series has been designed to help you reach your highest potential and achieve the best possible grade. Each book fully covers the syllabus and is written in syllabus order to help you prepare effectively for the exam. In contrast to traditional revision guides, these new books contain advice and guidance on how to improve answers, giving you a clear insight into what examiners are expecting of candidates.

Each of the titles in the Exam Success series contains common features to help you do your best in the exam. These include the following:

Key terms
These give you easy-to-understand definitions of important terms and concepts of the subject.

★ Exam tip
These give you guidance and advice to help you understand exactly what the examiners are looking for from you in the exam.

Worked Example
Each unit contains a Worked Example section. This provides an exam-style question and an example of an answer to this question to indicate what examiners are looking for from candidates in their answers.

Raise your grade
In these sections, you will be able to read answers by candidates who do not achieve maximum marks. This feature provides advice on how to improve the grade for these answers.

Dedications and acknowledgements

To mum. Love always.

Thanks to Seth, Susan and Andy for being an amazing team of authors to work with. It has been a total pleasure. Also, thanks to my family and Jav for seeing me through this book. Finally, thanks to all of the Modern Pentathletes I know who helped fight the fight to keep riding in the sport. We may have lost but we will remain strong, especially Alexandre Dällenbach, Danilo Fagundes, William Munihos, Joe & Henry Choong, Ilyha Miagkikh, Rodion Khripchenko, Pavel Ilyashenko, Denis Pavlyuk and Pentathlon United. Hopefully one day we will all meet at a real MP Competition.

Craig Roberts

Thank you to my family for the continued support. And to my fellow teachers and students for the motivation to continue down this path.

Seth Alper

There are lots of people I wish to thank. First of all Craig Roberts, my co-author for lighting this path into being an author. To Seth for all your advice and ideas as we wrote this book. My heartfelt thanks to my two beautiful daughters Makeba and Meka who were both my Psychology students. They shared so many ideas with me, read through my work and encouraged me through this difficult journey. I cannot forget my staff colleagues, especially John, Eric and Sarah and students at Brookhouse who were so positive about my journey and cheered me on. To all my family members and friends, thank you! Also, thanks to Oliver and Emily who made this happen through numerous meetings, emails and their general presence. This is dedicated to the whole team of Kenyan psychology teachers who diligently work to ensure the subject is held in high esteem in Africa.

Susan Bantu

Michelle, thank you for your continued love and support, and for your patience and understanding when I take on 'extra work'.

Andrew Gilbert-Dunnings

1 Approaches, Issues, and Debates

Introduction to the paper

For Paper 1 the structure is as follows:

- This paper requires candidates to demonstrate their knowledge of the core studies.
- There are two sections to this paper. For both sections, you should answer **all** questions.
- **Section A** includes short and medium answer questions. These include a range of questions broken down into 1-, 2-, 3-, 4-, and 5-mark parts, based on information from the core studies. This section is worth 38 marks.
- **Section B** includes extended response questions. These questions are also based on the core studies. This section is worth 22 marks.
- The paper is marked out of 60 in total.

Knowledge check

You are required to know the following information for your Paper 1 exam.

- **Red: I do not understand.**
- **Amber: I somewhat understand.**
- **Green: I do understand.**

Syllabus area	Red	Amber	Green
Dement and Kleitman's biological core study on sleep and dreams			
Assumptions of the biological approach and how they relate to this core study			
The psychology that is being investigated			
The background			
The aims			
The procedures			
The research method used			
The number of participants and where they are from			
The sampling method used			
The experimental design used			
The controls used			
Types of questions asked			
Data collection method used			
Independent and dependent variables used			
Ethical issues			
Results, including quantitative data, and/or qualitative data and how it is represented and interpreted			
Conclusions drawn			
Strengths, including methodological issues such as: research method, reliability, validity, generalisability, and control of variables			
Weaknesses, including methodological issues such as: research method, reliability, validity, generalisability, and control of variables			
The issue of application of psychology to everyday life and how it relates to the study			

★ **Exam tip**

This paper lasts 90 minutes. The 8-mark part-question and the 10-mark question will appear at the end of the paper. They are worth 30 per cent of the whole paper, so ensure you leave enough time to answer these. You may answer the questions in any order, so you may want to consider answering these questions first.

★ **Exam tip**

There will be questions that focus on new research scenarios **not** from the key studies. These will require you to think on your feet in demonstrating your knowledge of research methodology in psychology.

The individual and situational explanations debate and how it relates to the study			
The nature versus nurture debate and how it relates to the study			
Hassett *et al.*'s biological core study on monkey toy preferences			
Assumptions of the biological approach and how they relate to this core study			
The psychology that is being investigated			
The background			
The aims			
The procedures			
The research method used			
The number of participants and where they are from			
The experimental design used			
The controls used			
Data collection method used			
Independent and dependent variables used			
Ethical issues			
Results, including quantitative data, and/or qualitative data and how it is represented and interpreted			
Conclusions drawn			
Strengths, including methodological issues such as: research method, reliability, validity, generalisability, and control of variables			
Weaknesses, including methodological issues such as: research method, reliability, validity, generalisability, and control of variables			
The issue of application of psychology to everyday life and how it relates to the study			
The individual and situational explanations debate and how it relates to the study			
The nature versus nurture debate and how it relates to the study			
The issue of the use of animals in psychological research and how it relates to each study			
Hölzel *et al.*'s biological core study on mindfulness and brain scans			
Assumptions of the biological approach and how they relate to this core study			
The psychology that is being investigated			
The background			
The aims			
The procedures			
The research method used			
The number of participants and where they are from			
The sampling method used			
The experimental design used			
The controls used			
Types of questions asked			
Data collection method used			
Independent and dependent variables used			
Ethical issues			

Approaches, Issues, and Debates

Results, including quantitative data, and/or qualitative data and how it is represented and interpreted			
Conclusions drawn			
Strengths, including methodological issues such as: research method, reliability, validity, generalisability, and control of variables			
Weaknesses, including methodological issues such as: research method, reliability, validity, generalisability, and control of variables			
The issue of application of psychology to everyday life and how it relates to the study			
The individual and situational explanations debate and how it relates to the study			
The nature versus nurture debate and how it relates to the study			
Andrade's cognitive core study on doodling			
Assumptions of the cognitive approach and how they relate to this core study			
The psychology that is being investigated			
The background			
The aims			
The procedures			
The research method used			
The number of participants and where they are from			
The sampling methods used			
The experimental design used			
The controls used			
Types of questions asked			
Data collection method used			
Independent and dependent variables used			
Ethical issues			
Results, including quantitative data, and/or qualitative data and how it is represented and interpreted			
Conclusions drawn			
Strengths, including methodological issues such as: research method, reliability, validity, generalisability, and control of variables			
Weaknesses, including methodological issues such as: research method, reliability, validity, generalisability, and control of variables			
The issue of application of psychology to everyday life and how it relates to the study			
The individual and situational explanations debate and how it relates to the study			
The nature versus nurture debate and how it relates to the study			
Baron-Cohen et al.'s cognitive core study on the eye tests			
Assumptions of the cognitive approach and how they relate to this core study			
The psychology that is being investigated			
The background			
The aims			

The procedures			
The research method used			
The number of participants and where they are from			
The sampling methods used			
The experimental design used			
The controls used			
Types of questions asked			
Data collection method used			
Independent and dependent variables used			
Ethical issues			
Results, including quantitative data, and/or qualitative data and how it is represented and interpreted			
Conclusions drawn			
Strengths, including methodological issues such as: research method, reliability, validity, generalisability, and control of variables			
Weaknesses, including methodological issues such as: research method, reliability, validity, generalisability, and control of variables			
The issue of application of psychology to everyday life and how it relates to the study			
The individual and situational explanations debate and how it relates to the study			
The nature versus nurture debate and how it relates to the study			
Pozzulo *et al.*'s cognitive core study on line-ups			
Assumptions of the cognitive approach and how they relate to this core study			
The psychology that is being investigated			
The background			
The aims			
The procedures			
The research method used			
The number of participants and where they are from			
The sampling method used			
The experimental design used			
The controls used			
Types of questions asked			
Data collection method used			
Independent and dependent variables used			
Ethical issues			
Results, including quantitative data, and/or qualitative data and how it is represented and interpreted			
Conclusions drawn			
Strengths, including methodological issues such as: research method, reliability, validity, generalisability, and control of variables			
Weaknesses, including methodological issues such as: research method, reliability, validity, generalisability, and control of variables			

Approaches, Issues, and Debates — AS

The issue of application of psychology to everyday life and how it relates to the study			
The individual and situational explanations debate and how it relates to the study			
The nature versus nurture debate and how it relates to the study			
The issue of the use of children in psychological research and how it relates to each core study			
Bandura et al.'s learning core study on aggression			
Assumptions of the learning approach and how they relate to this core study			
The psychology that is being investigated			
The background			
The aim			
The procedures			
The research method used			
The number of participants and where they are from			
The sampling method used			
The experimental design used			
The controls used			
Data collection method used			
Independent and dependent variables used			
Ethical issues			
Results, including quantitative data, and/or qualitative data and how it is represented and interpreted			
Conclusions drawn			
Strengths, including methodological issues such as: research method, reliability, validity, generalisability, and control of variables			
Weaknesses, including methodological issues such as: research method, reliability, validity, generalisability, and control of variables			
The issue of application of psychology to everyday life and how it relates to the study			
The individual and situational explanations debate and how it relates to the study			
The nature versus nurture debate and how it relates to the study			
The issue of the use of children in psychological research and how it relates to the study			
Fagen et al.'s learning core study on elephant learning			
Assumptions of the learning approach and how they relate to this core study			
The psychology that is being investigated			
The background			
The aims			
The procedures			
The research method used			
The number of participants and where they are from			
The controls used			
Data collection method used			

Independent and dependent variables used			
Ethical issues			
Results, including quantitative data, and/or qualitative data and how it is represented and interpreted			
Conclusions drawn			
Strengths, including methodological issues such as: research method, reliability, validity, generalisability, and control of variables			
Weaknesses, including methodological issues such as: research method, reliability, validity, generalisability, and control of variables			
The issue of application of psychology to everyday life and how it relates to the study			
The individual and situational explanations debate and how it relates to the study			
The nature versus nurture debate and how it relates to the study			
The issue of the use of animals in psychological research and how it relates to the study			
Saavedra and Silverman's learning core study on a button phobia			
Assumptions of the learning approach and how they relate to this core study			
The psychology that is being investigated			
The background			
The aims			
The procedures			
The research method used			
The number of participants and where they are from			
The sampling method used			
The controls used			
Types of questions asked			
Data collection method used			
Ethical issues			
Results, including quantitative data, and/or qualitative data and how it is represented and interpreted			
Conclusions drawn			
Strengths, including methodological issues such as: research method, reliability, validity, generalisability, and control of variables			
Weaknesses, including methodological issues such as: research method, reliability, validity, generalisability, and control of variables			
The issue of application of psychology to everyday life and how it relates to the study			
The individual and situational explanations debate and how it relates to the study			
The nature versus nurture debate and how it relates to the study			
The issue of the use of children in psychological research and how it relates to the study			

Approaches, Issues, and Debates

Milgram's social core study on obedience			
Assumptions of the social approach and how they relate to this core study			
The psychology that is being investigated			
The background			
The aim			
The procedures			
The research method used			
The number of participants and where they are from			
The sampling method used			
The controls used			
Data collection method used			
Ethical issues			
Results, including quantitative data, and/or qualitative data and how it is represented and interpreted			
Conclusions drawn			
Strengths, including methodological issues such as: research method, reliability, validity, generalisability, and control of variables			
Weaknesses, including methodological issues such as: research method, reliability, validity, generalisability, and control of variables			
The issue of application of psychology to everyday life and how it relates to the study			
The individual and situational explanations debate and how it relates to the study			
The nature versus nurture debate and how it relates to the study			
Perry *et al.*'s social core study on personal space			
Assumptions of the social approach and how they relate to this core study			
The psychology that is being investigated			
The background			
The aims			
The procedures			
The research method used			
The number of participants and where they are from			
The sampling method used			
The experimental design used			
The controls used			
Types of questions asked			
Data collection method used			
Independent and dependent variables used			
Ethical issues			
Results, including quantitative data, and/or qualitative data and how it is represented and interpreted			

Conclusions drawn			
Strengths, including methodological issues such as: research method, reliability, validity, generalisability, and control of variables			
Weaknesses, including methodological issues such as: research method, reliability, validity, generalisability, and control of variables			
The issue of application of psychology to everyday life and how it relates to the study			
The individual and situational explanations debate and how it relates to the study			
The nature versus nurture debate and how it relates to the study			
Piliavin *et al.*'s social core study on subway Samaritans			
Assumptions of the social approach and how they relate to this core study			
The psychology that is being investigated			
The background			
The aims			
The procedures			
The research method used			
The number of participants and where they are from			
The sampling method used			
The experimental design used			
The controls used			
Data collection method used			
Independent and dependent variables used			
Ethical issues			
Results, including quantitative data, and/or qualitative data and how it is represented and interpreted			
Conclusions drawn			
Strengths, including methodological issues such as: research method, reliability, validity, generalisability, and control of variables			
Weaknesses, including methodological issues such as: research method, reliability, validity, generalisability, and control of variables			
The issue of application of psychology to everyday life and how it relates to the study			
The individual and situational explanations debate and how it relates to the study			

Approaches, Issues, and Debates AS

Section A

All short and medium answer questions in this section will relate to knowledge and understanding of features of any of the 12 core studies. This includes the strengths and weaknesses of them, application of knowledge of the studies to scenarios, assumptions of the four different approaches, and issues and debates. All questions will be worth between 1 and 6 marks.

★ Exam tip

Look at the space available on the question paper for you to answer each question. This will give you an indication of how much you should write. However, you do not need to fill this space and if required you can write on extra pages.

Activity or revision strategy

Activity: Using the Knowledge checklist, answer every possible question in relation to the features of each core study: the psychology being investigated, background, aim(s), all points relating to the procedures (as separate questions), ethical issues, results, conclusions, and strengths and weaknesses. For example: Describe the psychology being investigated in the study by *insert the name of each core study*. Describe the background of the study by *insert name of each core study*.

Short answer questions worked examples

Here are three examples of short answer questions for each of the four approaches: biological, cognitive, learning, and social. There are two sets of candidate responses for each question for you to compare. There is also detailed commentary related to each of the responses given by the candidates.

Worked example

Biological approach

1. Outline the aim of the study by Hassett *et al.* (monkey toy preferences). (2 marks)

Candidate A:

The aim was to see how monkeys played with toys.

Candidate B:

To see if there are sex differences in rhesus monkeys' preference for human gendered-stereotyped toys as seen in humans.

0 marks

The number of males and females is the wrong way around; there were in fact 10 females and six males. They were also not university candidates.

2. Describe the sample used in the study by Hölzel *et al.* (mindfulness and brain scans). (3 marks)

Candidate A:

Ten male and six female university candidates.

Candidate B:

There were 16 participants with a mean age of 38 years.

2 marks

Both features of the sample provided are correct; however, a third feature such as being enrolled on an MBSR course, ethnicity (mostly white) or mean years in education (17.7) is needed for full marks.

---

0 marks

Although the study did investigate monkeys and toys, how they played with them was not the aim, therefore this response is incorrect.

Key term

The **aim** of a study is what the psychologist(s) intended to investigate or the purpose of the study.

2 marks

The aim is correctly outlined.

Key term

A **sample** is a group of people from the target population who have been chosen to take part in a study; they are the participants.

★ Exam tip

This question is worth 3 marks, therefore you should try to include three points within your answer. Ensure you know the key features of the sample for each core study.

Approaches, Issues, and Debates

3. Suggest **one** real-world application for the study by Dement and Kleitman (sleep and dreams). (2 marks)

Candidate A:

If someone's eyes are moving when they are asleep, we shouldn't wake them because they are dreaming.

> **0 marks**
> What the answer proposes here is incorrect.

Candidate B:

It can help us understand people with sleep disorders like insomnia or those experiencing nightmares.

> **1 mark**
> The answer identifies some potential real-world application, but it fails to suggest how it would help us understand such individuals.

Activity or revision strategy

Activity: Suggest a real-world application for all 12 core studies and add them to your revision notes.

Worked example

Cognitive approach

1. Outline **one** result from the study by Andrade (doodling). (2 marks)

Candidate A:

The number of correct names remembered.

> **0 marks**
> This response does not answer the question. The candidate partially outlines how results were measured. No actual results are provided.

Candidate B:

In the doodling condition a mean of 7.8 names of partygoers were recalled correctly and one person made one false alarm. This was higher than the control condition who had a mean recall of 7.1 names.

> **2 marks**
> Although this answer is correct and would be awarded 2 marks, the amount of detail provided is unnecessary as the question only asks for one result.

2. Outline **one** conclusion from the study by Pozzulo *et al.* (line-ups). (2 marks)

Candidate A:

Children are good at remembering familiar things like cartoon characters.

> ★ **Exam tip**
> You may be asked to suggest a real-world application from any of the core studies. These questions will require you to consider what we can learn from the research and how it can be usefully used in real life outside of the study.

> ★ **Exam tip**
> Read the question! This may seem obvious, but the number of people who do not achieve marks because they do not read the question is surprisingly high. By using this exam success guide and practising answering exam-style questions, you will get to know the types of questions that will be asked and how you should answer them.

> **1 mark**
> This answer is just about enough for 1 mark. The focus of the answer needs to be fully on a conclusion rather than partly a result.

11

Approaches, Issues, and Debates

Candidate B:

Children are more likely to choose an incorrect face in a line-up rather than to reject the line-up compared to adults. This is because they believe the social demands of a situation are to make a selection, rather than cognitive reasons such as having a faulty memory.

2 marks

The candidate nicely outlines what we can conclude from the study in terms of a social rather than a cognitive explanation.

Activity or revision strategy

Activity: Answer question 2 a further 11 times but replace Pozzulo *et al.* with every other core study. If you are not confident, then use your notes to do this. Once you are familiar with every conclusion, see if you can write them all down in 10 minutes, without using your notes.

3. Outline **one** aim of the study by Baron-Cohen *et al.* (eye tests). (2 marks)

Candidate A:

To see if performance on the eye tests can be used to diagnose autism.

0 marks

This is incorrect, the study looked at how people with autism performed on the eye test, not to diagnose them with autism.

Candidate B:

To see if females had a higher score than males on the eyes test.

2 marks

This is one of many aims. Enough detail is provided through a comparison for 2 marks to be awarded.

Activity or revision strategy

Activity: Answer question 3 a further 11 times but replace Baron-Cohen *et al.* with every other core study. If you are not confident, then use your notes to do this. Once you are familiar with every conclusion, see if you can write them all down in 10 minutes, without using your notes.

Worked example

Learning approach

1. Suggest **one** real-world application for the study by Bandura *et al.* (aggression). (2 marks)

Candidate A:

You can make managers at work scarier by showing them violent films and therefore making them better bosses and their team members will obey their orders more.

0 marks

This answer is firstly unethical and then makes a suggestion about obedience which relates to Milgram rather than Bandura. Therefore, no marks can be awarded.

Candidate B:

Children can be shown TV shows where the role models are kind and helpful and are popular as a result. Bandura found that aggression is observed, and imitated – pro-social behaviour can also be learned this way.

2 marks

A good answer in which the candidate applies their knowledge of Bandura's research and social learning theory effectively.

AS Approaches, Issues, and Debates

2. Outline **one** result from the study by Fagen *et al.* (elephant learning). (2 marks)

Candidate A:
All elephants learned the trunk wash.

> **0 marks**
> The adult elephant did not successfully learn to trunk wash; therefore, the result is wrong, and no marks can be awarded.

Candidate B:
The elephants' performance improved from the beginning of the training to a mean success rate of 89 per cent at the end.

Activity or revision strategy

> **Revision strategy:** Trying to remember results from lots of different studies can be challenging and it is easy to confuse percentages from one study with another. Therefore, don't just remember the numbers on their own, link them to some information about the study. For example, 89 per cent trunk wash success, 65 per cent obedience to the maximum voltage.

3. Outline **one** assumption of the learning approach, using an example from the study by Saavedra and Silverman (button phobia). (3 marks)

Candidate A:
Button boy shows that we learn through reward and punishment, association, and watching others.

> **1 mark**
> The candidate briefly outlines an assumption, but no evidence is provided from the study.

Candidate B:
We learn through the processes of classical conditioning (association), the child's phobia was unlearnt by targeting the disgust and fear response reducing the distress associated with the button phobia. We also learn through operant conditioning (reward and punishment), the boy's mother provided positive reinforcement if he successfully completed the gradual exposure to buttons. Learning can be understood using the stimulus-response model.

> **3 marks**
> One assumption is clearly outlined, with accurate examples of both classical and operant conditioning from the study used.

Activity or revision strategy

> **Activity:** Write down the two assumptions for each of four approaches. Then link each of the three core studies within that area of psychology to one of these assumptions. How does each study support an assumption? If you can do this, then you'll be able to answer any assumption question in the exam.

★ **Exam tip**

In every question, further information about a study will be provided in brackets. For example, here you are reminded that Fagen *et al.* are the researchers who carried out the core study into elephant learning. Take a moment to think about this before answering the question, as you will not achieve any marks for writing about the wrong study, even if it is correct.

2 marks

A full result is provided with a meaningful comparison between performance at the beginning and at the end of training. Although data is not required, this supports the answer.

★ **Exam tip**

If a result from a core study is the mean (average) then you must include that within your answer; if you don't then you may not be awarded the mark.

Key term

An **assumption** is what is believed to be true. In the case of the approaches in psychology, it is what they think causes us to behave in a certain way.

13

Approaches, Issues, and Debates — AS

Worked example

Social approach

1. Outline **one** conclusion from the study by Milgram (obedience). (2 marks)

Candidate A:
65 per cent of people went to 450 volts.

> **0 marks**
> The answer is a result, rather than a conclusion.

Candidate B:
People will obey authority figures.

> **1 mark**
> The conclusion is correct but is not detailed enough for 2 marks.

⭐ **Exam tip**

Ensure you know the difference between a result and a conclusion. A result is a finding from the study, and this is likely to be qualitative or quantitative data. Whereas a conclusion is going beyond the results. Consider the following: what do the results tell us? What have we learnt from the study? How do they relate to the aims and hypotheses?

2. Outline **one** assumption of the social approach, using an example from the study by Piliavin *et al.* (subway Samaritans). (3 marks)

Candidate A:
Piliavin looked at how bystanders behave in different environments such as when a model helps after 70 seconds or 150 seconds in the critical or adjacent area and with drunk or ill victims.

> **1 mark**
> The answer focuses on describing the different conditions within the experiment, but this does not relate to the assumption. Some credit can be awarded for reference to 'different environments'.

Candidate B:
The social approach assumes that behaviour, cognitions, and emotions are influenced by our social environment, the context, and groups within it. This is shown in the Piliavin study in which helping behaviour was influenced by type of victim and other people around.

> **2 marks**
> A good answer in which the assumption is well described; however, the example does not clearly link to the assumption.

3. Describe the sample used in the study by Perry *et al.* (personal space). (3 marks)

Candidate A:
Participants were males and females from the University of Tel Aviv and were aged 25.

> **0 marks**
> All details provided are incorrect. Although the sample included males, there were no females so this cannot be credited.

Candidate B:
54 male undergraduates.

> **3 marks**
> Although the answer is brief, there are three correct pieces of information about the sample, so full marks can be awarded.

⭐ **Exam tip**

The more you write does not necessarily mean the more marks you will gain. Do not waste time writing irrelevant / extra information or when marks can be achieved with a short and focused answer.

AS Approaches, Issues, and Debates

Activity or revision strategy

Revision strategy and activity: Write the name of each core study on a piece of paper or card and place them in a pile and turn them over. On separate pieces of paper or card, write down the required features of each core study. For example, sample, conclusions, and ethics. Place these in a separate pile and turn them over. Pick one card from each pile and remember as much as you can about the feature of this core study.

Short answer questions raise your grade examples

Here there will be one set of candidate responses. There will be example candidate responses with check marks (✔) showing where the marks were awarded. A brief commentary is also provided.

↑ Raise your grade

Biological approach

1. Describe **one** methodological strength from the study by Hassett *et al*. (monkey toy preferences). (2 marks)

   A large sample of about 150 monkeys was studied, therefore the results can be generalised.

   The number of participants in the study is incorrect and it is unclear how the results could be generalised – 0 marks.

2. Outline **one** control used in the study by Dement and Kleitman (sleep and dreams). (2 marks)

   No coffee was drunk before the study. ✔

   This is correct; however, further information is required in terms of what is being controlled – 1 mark.

3. Explain how **one** finding from the study by Hölzel *et al*. (mindfulness and brain scans) supports **one** of the assumptions of the biological approach. (3 marks)

   There were increases in grey matter concentration in the left hippocampus ✔ *which is in our brain therefore supporting the biological assumption.*

   The result is correct; however, the answer needs to meet to the requirements of the question by explaining how it supports an assumption of the biological approach. An assumption is not identified – 1 mark.

   > ★ **Exam tip**
   >
   > A finding is a result or a conclusion from a study. Make sure you know how the findings/results of each of the core studies support an assumption from the approach that it is from.

This response could earn a total of 2 out of 7 marks.

Approaches, Issues, and Debates

> **Activity or revision strategy**
>
> **Activity:** Answer each of these questions in less than five minutes. Refer to the previous commentary about how to achieve full marks.
>
> - Explain how **one** finding from the study by Dement and Kleitman (sleep and dreams) supports **one** of the assumptions of the biological approach. (3 marks)
> - Explain how **one** finding from the study by Andrade (doodling) supports **one** of the assumptions of the cognitive approach. (3 marks)
> - Explain how **one** finding from the study by Bandura *et al.* (aggression) supports **one** of the assumptions of the learning approach. (3 marks)
> - Explain how **one** finding from the study by Milgram (obedience) supports **one** of the assumptions of the social approach. (3 marks)

↑ Raise your grade

Cognitive approach

1. Describe the sampling technique used in the study by Andrade (doodling). (2 marks)

   Opportunity sampling ✔ from those who were readily available from the Medical Research Council. ✔

   The sampling technique is correctly identified within the context of the Andrade study – 2 marks.

2. Outline **one** assumption of the cognitive approach, using an example from the study by Baron-Cohen *et al.* (eye tests). (3 marks)

   People have individual differences in their cognitive processing such as with attention, language, thinking, and memory. ✔ There are also differences in our abilities to understand emotions in others by observing expressions of their eyes, ✔ this cognitive process is impaired in people with autism. ✔

   An assumption is clearly and accurately outlined and is supported by an appropriate example from the Baron-Cohen study – 3 marks.

   > ★ **Exam tip**
   >
   > You can see from the commentary how the marks were awarded for this question. This is done throughout this section for all questions. Take note of this so that you are able meet the marking criteria within the exam.

3. Outline the experimental design used in the study by Pozzulo *et al.* (line-ups). (2 marks)

   Independent measures ✔ as children were in one condition and adults in another. ✔

   The experimental design is correctly identified within the context of the Pozzulo et al. study – 2 marks.

   This candidate could earn full marks – a total of 7 out of 7 marks.

↑ Raise your grade

Learning approach

1. Identify **two** independent variables in the study by Bandura *et al.* (aggression). (2 marks)

   Levels of aggression, ✘ and gender of the children. ✔

   Gender of the children is one of the three independent variables; however, the levels of aggression is a dependent variable – 1 mark.

16

AS Approaches, Issues, and Debates

2. Describe **one** conclusion from the study by Fagen *et al.* (elephant learning). (2 marks)

   It is possible to train elephants to voluntarily participate in a trunk wash ✔ using secondary positive reinforcement. ✔

   The conclusion is clearly and accurately described – 2 marks.

3. Explain how evaluative learning was used in the study by Saavedra and Silverman (button phobia). (3 marks)

   The boy learnt to negatively evaluate buttons without anticipating any threat. ✔ This negative evaluation leads to a feeling of disgust rather than fear. ✔

   A greater focus is required on exactly how this happened – 2 marks.

> **Key term**
>
> **Secondary positive reinforcement** does not naturally occur but is a stimulus that reinforces a behaviour after it has been associated with a primary reinforcer.

This candidate could earn a total of 5 marks out of 7.

★ **Exam tip**

You may be asked about specific information from a core study, such as evaluative learning—see Table 1.1 on page 24—make sure you are able to explain them in the context of the study.

⬆ Raise your grade

Social approach

1. Identify **two** features of the 'experimenter' in the study by Milgram (obedience). (2 marks)

   A 31-year-old ✔ American man ✔ dressed in a lab coat. ✔

   More than two features are correctly identified – 2 marks.

   Activity or revision strategy

   > **Revision strategy:** If you are revising with a friend, ask each other specific questions about each of the core studies, such as question 1. This will help you remember important details from each piece of research.

2. Describe the questionnaire used in the study by Perry *et al.* (personal space). (3 marks)

   A 28-item ✔ online ✔ questionnaire, consisting of four 7-item subscales ✔, each measuring a different aspect of empathy. ✔

   A detailed and accurate description of the questionnaire is provided – 3 marks.

3. Outline **one** qualitative result from the study by Piliavin *et al.* (subway Samaritans). (2 marks)

   The ill victims are more likely to be helped 62/65, compared to drunk ones 19/38.

   An excellent answer is provided; however, no marks can be awarded because the question asks for a qualitative result, not a quantitative result – 0 marks.

This response can earn a total of 5 out of 7 marks.

Activity or revision strategy

> **Activity:** Think about any other core studies which have qualitative data and answer this question in relation to these studies too.

17

Approaches, Issues, and Debates

Medium answer questions worked examples

Here are three examples of medium answer questions for each of the four approaches: biological, cognitive, learning, and social. There are a range of answers in terms of marks achieved and there is detailed commentary related to each of the responses given by the candidates.

Worked example

Biological approach

1. Outline two assumptions from the biological approach. (4 marks)

Candidate response:

One assumption is that our thoughts, behaviours, and emotions are a result of how our brain works, as well as genetics, hormones, and evolution. Secondly, similarities and differences between people are due to biological factors and their interaction with other factors.

4 marks

Both assumptions are outlined clearly and accurately. Each assumption has been awarded 2 marks.

Activity or revision strategy

Activity: See if you can write three other model answers for an outline of the assumptions of the social, cognitive, and learning approaches.

★ **Exam tip**

The answer to question 1 is an example of what should be written as an answer if this question appears in the exam. You will notice that psychological key terms are used, and the length of the answer is appropriate for an outline of the assumptions.

2a. Explain **one** weakness of the use of animals in psychological research, using an example from the study by Hassett *et al.* (monkey toy preferences). (3 marks)

2b. Explain one ethical strength of the use of animals in psychological research, using an example from the study by Hassett et al (monkey toy preferences). (3 marks)

Candidate response:

2a. Researchers should use the smallest number of animals possible that will still achieve the research aims. However, in this study more monkeys than the minimum were studied, therefore breaking this guideline, which is a weakness.

2b. A strength of the study was that it was carried out in line with the NIH Guide for the Care and Use of Laboratory Animals and was approved by Emory's Institutional Animal Care and Use Committee.

2 marks

The ethical weakness is explained; however, the link to the study is not clear. This answer just says 'more monkeys than the minimum', but if detail such as 'a potential of 82 monkeys were identified to take part', then the third mark would be awarded for the weakness.

Activity or revision strategy

Activity: For exam questions relating to the ethics of the use of animals in psychological research, you need to know about: minimising harm and maximising benefit; replacement; species; numbers; pain, suffering, and distress; housing; reward, deprivation, and aversive stimuli. Write a definition of each of these terms. Then identify whether they are a strength or a weakness in relation to the Fagen *et al.* study and the Hassett *et al.* study and explain why.

2 marks

The strength is explained in the context of the study; however, it is not clear what the strength actually is. Again, this prevents the third mark being awarded.

3. Describe **one** methodological strength and **one** methodological weakness from the study by Dement and Kleitman (sleep and dreams). (4 marks)

Candidate response:

The sample was small, with only five participants being studied in detail, therefore the results cannot be generalised to a wider population.

AS Approaches, Issues, and Debates

The study was reliable as standardised procedures such as waking participants with a doorbell were used, therefore it can be easily replicated.

> **4 marks**
>
> Both the strength and the weakness are clearly and accurately described within the context of the study. Each has been awarded 2 marks.

Worked example

Cognitive approach

1. Two friends, Ada and Amara, are discussing the study by Pozzulo *et al.* (line-ups) in terms of the debate about individual and situational explanations.

   Ada believes this study supports the individual explanation, but Amara believes this study supports the situational explanation. Outline why you think either Ada or Amara is correct, using evidence from the study. (4 marks)

Candidate response:

The situational debate argues that behaviour is a result of the context or the environment we are in. Children falsely identified humans in line-ups because they thought they should give an answer because of the situation, not because of their cognitive inability to recall.

2. Describe the background to the study by Andrade (doodling). (6 marks)

Candidate response:

When attention is divided, performance is poor. However, researchers have found that doodling actually enhances concentration because it reduces the chance of daydreaming. This supports the working memory model.

> **3 marks**
>
> The background to the Andrade study is accurately described. However, as the question is worth 5 marks, the amount written is not enough. Further description of, for example, how the study relates to the working memory model would be useful.

> **Key terms**
>
> The **background** of a study refers to any underpinning theory or related research which informs and influences the study.

Activity or revision strategy

> **Revision strategy:** You may be asked about the background of any of the core studies. There is often quite a lot of background to choose from, so make sure you know enough.

3. Explain **two** weaknesses of the research method used by Baron-Cohen *et al.* (eye tests) using examples from the study. (4 marks)

> ★ **Exam tip**
>
> A methodological strength or weakness can be anything in relation to a study, such as research method, experimental design, participants, or procedures. But this does not include ethics, if you include ethical strengths or weaknesses when answering such a question you will not get any marks.

> **2 marks**
>
> This answer outlines why the results may have been due to situational factors. However, only 2 marks can be awarded as the answer does clearly specify that they think Amara is correct. Moreover, the description of the situational explanation is of limited value in isolation; a clear link needs to be made to the study (and Amara's belief).

> **Key term**
>
> A **debate** in psychology is an important argument about what is the cause of a behaviour. These are opposite viewpoints and evidence can be found to support each side of the debate.

> ★ **Exam tip**
>
> In a scenario question like question 1, you may be asked to make a judgement on which person you believe or which side of a debate you agree with. You must clearly state who or what you agree with, or your marks will be limited. When describing a debate, you must also clearly state which side of the debate your description relates to.

19

Approaches, Issues, and Debates AS

Candidate response:

One weakness is that it is an artificial environment, and the task lacks ecological validity.

Another weakness is that there may have been demand characteristics as participants may have changed their behaviour because they knew they were taking part in a study, making results invalid.

Activity or revision strategy

Activity: For each core study identify the research method(s) used, for example lab experiment, questionnaire, case study. Then note down the strengths and weaknesses of each these methods in the context of the study, for example completing the eye test task in an artificial lab environment is not an everyday task so it lacks mundane realism. By doing this, you will avoid the mistake that this candidate made.

2 marks

Two weaknesses are explained well, but there is no clear reference to the Baron-Cohen study. Simply adding what the artificial task was would allow a second mark to be achieved for the first weaknesses. The point about demand characteristics is true about lab experiments. However, it is unclear how this would be an issue in this particular study.

Key term

Demand characteristics are the features of a study that somehow inform the participants about the true aim and this influences their behaviour independently of the independent variable.

Worked example

Learning approach

1. In the study by Fagen *et al.* (elephant learning), the psychology being investigated included shaping.

   Describe what is meant by shaping. (4 marks)

Candidate response:

Shaping is when behaviour is modified to what you want it to be. Fagen *et al.* found that target behaviour can easily be shaped as the elephants learnt to trunk wash through rewards which are positive and negative reinforcement and behavioural chaining in which associations between behaviours are developed. Shaping was really effective as there was about 90 per cent success in learning to trunk wash.

2 marks

Two features of shaping are identified: behaviour being modified and the use of reinforcement. The point about behavioural chaining is not relevant to shaping, and the result from the study, although showing that shaping is effective, does not describe what is meant by shaping.

Activity or revision strategy

Activity: Now that you know that the candidate response on what is meant by shaping would only achieve 2 marks, write your own answer with enough detail to achieve 4 marks. You could then do this with every answer in this chapter where you did not get full marks.

2. Michelle believes that the study by Saavedra and Silverman (button phobia) is unethical. Explain why Michelle is correct, using evidence from the study in your answer. (4 marks)

Candidate response:

Michelle is correct because the boy did not give consent to take part. It was also proved that he had long-term psychological harm as they made him distressed in the study. He was also not debriefed and there was no follow-up. Also, it is unethical because he was the only participant so results cannot be generalised to children with other phobias.

0 marks

The answer is totally inaccurate. The boy did give consent to take part (and so did his mother), there is no evidence of long-term psychological harm, and there was a debrief and follow-up. The final point about generalisability is a methodological issue not an ethical issue and is therefore irrelevant.

AS Approaches, Issues, and Debates

Activity or revision strategy

Activity: For each of the 12 core studies write down whether each of the ethical issues detailed in the Key term explanation is a strength or a weakness. Give a brief explanation of why. For example, a weakness of Piliavin et al. is that participants did not provide informed consent to take part in the study, while in Dement and Kleitman a strength is that participants were referred to by initials and therefore their identities remained anonymous.

3. Two friends, Jasmine and Tom, are discussing the study by Bandura et al. (aggression) in terms of its validity. Jasmine believes that this study has validity, but Tom disagrees.

   Explain **one** reason why you think Jasmine is correct and **one** reason why you think Tom is correct. (4 marks)

Candidate response:

Jasmine is correct; Bandura et al.'s study has high levels of ecological validity, population validity, and internal validity because it is a well-designed study. Tom is correct because we don't know the long-term impact on the children.

★ Exam tip

Validity and reliability are terms that are often used by candidates, but they are not always used correctly. Make sure you understand what these terms mean, the different types of them, and what the causes and consequences of these terms are.

Key term

Being **ethical** or **unethical** refers to what is good and bad in relation to morals and standards of conduct. This includes issues such as: minimising harm (and maximising benefit), valid consent (including informed consent), right to withdraw, lack of deception, confidentiality, privacy, and debriefing.

1 mark

The answer relating to Jasmine is very generic. It simply lists types of validity and doesn't explain why the study possesses these types of validity. It is questionable whether some of these are true (without an explanation). The answer about Tom needs to explain why this is an issue in relation to validity.

Worked example

Social approach

1. Describe what is meant by the nature versus nurture debate using examples from the study by Perry et al. (personal space). (4 marks)

Candidate response:

The nature argument supports the influence of genetics and innate characteristics, while nurture is about environmental factors and how they influence behaviour. Perry supports the nature debate because interpersonal distance preferences are affected by our natural levels of empathy. This is enhanced by levels of oxytocin that is produced in certain social situations, which supports the nurture debate.

★ Exam tip

For any question in which you need to use examples from a study to support an argument, you should describe the debate/assumption/issue, etc. and then describe *how* the study supports the point you are making.

2. Delilah believes that the study by Piliavin et al. (subway Samaritans) is valid. Explain why Delilah is correct, using evidence from the study in your answer. (4 marks)

Candidate response:

Delilah is correct because it took place on the New York subway in which people were going about their day-to-day lives, which makes it ecologically valid.

4 marks

This answer demonstrates how maximum marks can be awarded without writing too much. Both sides of the debate are described succinctly, with accurate research evidence to support the argument.

2 marks

What is written here is correct. However, further expansion of the point is required, such as whether results can be generalised outside of the study and, if so, why and where to.

Approaches, Issues, and Debates

Activity or revision strategy

Activity: For the question about Delilah, replace Piliavin *et al.* with each of the other core studies and write an answer which would achieve full marks based on the commentary provided. For example, 'Delilah believes that the study by Dement and Kleitman (sleep and dreams) is valid. Explain why Delilah is correct, using evidence from the study.'

3. Evaluate the use of laboratory experiments in terms of **two** strengths using examples from **one** study from the social approach. (6 marks)

Candidate response:

Lab studies have high levels of control, which means that confounding variables are minimised. For example, in the Perry *et al.* study, each participant waited 45 minutes after being given the oxytocin before starting the experiment. This was to ensure that the oxytocin levels in the central nervous system had reached a plateau, otherwise the results may not have been due to oxytocin levels. Another confounding variable could have been social interaction during the 45-minute wait; however, this was overcome by being seated in a quiet room with magazines to read. This makes the study high in internal validity.

3 marks

A thorough evaluation of the lab experiment in the context of the Perry *et al.* study. However, although two examples of confounding variables being controlled are provided from the study, these relate to the same strength. A second strength is not provided, which is what the question asks for.

Key term

Validity refers to whether something measures exactly what it claims to be measuring.

★ Exam tip

If a question asks about validity, you can choose which type of validity to include within your answer. The most suitable type will depend on the core study, but ecological and population validity are often the most suitable. However, you could consider internal validity and even temporal validity if appropriate.

Medium answer questions raise your grade examples

↑ Raise your grade

Biological approach

1. From the study by Dement and Kleitman (sleep and dreams), describe the procedure from the point when the participants reported to the sleep laboratory until they were asked to describe a dream. (5 marks)

Participants had electrodes attached to their scalp ✔ and the wires were arranged in a ponytail. ✔ They then went to bed in a dark room. ✔ They were woken up at different times during the night by a loud doorbell in either REM or nREM sleep. ✔ Once awake they spoke into a recording device and reported whether they had been dreaming, ✔ and whether the dream had lasted 5 or 15 minutes, they then described their dream. ✔

A detailed answer which includes a large number of correct pieces of information about the procedure – full marks.

Activity or revision strategy

Activity: Write down the procedures for each of the core studies with as much detail as possible.

★ Exam tip

For a procedure question on a core study, you will be awarded 1 mark for each correct point that you make. You are also likely to be asked about the procedure from a certain point in the procedure until another point. Therefore, you must ensure that you know what happened throughout the procedure for each study.

22

AS Approaches, Issues, and Debates

2. Describe what is meant by the nature versus nurture debate using examples from the study by Hassett *et al.* (monkey toy preferences). (4 marks)

This debate argues that behaviour is result of nature which is biological or genetic inheritance ✔ or nurture which is environmental factors such as upbringing. ✔ Hassett *et al.*'s study supports the nature debate as male monkeys, like human boys, prefer wheeled toys, these preferences developed without gendered socialisation because we are born with toy preferences. ✔

Both nature and nurture are described well. However, there is only an example of nature from the Hassett *et al.* study. An example of nurture is also required for full marks, so this gets 3 marks.

> **Key term**
>
> **Socialisation** is the process in which individuals learn and develop social skills, values, beliefs, and behaviours necessary to be an accepted member of a social group.

Activity or revision strategy

Activity: Write an additional sentence with an example from the Hassett *et al.* study about the nurture debate.

3. Pedro believes that the study by Hölzel *et al.* (mindfulness and brain scans) is ethical. Explain why Pedro is correct, using evidence from the study in your answer. (4 marks)

Pedro is correct as all participants gave written informed consent. ✔ The procedures were also approved by the IRBs of Massachusetts General Hospital and the University of Massachusetts Medical School, ✔ thus the rights and welfare of those taking part were protected. ✔ Participants also had the right to withdraw ✔ as two participants did not return for the second session due to experiencing discomfort. ✔

A range of ethical issues are explained, with evidence from the study to support why Pedro is correct – full marks.

This candidate could earn a total of 12 out of 13 marks.

Activity or revision strategy

Activity: Answer question 3 but replace Hölzel *et al.* with one study from the cognitive approach, one from the learning approach, and one from the social approach. Use the sample answer to help you structure your answers and to achieve 4 marks.

↑ Raise your grade

Cognitive approach

1. Marek believes that the study by Pozzulo *et al.* (line-ups) is not ethical. Explain why Marek is correct, using evidence from the study in your answer. (4 marks)

Marek is correct because children would have been upset as they could not recall human faces very well. ✔ This is an example of psychological harm as they were worried about their memory. ✔

One issue is briefly explained in relation to Marek, with evidence from the study – 2 marks.

Approaches, Issues, and Debates

2. From the study by Andrade (doodling) describe the procedure from the point when the participant had to start listening to the phone call until the recall task. (5 marks)

Participants listened to a boring phone call about a birthday party including information about who attended and who didn't. ✔ The phone call lasted about 5 minutes. ✔ They were told they would have to recall this information to make them pay attention. ✔

Three pieces of information from the study are described clearly and accurately – 3 marks.

3. In the study by Baron-Cohen *et al.* (eye tests), the psychology being investigated included theory of mind.

Describe theory of mind. (4 marks)

This is mind reading, which is an understanding of what other people are thinking and feeling and know. ✔ People with autism lack this. ✔

The answer provides a brief description of theory of mind – 2 marks.

This candidate could earn a total of 7 out of 13 marks.

Activity or revision strategy

Activity: For each core study, you are required to know about the psychology being investigated. These are identified in Table 1.1. Describe each of these areas of psychology in the context of their core study as a 4-mark question.

Core study	Psychology being investigated
Dement and Kleitman	• Sleep – Dreaming – Ultradian rhythms
Hassett *et al.*	• Sex differences – Socialisation – Play – The role of hormones
Hölzel *et al.*	• Mindfulness – Localisation of function
Andrade	• Attention – Memory
Baron-Cohen *et al.*	• Theory of mind – Social sensitivity
Pozzulo *et al.*	• False positive responses – Eyewitness testimony
Bandura *et al.*	• Social learning theory – Aggression
Fagen *et al.*	• Operant conditioning – Reinforcement (positive, negative, primary, and secondary) – Shaping – Behavioural chaining
Saavedra and Silverman	• Operant conditioning – Classical conditioning – Phobias
Milgram	• Obedience – Social pressure
Perry *et al.*	• Interpersonal distance (personal space) – Social hormones – Empathy
Piliavin *et al.*	• Bystander apathy – Diffusion of responsibility

Table 1.1

Key term

Eyewitness testimony is the evidence provided by a person who saw a crime take place, with a view to identifying the perpetrator.

Approaches, Issues, and Debates

⬆ Raise your grade

Learning approach

1. Describe what is meant by the debate about individual and situational explanations using examples from the study by Fagen *et al.* (elephant learning). (4 marks)

   The individual debate suggests that behaviour is due to dispositional factors within the individual. ✔ While the situational side of the debate argues that behaviour results from factors within the external environment. ✔

   The success of operant conditioning to teach four elephants to trunk wash shows that behaviour can be learnt from the environment and is due to nurture. ✔ While Elephant 5 had difficulties learning due to visual impairment, trunk weakness, and age, this supports the individual explanation. ✔

   Both individual and situational explanations are described with appropriate evidence provided to support both explanations – full marks.

   ### Activity or revision strategy

   > **Revision strategy:** Have a debate when revising with a friend! Write down an individual explanation on one piece of paper and a situation explanation on another. Go through each of the core studies and then each of you pick of piece of paper to decide which side of the debate you are arguing for. Take it in turns to put forward an argument as to why that study supports that side of the debate. The person who is unable to put forward an argument loses that debate. Repeat this for the nature versus nurture debate. Please note: it is difficult to argue for certain sides of a debate for some core studies.

2. Romilly believes that the study by Bandura *et al.* (aggression) is reliable. Explain why Romilly is correct, using evidence from the study in your answer. (4 marks)

   Bandura et al.'s procedures were standardised. ✔ For example, all children in the experimental conditions were taken to a room, sat at a table, and played with potato prints and picture stickers for 10 minutes. ✔

   The answer is good, but doesn't clearly link to reliability and replicability, or to what Romilly believes – 2 marks.

   > **Key term**
   >
   > **Replicability** is the ability to repeat an investigation under the same conditions in order to check the method used and to compare the results.

3. Outline **two** assumptions from the learning approach. (4 marks)

   The learning approach says that we are born as a blank slate, ✔ and experiences and interactions shape our behaviour. ✔ It is also assumed that we learn through social learning. ✔

   Assumption one is clear and detailed, assumption two is a little vague and lacks detail – 3 marks.

   > **Key term**
   >
   > **Social learning** is where behaviour is learnt through the observation of a role model; a mental representation of what is seen is developed and rehearsed, and this behaviour is then imitated in a similar situation.

   This candidate could earn a total of 9 out of 12 marks.

Activity or revision strategy

> **Activity:** Write down how the assumptions of learning approach can be explained by examples from the studies by Bandura *et al.*, Fagen *et al.*, and Saavedra and Silverman.

Approaches, Issues, and Debates

⬆ Raise your grade

Social approach

1. From the study by Milgram (obedience), describe the procedure from the point when the participant met the 'learner' until they administered a shock of 300 volts. (5 marks)

Participants were 40 men aged between 20 and 50 and they were paid $4.50 for taking part. **NAQ**

The learner was a confederate and roles were always fixed. The experimenter gave prods to the teacher ✔ *which made all participants go to 300 volts.*

The majority of the answer is not answering the question (**NAQ**) as it does not describe the procedures, instead it identifies participants and results – 1 mark.

Activity or revision strategy

Activity: Answer question 1, ensuring you include the details from between the two points stated and then add five pieces of information.

★ Exam tip

Milgram's study is one of the most well-known and interesting studies in psychology and candidates often have lots to write about this piece of research. However, it is not always relevant to the question. When answering a question about Milgram, make sure you read what the question is asking, look at the number of marks available, and do not get carried away with unnecessary details.

2. In the study by Perry *et al.* (personal space) the psychology being investigated included social hormones.
   Describe social hormones. (4 marks)

Oxytocin is a social hormone. Perry found that oxytocin promotes the choice of closer interpersonal distances in individuals. ✔

The answer gives an example of a social hormone and then focuses on the results from the Perry *et al.* study, rather than describing social hormones – 1 mark.

Key term

Social hormone – Hormones are chemical substances that are produced in the body that regulate the activity of organs. Social hormones influence our interactions with others.

3. Outline **two** assumptions from the social approach. (4 marks)

One assumption is that behaviour is influenced by society around us. ✔ *Another is that everyone's social behaviour is influenced by what is inside our brain, which is like a computer, this route is input, process, and output.* ✘

The first assumption is brief. The second assumption is not correct as it is from the cognitive approach – 1 mark.

This candidate could earn a total of 3 out of 13 marks.

Revision tip

You are required to know the assumptions from the following four approaches. You may be required to describe some of these assumptions or use examples from the core studies to explain them.

Biological assumptions
Cognitions, emotions, and behaviours can be explained in terms of the workings of the brain and the effect of genetics, hormones, and evolution.
Similarities and differences between individuals can be explained by biological factors and their interaction with other factors.
Cognitive assumptions
Information is processed in the same way and through the same route in every human: input – process – output, this is similar to how information is processed by a computer.

26

People have individual differences in their cognitive processing such as with thinking, memory attention, and language. These processes can also help to explain our emotions and behaviours.
Learning assumptions
Everyone starts life as a blank slate. Experiences and interactions with the environment shape our behaviour and these changes are directly observable.
Everyone learns through the processes of social learning, operant conditioning, and classical conditioning. This can be understood using the stimulus–response model.
Social assumptions
Cognitions, emotions, and behaviours are affected by social contexts, environments, and groups.
Cognitions, emotions, and behaviours are affected by the actual, imagined, or the implied presence of others.

Activity or revision strategy

Revision strategy and activity: Highlight key words from each of the assumptions to help you remember them.

Close the page and write down a description of each of the assumptions. How closely does your description match?

Answer these questions:

- Outline **one** assumption of the biological approach, using an example from the study by Hölzel *et al.* (mindfulness and brain scans). (3 marks)
- Outline **one** assumption of the cognitive approach, using an example from the study by Pozzulo *et al.* (line-ups). (3 marks)
- Outline **one** assumption of the learning approach, using an example from the study by Fagen *et al.* (elephant learning). (3 marks)
- Outline **one** assumption of the social approach, using an example from the study by Perry *et al.* (personal space). (3 marks)

Section B

The section will always include:

- A 4-mark part-question.
- An 8-mark part-question on two similarities between two core studies, two similarities between two core studies, or on one similarity and one difference between two core studies. At least one of the core studies will be named.
- A 10-mark essay on the evaluation of a specific core study, in which you are required to include two strengths and two weaknesses of the study, including a named evaluation issue.

Similarities and differences – 8 marks

The similarities and/or differences can be about anything about the core studies and the most appropriate similarities/differences would be dependent on the two studies in the question. However, typically it would be expected that the most likely answers would be about any of the following:

- Research methods
- Sample size
- Sample demographics
- Sampling technique

- Experimental design (if both studies are experiments)
- Controls
- Variables
- Data collection methods
- Ethical issues
- Results, including qualitative or quantitative data
- Conclusions.

Strengths and weaknesses – 10 marks

You will be required to evaluate two strengths and two weaknesses of a named study in the essay question. There will be a named issue that you must write about as either a strength or weakness, while the other evaluation points are of your choice. They are likely to include:

- Reliability
- Validity
- Generalisability
- Ethics
- Research method (experiment, observation, self-report, case study, correlation or longitudinal, depending on the core study)
- Experimental design
- Controlling of variables
- Sample (including animals or children if relevant)
- Sampling technique
- Data (qualitative and/or quantitative data).

The strengths and weaknesses chosen, and the named evaluation point, will depend on the nature of the study and certain ones will be more appropriate or only relevant for certain studies.

Long answer questions worked examples

Here are two examples of long answer questions for each of the four approaches: biological, cognitive, learning, and social. One example is an 8-mark question, and the other example is a 10-mark essay. There are a range of answer in terms of marks achieved and there is detailed commentary related to each of the responses given by the candidates.

Worked example

Biological approach

1. Explain **one** similarity and **one** difference between the study by Dement and Kleitman (sleep and dreams) and the study by Hölzel *et al.* (mindfulness and brain scans). (8 marks)

Candidate response:

One similarity is that both studies are in the biological area of psychology which is scientific. It looks at topics such as sleep and dreaming and brain scans which are to do with our biology, brains, and neurology.

One difference between the studies is that one studies participants when they are awake and the other studies them when they are asleep.

1 mark

This answer is very weak. The similarity given is just an attempt to describe the biological approach. The topics being named are taken from the question within the named studies. The difference would be awarded 1 mark at most. Very little psychological knowledge is demonstrated and there are no clear examples from the studies; however, what is written is correct and is a difference.

AS Approaches, Issues, and Debates

> ★ **Exam tip**
>
> For the 8-mark similarity and/or difference questions, each similarity and/or difference is marked separately out of 4 marks. When marking your answer, examiners will award marks for the following:
>
> - **Level 1: 1 mark** will be given if the similarity or difference is briefly explained, but without including any specific evidence from the named studies.
> - **Level 2: 2 marks** will be given if the similarity or difference is explained clearly, accurately, and in detail, but without including any specific evidence from the named studies OR if the similarity or difference is briefly explained and includes some specific evidence from one of the named studies.
> - **Level 3: 3 marks** will be given if the similarity or difference is explained clearly, accurately, and in detail, with good use of specific evidence from one of the named studies OR if the similarity or difference is explained clearly, accurately, and in detail, with specific evidence from both of the named studies, but the evidence lacks detail.
> - **Level 4: 4 marks** will be given if the similarity or difference is explained clearly, accurately, and in detail, with good use of specific evidence from both of the named studies.

Activity or revision strategy

Revision strategy and activity: Write down all core studies on pieces of card. Shuffle the cards and pick two studies. For these two studies recall two similarities and two differences.

Put the cards back in the pile, shuffle, and repeat the process.

After every three pairs that you pick, write your answer down (this can be one similarity and one difference, or two similarities and two differences – you choose). Make sure your answer includes everything that is needed to achieve two lots of 4 marks, as outlined in the Exam tip.

2. Evaluate the study by Hassett *et al.* (monkey toy preferences) in terms of **two** strengths and **two** weaknesses. One of your evaluation points must be about **quantitative data**. (10 marks)

> **Key term**
>
> **Quantitative data** is numerical data that can be analysed statistically.

There are a number of strengths and weaknesses in the monkey toy preferences study that I am going to discuss. A strength is something good about a study, while a weakness is something bad.

Hassett et al. carried out an experiment about sex differences for toy preferences in monkeys' toy preferences. Hassett believed that their preferences were more biologically controlled than that of children. This is a strength as the study has an aim.

The researchers observed interactions with stereotypical girls' toys and boys' toys observed. These behaviours were coded using a behavioural checklist which is a strength because it makes the study valid and reliable.

Human participants were not included in this study. This is a weakness as humans and monkeys are biologically and cognitively different. We can therefore say that the study lacks population validity. To compare, monkey toy preferences data of children from another study was used; this is good as it saves time and money.

Approaches, Issues, and Debates AS

Quantitative data was used in the study. This is a strength because it is objective data and is not open to biased interpretation. We can also compare data and make charts and graphs so results can be seen visually. However, it is also a weakness as it doesn't explain reasons for the results, which qualitative data does.

Overall, the study has both strengths and limitations, and the results show that biological factors and socialisation play a part in preferences for toys.

Level 1: 2 marks

One the face of it, this answer may look good, and the learner clearly has some sound knowledge; however, the question is not answered properly and therefore few marks would be awarded.

The first paragraph sets the scene nicely, but this is not required and would just be wasting valuable exam time.

The second paragraph is also not required, the question is about the evaluation of the study, not describing what it is about. Furthermore, a study having an aim is not a strength.

The third paragraph is also mainly descriptive, with an attempt at evaluation at the end. However, it is not clear that the learner understands what reliability and validity are.

The fourth paragraph is partially correct but fails to understand the reasons for the monkeys being used.

The fifth paragraph evaluates the strengths and weaknesses of quantitative data, which is the named issue. However, it is not evaluated in the context of the study. Examples of this type of data, for example the amount of time they interacted with different toys, is required to achieve more marks.

The final sentence is also unnecessary as it does not provide any strengths or weaknesses, which is what the question requires.

★ Exam tip

For the 10-mark essay, you will be required to evaluate a specific core study in terms of two strengths and two weakness. When marking your answer, examiners will assess each strength and weakness separately, before making an overall judgement about the level of your response.

Mark descriptors:

- **Level 5: 9–10 marks** – All four evaluation points are detailed and are in the context of the study.
- **Level 4: 7–8 marks** – Three of the evaluation points are detailed and are in the context of the study, one is brief and in the context of the study.
- **Level 3: 5–6 marks** – All four evaluation points are brief and are in the context of the study. Or only two evaluation points are in the context of the study, but they are both detailed.
- **Level 2: 3–4 marks** – Up to three evaluation points that are brief and in the context of the study. Or one detailed evaluation point in the context of the study. Other evaluation points will be poor and lack context.

- **Level 1: 1–2 marks** – Generic evaluation points, with none in the context of the study.

Worked example

Cognitive approach

1. Explain **two** differences between the study by Pozzulo *et al.* (line-ups) and **one** other study from the cognitive approach. (8 marks)

Candidate response:

One difference between Pozzulo *et al.* and another cognitive study is that the participants had to remember faces of cartoon characters and human faces, while in Andrade's study they had to remember names of people who went to a party.

While a difference between Pozzulo and the other cognitive study by Baron-Cohen is that those taking part were both shown faces, those in the Pozzulo study had to correctly identify them later, while Baron-Cohen's just had to identify the emotions in faces they were shown.

2. Evaluate the study by Baron-Cohen *et al.* (eye tests) in terms of **two** strengths and **two** weaknesses. One of your evaluation points must be about **reliability**. (10 marks)

> **Key terms**
>
> **Reliability** relates to whether something is consistent, which means it stays the same. When evaluating core studies, you may consider their **internal reliability** which refers to the consistency of a measure, such as whether questions in a questionnaire or items on an observation checklist are all measuring the same thing, such as aggression or helping behaviour.
>
> Strengths or weaknesses of studies may also refer to **external reliability**, which assesses the consistency of a test or a measure. If a test is repeated and similar results are achieved, it would have external reliability.

One strength of the Baron-Cohen study is that the study is reliable. This is because the procedures of the study were standardised for everyone, all participants saw the same set of eyes during the eye tests, therefore we can be sure that the IV is causing the DV and also the study can be easily replicated. Moreover, this increases the validity of the study and we can generalise the results to all people with autism or Asperger syndrome.

Another strength is that a large sample was used, including 122 adults in group 2, 103 in group 3 adults using different sampling methods, therefore results can be generalised to a wider population.

A weakness of this study is that it is a highly controlled lab experiment that lacks ecological validity because the images were static and the whole faces were not shown; this is an artificial situation.

Level 3: 3 marks

Unfortunately, this answer can only be awarded a maximum of 4 marks as the requirements of the question are not met. The question asks the learner to compare Pozzulo *et al.* with one other study from the cognitive approach, but the answer uses Andrade for the similarity and Baron-Cohen for the difference. In these circumstances, marks would be awarded for the best answer. Both of these differences are Level 3 responses. However, they have used two different studies. Only the best can be credited in these instances, so 3 marks awarded overall.

> ★ **Exam tip**
>
> Before answering a question, take a moment to consider what is required. Underline or highlight any key words in the question. You will notice that certain words within a question are deliberately made bold. In question 1, this is to alert you that **two differences** are required and **one other study from the cognitive approach** needs to be compared.

Approaches, Issues, and Debates AS

Another weakness is that the study is unethical. The people with autism would have been upset because they found the task hard and would have psychological harm and long-term damage thinking they are less intelligent. This gives psychology a bad name and once people hear about the treatment of these participants, they wouldn't want to take part in research studies themselves, which makes it difficult for other psychologists to find a sample and any more research to take place.

> ★ **Exam tip**
>
> If you are required to write about reliability, you should consider whether a core study has standardised procedures. If this is the case, then it is a good opportunity to include a detailed strength. Please note, that standardisation is not a strength on its own, reliability is the strength, because it is standardised, and this can lead to replicability which provides a more in-depth answer. Also, as seen in the answer above, validity and the IV and DV do not relate to reliability.
>
> This example shows a detailed strength:
>
> Dement and Kleitman used a standardised procedure. For example, being attached to an EEG machine and being in a quiet, dark room. This increases the reliability of the study, and it makes it easier for someone else to replicate the study to test for comparable findings.

Activity or revision strategy

Activity: Rewrite the Dement and Kleitman example in the Exam tip but replace it with examples from other core studies. See how many studies you can do this for.

Level 3: 5 marks

All strengths and weaknesses are brief. The first paragraph identifies the named issue of reliability as a strength with an example of standardisation in the context of the study. However, there is then some confusion around reliability and validity = Brief strength.

The second paragraph also provides contextualised evidence from the study to support the identified strength. However, in order for it be a detailed strength the learner must explain why the results can be generalised and to whom = Brief strength.

As with the strengths, the third paragraph offers a brief evaluation point with evidence from the study. An explanation of the implications of a lack of ecological validity is needed = Brief weakness.

The fourth paragraph explains the ethical implications of the study as a weakness with a good example. There is also an attempt at making the weakness detailed, but the point being made is a little exaggerated = Brief weakness.

Worked example

Learning approach

1. Explain **one** similarity and **one** difference between the study by Saavedra and Silverman (button phobia) and **one** other study from the learning approach. (8 marks)

Candidate response:

One similarity between Saavedra and Silverman and Fagen et al. is that they both used principles of operant conditioning to change behaviour. In the Saavedra and Silverman study the boy was rewarded when his fear levels when touching the buttons dropped – his mother gave him positive reinforcement when he successfully completed the gradual exposure to buttons. Similarly, Fagen et al. used (secondary) positive reinforcement when training the elephants. The primary reinforcer used was chopped banana, and the secondary reinforcer was a short whistle blow. Essentially the elephants learnt a desired behaviour, the trunk wash, as they knew they would be rewarded with food they liked.

One difference between the studies is the sample used, both in terms of numbers and characteristics. The button phobia study used one human participant; a Hispanic boy who was nine years old. In contrast, Fagen et al. used more than one participant who were animals, specifically five female elephants from Nepal of which four were juveniles and one was in her 50s.

Level 4: 8 marks

This is an excellent answer and would comfortably be awarded full marks. Both the similarity and difference are clearly identified, then explained using accurate and detailed examples from both studies. The similarity and the difference are both Level 4, so the responses would be awarded 8 marks in total.

AS Approaches, Issues, and Debates

2. Evaluate the study by Fagen *et al.* (elephant learning) in terms of **two** strengths and **two** weaknesses. One of your evaluation points must be about the **controlling of variables**. (10 marks)

> **Key terms**
>
> Understanding these will help with the named issue in this essay:
>
> **Independent variable (IV):** The variable that is manipulated to see if there is a change on the DV.
>
> **Dependent variable (DV):** The variable that is measured and is impacted by the IV.
>
> **Extraneous variables:** Variables that need to be controlled to prevent them from affecting the DV.
>
> **Confounding variables:** Variables that have not been controlled that have affected the DV.
>
> **Cause and effect:** In experiments where variables are well controlled, we can assume that the IV causes the DV and it is not due to confounding variables.
>
> **Internal validity:** Results are due to the IV being manipulated in a cause-and-effect relationship and because of the controlling of extraneous variables.

One weakness of the study is the lack of control of confounding variables which may have influenced the elephants being able to learn to trunk wash or not, rather than the effectiveness of the positive reinforcement training that they had received. Therefore, reducing the internal validity of the results. For example, other animals in the neighbouring jungle, the presence of audiences of tourists including some who took photographs during the training sessions, and the proximity of the afternoon sessions to their evening meal – all of which were not controlled for and may have impaired the elephants' performance. While Elephant 5 had visual impairment and trunk weakness, which could explain why she didn't learn the trunk wash and thus making the results invalid.

Another weakness is the subjective analysis of the elephants' performance. The trainer had to decide whether the behaviour was "of high enough quality to be successful in a full trunk wash." This criteria was not very strict and should have included the time a position is held with exact positions such as the trunk at a certain height. Furthermore, the behaviours were not recorded and therefore could not be reviewed by other researchers. Therefore, the results may have been subject to experimenter bias making the results less accurate and based on a single individual's opinion of what a trunk wash is and lacks inter-rater reliability, as they are not compared to that of another 'rater'.

One strength of the study is that quantitative data was used which made the results easy to analyse. For example, we know the number of sessions that it took each elephant to learn the trunk wash. Elephant 1 passed her test after 30 training sessions with a mean duration of 12.42 minutes, while Elephant 2 passed her final test after only 25 training sessions and Elephants 3 and 4 did so after 35 sessions.

A final strength is that the research has high levels of ethics which has real-world application when training other elephants. Traditionally, elephant training is based on punishment and negative reinforcement and relies on aversive

> **Level 4: 8 marks**
>
> The first paragraph is a detailed evaluation of the named issue. A number of excellent examples are provided to support the weakness and understanding of how this impacts the results and the validity of the study = Detailed weakness.
>
> The second paragraph demonstrates a strong understanding of the research as well as terminology in relation to reliability, bias, and subjectivity = Detailed weakness.
>
> The third paragraph is a good evaluation of quantitative data with examples from the study. However, it could be improved by explaining why it made the results easy to analyse and why this is a strength such as what can be concluded from this data = Brief strength.
>
> The fourth paragraph is an excellent strength which is highly contextualised with some detailed evidence from research to support the argument being made = Detailed strength.
>
> Level 4: 8 marks out of 10 would be awarded as there are three detailed evaluation points and one brief evaluation point.

33

Approaches, Issues, and Debates **AS**

stimulus, such as pain or fear of pain, to elicit avoidance behaviours. In some areas of Southeast Asia, pain is inflicted on elephants using the sharp end of a whittled bamboo stick, this motivates them to perform certain actions to avoid the pain which is highly unethical. The success of this positive reinforcement training demonstrates that techniques that punish animals are not required and these reward-based strategies can improve animal welfare as well as keep safety, with animals still being trained as required.

Worked example

Social approach

1. Explain **two** similarities between the study by Milgram (obedience) and the study by Piliavin *et al.* (subway Samaritans). (8 marks)

Candidate response:

One similarity is that both studies were unethical. Milgram's participants thought they'd seriously injured another man, therefore causing psychological harm, while in Piliavin's study seeing someone collapse may have affected them mentally, especially if they had not helped, they may have felt guilty. Neither study had informed consent either, as Milgram's participants were not aware that they were in a study about obedience, while in Piliavin they didn't know they were taking part in a study at all, as they were just going about their normal lives.

Another similarity is that all of the participants were from the USA. Milgram only used 40 male participants who were all from the New Haven area, while Piliavin's large sample were from New York as they were on the subway there.

2. Evaluate the study by Perry *et al.* (personal space) in terms of **two** strengths and **two** weaknesses. One of your evaluation points must be about **experiments**. (10 marks)

This study lacks population validity. The sample consisted of 44 male undergraduate candidates all from the University of Haifa, with a small age range of 19 to 32. This limited sample makes results difficult to generalise to different populations, particularly females who we know are affected differently by oxytocin, for example it plays a part in lactation. Therefore, we cannot conclude from this study how oxytocin would affect interpersonal distance preferences in females.

However, a strength is that the sample size was quite large, so results can be generalised.

A second weakness is that because the study was a computerised experiment in which participants had to choose a preferred room based on the distances and angles between chairs, a table and a plant, which was repeated a week later, it lacks ecological validity. This experiment does not represent a real-life situation about personal space and people's preferred interpersonal distance from strangers. Because of this, participants may behave differently to what they would in a real-life situation, they may also demonstrate demand characteristics as they could work out the aims of the study. Therefore, the results from this experiment cannot be generalised.

Level 4: 7 marks

A very good response is provided here. The first similarity gives more than enough detail for 4 marks, with two examples from each study given as to why they are unethical. The second similarity is well explained, but lacks the detail required for full marks. Simply naming whereabouts in the USA the participants are from is not enough. A choice of an alternative similarity such as the use of controls, a confederate, or the collection of quantitative data would provide the opportunity for sufficiently detailed examples.

★ Exam tip

Before answering the questions on similarities and/or differences, don't just write about the first ones that come into your head. Think about different possibilities and whether you are able to provide sufficient detail in your evidence from the core studies to achieve maximum marks.

Approaches, Issues, and Debates

However, the experimental method is also a strength because of high levels of controls, standardisation, reliability, and replicability.

An additional strength of the study is that we can make some clear conclusions based on the large amount of quantitative data, which cannot be interpreted in a biased way in the study. Researchers found that although oxytocin decreased the mean distance from self to other in the high empathy group, from 26.11 cm to 23.29 cm. It had the opposite effect in the low empathy group, the preferred distance between self and other increased from 26.98 to 30.20 with oxytocin. This data was crucial in providing evidence to support the hypothesis.

Level 4: 7 marks

The first paragraph is a good example of an in-depth weakness. The evaluation point is identified and explained through examples from the study; by discussion about who it cannot be generalised to with reasons why, again in the context of the study = Detailed weakness.

The second paragraph unfortunately then only offers a strength that lacks detail relating to the sample, without any context = Strength not in context.

The third paragraph is a very detailed weakness of the named issue. It explains in the context of the experiment why it lacks ecological validity and why it can't be generalised. A second reason, that is demand characteristics, is also then effectively added to further elaborate on this point = Detailed weakness.

Although the fourth paragraph uses relevant terminology, much like the second paragraph it is brief and not in context, therefore limited credit can be given = Strength not in context.

However, the fifth paragraph does provide a detailed strength, making the majority of the points within this essay in-depth. The benefits of quantitative data are made clear with some impressive examples from the study of this type of data added to support the argument = Detailed strength.

This is a Level 4 answer and would be awarded 7 marks out of 10 as there are three detailed evaluation points but two points not in the context of the study.

★ Exam tip

When evaluating experiments, many candidates will state that a strength is that they are well controlled or standardised and a weakness is that they are conducted in an artificial environment. These statements are descriptive, factual statements which are not evaluative and therefore would not gain any marks. In order to be evaluative, you must make a judgement such as the results are not generalisable, they lack ecological validity or mundane realism, which are weaknesses. Or they are reliable and replicable or have high internal validity, which are strengths.

Key term

Mundane realism is the extent to which research reflects everyday life and experiences encountered in the environment will occur in the real world. Experiments often lack mundane realism.

Approaches, Issues, and Debates

Long answer questions raise your grade examples

> ## ↑ Raise your grade
>
> ### Biological approach
>
> 1. Explain **two** differences between the study by Hassett *et al.* (monkey toy preferences) and the study by Hölzel *et al.* (mindfulness and brain scans). (8 marks)
>
> The first difference between these studies relates to how long the research took. ✔ The Hölzel et al. study was longitudinal ✔, as participants took part in mindfulness practice over an 8-week period, for an average of 22 hours ✔ to see what impact it had on people's brains. Meanwhile, Hassett et al.'s research on monkeys took place over a shorter period of time ✔, with seven trials each lasting only 25 minutes ✔, to see what toy preferences they had during this short time.
>
> The second difference is that although both are biological studies, they investigated different assumptions from the biological approach. ✔ Hassett et al. studied the role of different hormones in males and females ✔, while Hölzel et al. looked at localisation of brain functions. ✔
>
> The first difference is well explained using both studies as examples – 4 marks. The second difference is explained clearly with both studies being used briefly – 3. Total marks = 7 out of 8.

> ## ↑ Raise your grade
>
> ### Cognitive approach
>
> 1. Explain **one** similarity and **one** difference between the study by Baron-Cohen *et al.* (eye tests) and the study by Andrade (doodling). (8 marks)
>
> A similarity is that both studies took place in a lab and used standardised procedures for all participants ✔ making them both reliable. ✔
>
> A difference is the sampling method used in the studies. ✔ Baron-Cohen used different ones, while Andrade only used opportunity. ✔
>
> The similarity is well explained but there is no study evidence – 2 marks. The difference is brief with an attempt at using both studies as examples – 2 marks. Total marks = 4 out of 8.
>
> **Activity or revision strategy**
>
> **Revision activity:** Can you remember the sample and sampling method used in every core study in five minutes? Start your clock or stopwatch and write them all down. Any that you can't remember, revise the study, then repeat the task again.

Key terms

Sampling method: The technique used to recruit participants for a study.

Opportunity sampling: Participants who are most easily available are selected to take part, also known as convenience sampling.

Random sampling: All members of the target population have an equal chance of being selected and are chosen using a random method such as a random number generator.

Volunteer sampling: Participants select themselves to take part, for example by responding to an advertisement.

AS Approaches, Issues, and Debates

⬆ Raise your grade

Learning approach

1. Evaluate the study by Bandura *et al.* (aggression) in terms of **two** strengths and **two** weaknesses. One of your evaluation points must be about the **experimental design**. (10 marks)

   Bandura's study is good because it has real-world application. ✔ We have learnt from the research that children imitate role models, so exposing them to violent films and video games will make them aggressive, so this should be avoided. This is helpful to parents and teachers and therefore the study is useful. ✔

   Another strength is the sample is large and includes different types of kids, therefore results can be generalised to all children across the world. We can therefore say it has population validity. ✘

   A weakness is that the experimental design is a lab study ✘, this is an artificial environment, participants may act differently to what they would in real life and show demand characteristics. ✔

   Another weakness is that this is unethical, there was no informed consent psychological harm was inflicted, and we can't be sure a debrief happened. ✔

   Weak evaluation which does not include the named issue. Addresses one strength in detail. Other evaluation points are brief and/or have no context. Level 2: 4 marks out of 10.

   > ★ **Exam tip**
   >
   > The 10-mark essay question in your exam will always ask you to include a named evaluation issue. You can choose to discuss this as either a strength or a limitation. No matter how good your answer is, if you fail to include this then you will only be able to achieve a maximum of 6 marks out of 10.

   > **Key terms**
   >
   > **Experimental design:** This is how participants are allocated to different conditions within an experiment. This should not be confused with an experimental method, such as laboratory, field, or natural experiments.
   >
   > **Repeated measures:** A type of experimental design in which all participants take part in all experimental conditions.
   >
   > **Independent measures:** A type of experimental design in which different participants take part in different experimental conditions.
   >
   > **Matched pairs:** A type of experimental design in which different participants take part in different experimental conditions, but they match on important characteristics.

   ### Activity or revision strategy

   Activity: Out of the 12 core studies, identify which of these are experiments. Then write a detailed strength or weakness about the experimental method in the context of the study. Identify the experimental design of the experiments and write a detailed strength or weakness about it in the context of the study.

37

Approaches, Issues, and Debates **AS**

⬆ Raise your grade

Social approach

1. Evaluate the study by Milgram (obedience) in terms of **two** strengths and **two** weaknesses. One of your evaluation points must be about **generalisability**. (10 marks)

   One strength of the study by Milgram is that it included both quantitative and qualitative data. ✔

   Quantitative data is easy to analyse, and comparisons can be made, for example 65 per cent of participants went to 450 volts and 100 per cent went to at least 300 volts, we can therefore conclude that obedience levels are high in the presence of a legitimate authority figure. *[CONT]*

   Qualitative data can help us understand reasons for behaviours. Comments by participants such as 'I'm sorry I can't do that to a man. I'll hurt his heart' provide further insight into the quantitative data in that the 'prods' from the experimenter made them continue. Participants didn't always willingly obey, however despite these concerns obedience levels were still high, which tells us that the pressure from the authority figure caused obedience rather than a dispositional explanation. ✔ *D*

   One weakness of Milgram's study is that it is unethical. Participants experienced psychological harm, they left the study in a different mental state to what they had been in before the study. ✔ Participants were very distressed because they believed they had seriously harmed or even killed another man, as a result they showed signs of anxiety with a number of them sweating, shaking, and groaning. *[CONT]* Over a third exhibited nervous laughing and one even had a violent seizure. The electrical shocks were however not real which highlights another ethical issue of deception, they were also deceived about the nature of the study as they were told it was about punishment on learning. ✔ *D*

   Another weakness is that the sample was biased ✔ – all 40 participants were male, and all were from New Haven. Results therefore cannot be generalised to females or people from different places, because these men may have unique characteristics that make them more likely to obey. *[CONT]* Furthermore, the participants were all volunteers, people who volunteer for psychology experiments are a certain type of person and by nature may be more obedient compared to those who are not interested in volunteering. Therefore, we can conclude that the study lacks population validity and the results are not generalisable to a wider population. ✔ *D*

   Finally, a second strength is that the study has good reliability, ✔ this is because of standardisation as all participants went through the same procedure. This started from the allocation of roles and the use of the same four prods if participants didn't want to continue, such as 'you must continue'. *[CONT]* The same voice recorded responses from the learner were also played such as pounding on the wall at 300 volts. This procedure was easy to replicate and made the result reliable. Milgram went on to carry out more studies using these procedures to compare results. ✔ *D*

   Very good evaluation including the named issue. The answer addresses both strengths and both weaknesses in detail. Selection of evidence is very thorough and effective. Level 5: 10 marks out of 10.

   ### Activity or revision strategy

   Revision strategy: Take a large a piece of paper, draw out the table on page 39 and add strengths and weaknesses to each of the most common evaluation points that you could use in a 10-mark essay. Alternatively, you may wish to use a separate piece of paper for each core study or separate paper for strengths and for weaknesses.

   > ★ **Exam tip**
   >
   > Although in some circumstances it might be difficult, you could include the same evaluation point as a strength and a weakness. For example, in Milgram's study there were several ethical problems, but it could also be argued that there were ethical strengths such as a full debriefing. It is also important to be aware that if more than one ethical issue is discussed as a weakness (or a strength) such as psychological harm and lack of informed consent then it will only be credited as a single weakness, rather than two separate weaknesses.

   Note: *[CONT]* means context: The strengths and weaknesses must be in the context of the study to be able to gain top marks.

   ✔ *D* means detailed: The evaluation point is elaborated on and a conclusion is made from this.

38

	Reliability	Validity	Generalisability	Ethics	Research method	Data (qualitative and/or quantitative)	Controlling of variables	Sample	Sampling technique	Experimental design
Dement and Kleitman										
Hassett et al.										
Hölzel et al.										
Andrade										
Baron-Cohen										
Pozzulo et al.										
Bandura et al.										
Fagen et al.										
Saavedra and Silverman										
Milgram										
Perry et al.										
Piliavin et al.										

2 Research Methods

Introduction to the paper

For Paper 2 the structure is as follows:

- This paper requires candidates to demonstrate their knowledge and skills of research methodology.
- There are two sections to this paper. For both sections, you should answer **all** questions.
- **Section A** includes questions based on (a) the research of selected core studies and (b) novel research scenarios. Within this section, questions are based on definitions, examples, and strengths and weaknesses of research methodology. This section is worth 46 marks.
- **Section B** includes a 'design a study' prompt worth 10 marks, followed by two questions about your design (worth 2 marks each). The 'design a study' prompt will give you a research technique to use to investigate a novel research idea. This section is worth 14 marks.
- The paper is marked out of 60 in total.

> ★ **Exam tip**
>
> This paper lasts for 90 minutes and there are 60 marks available. This equates to 1 mark every 1.5 minutes. Therefore, a 10-mark question should take you around 15 minutes to complete.

Knowledge check

In addition to the checklist for Paper 1, you also need to know the following extra research methods for your Paper 2 exam.

■ Red: I do not understand.   ■ Amber: I somewhat understand.
■ Green: I do understand.

Syllabus area	Red	Amber	Green
Describe the main features of a laboratory experiment, plus evaluation in terms of reliability, validity, and ethics			
Describe the main features of a field experiment, plus evaluation in terms of reliability, validity, and ethics			
Describe and evaluate independent measures as an experimental design			
Describe and evaluate matched pairs as an experimental design			
Describe and evaluate repeated measures as an experimental design			
Describe and evaluate, random allocation, counter balancing and order effects (both fatigue and practice)			
Evaluate the use of experimental and control conditions			
Apply knowledge of experiments to any given novel (new) research scenario			
Questionnaires: describe techniques (paper and pencil; online)			
Questionnaires: describe question format (open; closed)			
Evaluate the use of self-reports			

Describe interviews (unstructured/structured/semi-structured), including technique (telephone or face-to-face) and question format (open/closed)			
Apply knowledge of self-reports to any given novel (new) research scenario			
Case studies: describe the method, including a single participant/single unit of people, studied in depth/in detail			
Evaluate the case study method			
Apply knowledge of case studies to any given novel (new) research scenario			
Observations: describe main features, including overt/covert, participant/non-participant, structured/unstructured, naturalistic/controlled			
Evaluate the use of observations			
Apply knowledge of observations to any given novel (new) research scenario			
Correlations: describe positive and negative correlations, and strength of a correlation			
Identify and operationalise co-variables			
Evaluate the use of correlations, including lack of causality			
Apply knowledge of correlations to any given novel (new) research scenario			
Longitudinal studies: describe longitudinal experiments and longitudinal designs			
Evaluate the use of longitudinal studies			
Apply knowledge of longitudinal studies to any given novel (new) research scenario			
Describe and write an aim to a study			
Describe and recognise a null hypothesis and alternative hypothesis, including a directional (one-tailed) hypothesis and a non-directional (two-tailed) hypothesis			
Describe what is a dependent variable (DV) and an independent variable (IV) and a dependent variable (DV)			
Describe how a DV can be measured			
Identify IV and DV in studies, known and new			
Understand 'operational definition'			
Operationalise IVs and DVs			
Apply knowledge of variables to any given novel (new) research scenario			
Describe how variables can be controlled			
Understand the difference between controls and standardisation			
Understand uncontrolled variables, participant variables, and situational variables			
Apply knowledge of controlling variables to any given novel (new) research scenario			
Describe quantitative and qualitative data			
Describe subjective and objective data			
Evaluation types of data			
Apply knowledge of types of data to any given novel (new) research scenario			

Research Methods — AS

Describe sample and population			
Describe sampling techniques: opportunity, volunteer (self-selecting) and random.			
Evaluate sampling techniques: opportunity, random, and volunteer (self-selecting). This must include generalisations			
Apply knowledge of sampling techniques to any given novel (new) research scenario			
Describe ethical guidelines for humans: minimising harm, valid consent (and informed consent), privacy confidentiality, debriefing, right to withdraw, lack of deception			
Describe ethical guidelines for the use of animals: minimising harm, replacement, species, numbers, pain (suffering and distress), housing, reward, deprivation, use of aversive stimuli			
Evaluate studies based on ethical guidelines			
Apply knowledge of ethical guidelines to any given novel (new) research scenario			
Describe validity, including ecological			
Evaluate studies on validity: subjectivity and objectivity, demand characteristics, generalisability			
Apply knowledge of validity to any given novel (new) research scenario			
Describe types of reliability: inter-rater, inter-observer, test–retest			
Evaluate studies on reliability			
Apply knowledge of reliability to any given novel (new) research scenario			
Understand replicability, including when planning studies			
Present and interpret data from tables			
Understand the term 'measure of central tendency'			
Name, recognise, and know how to calculate the mode, the median, and the mean			
Understand the term 'measure of spread'			
Name, recognise, and know how to calculate range			
Recognise, interpret, and understand the standard deviation			
Name, recognise, draw, and change bar charts, histograms, and scatter graphs			

Activity or revision strategy

Activity: Using the Knowledge checklist, on a separate paper (like the example in the table) write down the top 10 concepts that are the most challenging for you (marked as 'red' on the checklist). For each, write down your current understanding of the concept. Then go through your notes and the textbook, and write down your revised knowledge of the concept. You can continue with this for the 'amber' concepts you identified from the checklist as well. Included in the table are a few concepts that candidates often find to be challenging.

'Red' challenging subject	Current knowledge	Revised knowledge
How to operationalise an IV and DV		
How to control variables		
Validity vs. reliability		
Standard deviation		
Measure of speed		
Hypotheses – directional vs. non-directional		

Section A

Section A focuses on (a) the research methodology of a few selected core studies (usually 4–5 of the 12), (b) applying research methodology to novel research scenarios, and (c) defining and discussing strengths and weaknesses of research methodology in general. Marks available will range from 1 to 6.

Activity or revision strategy

Activity: Using Chapter 1 of the textbook, create flashcards for the definitions, strengths, and weaknesses of the terminology. You can add to this by creating your own questions that you can then answer and score yourself to check your understanding.

Short answer questions worked examples

Here are five examples of short answer questions for this paper. There are two sets of candidate responses for each question for you to compare. There is also detailed commentary related to each of the responses given by the candidates.

★ Exam tip

There are lines in the answer booklet for you to write your answer on. You should be able to fit your response to earn full marks for each question in this space. If you need more space, use an extension booklet, and make sure to note 'continued' in your original answer booklet and then number the extension booklet with the same question number you are continuing to answer.

Worked example

1. From the study by Milgram (obedience):
   (a) Describe the sampling technique used to recruit participants in this study. (2 marks)

Candidate A:

Milgram used a sample of recruited participants so he could conduct the study and get the results he was looking for.

0 marks

The question requires the identification of the type of sampling (volunteer) and how it was accomplished in the study (via newspaper adverts and direct mailings). The candidate does not provide either aspect.

Candidate B:

A volunteer sample was obtained through a newspaper advert and direct postal mailings.

(b) Explain **one** strength of the sampling technique you described in part (a). (2 marks)

Key term

Describe means to provide the main features of a particular topic.

2 marks

This response properly identifies the use of a volunteer sample (1 mark) and specifies the newspaper advertisement and the use of direct-mail solicitation (1 mark).

Research Methods — AS

Candidate A:
A strength of the sample was that it was 40 males and this makes the data reliable because they are all the same.

> **0 marks**
> The question requires a strength of the volunteer sample, either in general or applied to the Milgram study. The candidate instead states the makeup of the participants.

Candidate B:
When using a volunteer sample, experimenters can advertise for specific qualities of participants, such as certain ages, occupations, or similar. In the case of the Milgram study, he specified the age range of 20–50 years old and males from jobs such as businessmen and factory workers.

2. Describe what is meant by a 'measure of central tendency'. (2 marks)

Candidate A:
This is when we can see what the typical score would be from a set of data.

Candidate B:
Central tendency can be looked at using the mean, mode, median, and other numerical ways in which data can be displayed. The central tendency tells us how close the data is to a typical, centered score when all the data is clustered and represented together.

> **2 marks**
> The response begins with describing ways to measure central tendency rather than describing what it is, as the question requires. This portion of the response does not earn any marks. However, the next part of the response does earn 1 mark for the 'typical score' and 1 mark for the 'data clustered'.

3. From the study by Hölzel *et al.* (mindfulness and brain scans):

   (a) Explain the experimental design used in this study. (2 marks)

Candidate A:
The study used an independent measures design because the participants were only in one group.

Candidate B:
In the Hölzel study, an independent measures design was implemented with two distinct groups (mindfulness and control) who only experienced one level of the IV during the procedure.

> **2 marks**
> This response would earn both marks as it properly identifies the independent measures design (1 mark) and specifies the two possible groups (1 mark).

★ **Exam tip**
Provide an example and/or additional detail when asked a strength or weakness question.

2 marks
The response addresses a general strength of a volunteer sample (looking for specific characteristics) (1 mark) and properly applies this with valid examples from the Milgram study (1 mark).

1 mark
This would earn 1 mark as it identifies knowledge of the typical score in a cluster of data.

★ **Exam tip**
It is not necessary to 'show off' your content knowledge. Just answer the question asked and continue.

1 mark
The response properly identifies the type of experimental design (independent groups) for 1 mark, but does not include additional details from the study, such as the different groups.

★ **Exam tip**
Look at how many marks are available for each question to ensure that you are giving a response that has enough detail to be awarded the maximum marks.

(b) Explain **one** weakness of using this type of experimental design. (2 marks)

Candidate A:

Researchers need more participants.

> **1 mark**
> This response earns 1 mark as it properly identifies a weakness of an independent measures design (but does not elaborate for a second mark).

Candidate B:

One weakness of Hölzel using this design is that it may not account for individual differences of the participants within each group.

> **1 mark**
> This response earns 1 mark as it properly identifies a weakness of an independent measures design (but does not elaborate for a second mark).

4. From the study by Pozzulo *et al.* (line-ups):

   (a) Describe how qualitative data was collected in the study. (2 marks)

Candidate A:

Quantitative data was collected by the number of correct identifications in the line-up presentation. Results showed that the adults performed better on these tasks, such as 70 per cent vs 45 per cent in correctly rejecting the human faces.

> **0 marks**
> No marks can be awarded as the response describes quantitative content instead of qualitative content.

Candidate B:

Qualitative data was collected by the participants answering open-ended questions about what they watched.

   (b) Suggest **one** strength of collecting qualitative data in this study. (2 marks)

Candidate A:

Quantitative data collection is seen as being more 'scientific' and allows for an easier comparison of data, such as the percentages between the adults and children in the study.

Key term

Explain means to describe with additional details and tell the examiner 'why it is this'.

★ Exam tip

It is common to answer about the wrong type of data; make sure to double check before writing your answer.

1 mark

This response would earn 1 mark as it identifies one way that qualitative data was collected but does not earn the second mark as there is no elaboration on the open-ended questions.

0 marks

No marks can be awarded as the response describes quantitative content instead of qualitative content.

Candidate B:

A strength of qualitative data in this study is that it could allow the child participants to explain their response in their own words, rather than having to respond to specific pre-set questions that may be misleading.

> **2 marks**
>
> The candidate provides a strength of qualitative data in responding with their own words (1 mark) and earns an additional 1 mark for the elaboration of such open-ended questions not being misleading. Although this last part could be a little clearer and/or more detailed, it is sufficient to understand the point that the candidate is trying to make.

> ★ **Exam tip**
>
> In this question type, the noted strength must be accurate and properly applied to the named study for full marks.

> **Key term**
>
> **Suggest** means to apply the named topic to the content of the question by using the knowledge you have.

5. From the study by Perry *et al.* (personal space):

   Describe **two** self-reports that were used in this study. (4 marks)

Candidate A:

One self-report in the study was the comfortable interpersonal distance (CID) scale; the person had to say when they wanted the figure to stop so they would still be comfortable. Another self-report was when the participants were part of the oxytocin or placebo condition that was counterbalanced and double-blind.

> **2 marks**
>
> The candidate properly identified a self-report method in the study (CID) for 1 mark and provided a brief description to earn a second mark for this self-report. However, the administration of the oxytocin or placebo is not a self-report technique itself and no marks can be awarded for this portion of the response.

Candidate B:

The IRI was used as a self-report data collection technique where participants completed the online version and received an overall empathy score based on the four components of the questionnaire. Afterwards, the participants completed the CID and the room choosing activity.

> **3 marks**
>
> The candidate properly identifies one self-report method (IRI) for 1 mark and provides additional details of the questionnaire (1 mark). The candidate then properly identifies another self-report method (CID) for 1 mark but does not provide details about this self-report method.

Activity or revision strategy

Activity: Answer each of these questions in less than five minutes. Refer to the previous commentary about how to achieve full marks.

- Explain how inter-rater reliability was used in the study by Bandura *et al.* (aggression) to pre-rate the children on their level of aggression before the study took place. (4 marks)

- Explain how quantitative data and qualitative data was collected in the study by Dement and Kleitman (sleep and dreams). (4 marks)

- Explain the difference between directional and non-directional hypotheses. (4 marks)

Short answer questions raise your grade examples

Here are five examples of short answer questions for this paper, with a candidate's responses. The candidate's responses have check marks/ticks (✔) showing where the marks were awarded. There is also a brief commentary related to each of the responses given.

Raise your grade

1. (a) Outline what is meant by the ethical guideline of 'debriefing'. (2 marks)

Debriefing is when the participant is informed of any information that was not made known before going through the study ✔, *such as any use of deception or what the real aim of the study was.* ✔

The definition of debriefing is sufficient and the example of what may be revealed helps to show understanding of the concept. It is therefore awarded 2 marks.

(b) Explain how 'debriefing' was completed in the study by Milgram. (2 marks)

In the Milgram study, participants were told that they really were not shocking anybody ✔, *and the purpose was to look at obedience to an authority figure.* ✔ *They also met the stooge who was part of the experiment.*

This response properly applies two aspects of debriefing to the Milgram study. It is therefore awarded 2 marks.

Activity or revision strategy

Activity: Think of how the ethical issue of 'deception' can be applied to other core studies. As shown in 1(b) here, write down how deception can be applied to two other studies of your choice.

2. Describe what is meant by a 'positive correlation', using any example. (2 marks)

A positive correlation is when one variable influences another variable to go the same way (both increasing or both decreasing). ✔ *For example, when the temperature increases, the number of people drinking cold drinks also increases.* ✔

The response describes the correlation with identifying that the variables both increase or both decrease together. The provided example demonstrates understanding of the concept. It is therefore awarded 2 marks.

★ Exam tip

If a question notes that you can use any example, either refer to an example from a core study or a generic example that would be universally understood.

Activity or revision strategy

Activity: Think of two key studies that have positive correlations, such as Baron-Cohen *et al.* (eyes test). Write down what the positive correlation was in each study. Make sure to use terminology and details.

Activity or revision strategy

Activity: Copy the following table and add your own definitions and examples from these research aspects of the syllabus. Try to complete this first without notes or the use of the text. If needed, go back and add to the chart using these resources.

Term	Your own definition	Your own example
Positive correlation		
Negative correlation		
Directional (one-tailed) hypothesis		
Non-directional (two-tailed) hypothesis		
Null hypothesis		

Research Methods AS

3. From the study by Baron-Cohen *et al.* (eyes test):

   (a) Describe **one** way that quantitative data was collected in this study. (2 marks)

   Quantitative data was collected via the number of correct target words (out of 36) ✔ for each participant when completing the paper-and-pencil R-ET. ✔ This data was used for comparisons among the four groups of participants.

   This response provides how the data was collected with additional details for both marks.

   (b) Suggest **one** weakness of collecting quantitative data in this study. (2 marks)

   A weakness of collecting quantitative data is it does not provide the 'full picture' ✔ of why the data was the way that it was.

   This response earns a 'benefit of the doubt' (BOD) mark, but does not elaborate or provide an example to earn the second mark. It is therefore awarded 1 mark. Note: BOD is used to indicate material considered by the Examiner and judged to be more correct than incorrect.

   ### Activity or revision strategy

   Activity: The answer in question 3 (b) received a 'BOD' mark as it was vague. Write your own answer that would earn both marks.

4. (a) Describe what is meant by the ethical guideline of 'housing', in relation to animals. (2 marks)

   When housing animals, the enclosure (cage) should not be overpopulated ✔ to avoid problems.

   The notion of avoiding crowding is marked, but the 'problems' are not identified or elaborated upon. This response therefore gets 1 mark.

   (b) Explain why the ethical guideline of 'housing' was **not** broken in the study by Fagen *et al.* (elephant learning). (2 marks)

   The elephants were allowed to graze in parts of the jungle with the handler or were leg-chained with room to move when in the enclosure. ✔ This setup could reduce housing problems and stress. ✔

   The response identifies housing conditions and links to the reduction of stress. It is therefore awarded 2 marks.

5. From the study by Perry *et al.* (personal space), describe **two** of the independent variables. (4 marks)

   One IV was the condition to which the participants were assigned, ✔ either the oxytocin or the placebo ✔ (that was counterbalanced). Another IV was in the CID experiment where the approaching figure ✔ was a person or a ball.

   The first IV is clearly explained with details but the second IV lacks additional details. This response is therefore awarded 3 marks.

   This candidate may earn a total of 15 marks out of 18.

Activity or revision strategy

Activity: Think about how you can use the examples in the raise your grade box to apply data collection techniques to each one. Based on these examples, have a go at making five of your own questions and answering each one.

48

AS Research Methods

6-mark questions worked examples

Here are two examples of 6-mark questions for this paper. There are two sets of candidate responses for each question for you to compare. There is also detailed commentary related to each of the responses given by the candidates.

Worked example

1. Describe **two** types of self-reports, using any examples. (6 marks)

Candidate A:

One self-report is when participants answer questions about a particular topic, such as their favourite foods. Another self-report is when participants discuss what they were thinking about during an interview.

> **2 marks**
> The first mark is awarded for a general description of self-reports and the second mark is awarded for identifying an interview as a form of self-report.

Candidate B:

Interviews are a style of self-report when the researchers directly ask participants about a certain topic, such as viewing a funny movie and then asking what they found to be funny and not funny and why they thought that way. Another self-report is a survey where the researcher can use emails or flyers to gather lots of information in a fast manner about a subject, such as sending emails to candidates at university, asking them to complete three questions about housing on campus. Both interviews and surveys allow participants to provide their opinions, but sometimes that data may be unreliable as participants can lie due to demand characteristics.

2. Describe directional (one-tailed) and non-directional (two-tailed) hypotheses, using any examples. (6 marks)

Candidate A:

A directional hypothesis states that there will be one-direction with the results, like one condition working better than a different condition. A non-directional hypothesis predicts that all conditions will be the same.

Candidate B:

A one-tailed hypothesis predicts a significant difference and direction within the results of a study. For example, if an experimenter was looking to see if sitting in the front, middle, or back of the classroom influences test scores, predicting that 'learners who sit in the front of the class will score higher on the test than others' indicates that where a learner sits in the class will influence the results and that the 'front condition' will be the most influential when looking at test scores. In comparison, a two-tailed hypothesis predicts that there will be a difference among the conditions and results. However, it does not predict one condition to have more influence than another. For example, 'there will be a difference in test scores between those who sit in the front, middle, and back of the classroom' predicts that the results will be influenced by where the learner sits, but does not predict which location would have a greater difference in scores.

★ **Exam tip**
Make sure to provide enough content for 6-mark questions. That is roughly a paragraph in coverage rather than a two-line response.

> **5 marks**
> The first mark is for identifying the interview, the second mark for a brief description of the interview, the third mark for identifying a survey, the fourth mark for general description of a survey, and the fifth mark for a survey example.

> **1 mark**
> This would receive a 'generous' mark for the directional hypothesis notion that one variable will have more influence than another variable. The non-directional hypothesis content is incorrect, receiving no marks.

> **6 marks**
> This is an excellent response that would earn the full marks. For both hypotheses noted, there is a clear definition and well-defined examples that demonstrate a solid understanding.

Research Methods AS

Activity or revision strategy

Activity: Answer each of these questions in under 10 minutes. Refer to the previous commentary about how to achieve full marks.

- Describe **two** types of interviews, using any examples. (6 marks)
- Describe **two** types of observation, using any examples. (6 marks)
- Describe positive and negative correlations, using any examples. (6 marks)
- Describe independent groups and repeated measures designs, using any examples. (6 marks)
- Describe **two** types of validity, using any examples. (6 marks)

6-mark questions raise your grade examples

Here are two examples of 6-mark questions for this paper, with two candidate responses. The candidate responses have check marks (✔) showing where the marks were awarded. There is also a brief commentary related to each of the responses given.

↑ Raise your grade

1. Describe **two** types of experiments, using any examples. (6 marks)

   Candidate A:

   One style of experiment is in a laboratory ✔ and another is outside of the laboratory. These are the same in that they both have an IV and DV. ✔

   The response identifies a laboratory study as one type of experiment and notes the presence of an IV and a DV. This response therefore is awarded 2 marks.

   Candidate B:

   A lab experiment takes place in a controlled setting ✔ where the researcher manipulates an IV and measures a DV. ✔ For example, in the study by Perry on interpersonal space and empathy, the researchers were able to manipulate whether the participants received oxytocin or a placebo and the setup of the digital rooms for preference. ✔ A field study takes place outside of the lab, such as in a subway, with less control of variables ✔ and still manipulates an IV and measures a DV. ✔ For example, the Piliavin study in the subway system would have stooges act drunk or ill and see how many people would help when they fell on purpose. ✔

   The response clearly identifies two types of experiments, provides features of each, and provides clear examples from core studies. This response is therefore awarded all 6 marks.

2. Describe the mean and the median, using any examples. (6 marks)

   Candidate A:

   Both the mean and the median collect data in a study. The mean is the average of all the data combined ✔ and the median in the score that repeats the most.

   One mark is awarded for a basic description of the mean in data collection.

AS Research Methods

Activity or revision strategy

Activity: Draw out the following table and add your definitions, examples, and (as applicable) ways to calculate the following mathematical concepts of the syllabus. Try to complete this first without notes or the use of the text. If needed, go back and add to the chart using these resources.

Term	Own definition	Own worked example (How to calculate)
Measures of central tendency		
Mean		
Mode		
Median		
Range		
Standard deviation		

Candidate B:

The mean is the arithmetic average of the data set. ✔ For example, if a candidate takes four quizzes (with scores of 80, 85, 90, 95), the mean would be calculated by adding the scores together (350) and dividing by 4 to give an average quiz score of 87.5. ✔✔ The median is the middle score after ranking all the data. ✔ For example, if quiz scores were 89, 82, 85, 87, and 80, the median would be 85, the score in the middle when ranked in order (80, 82, 85, 87, 89). ✔✔

Full marks are given as there are sufficient descriptions of both ideas, with clear examples including demonstrating knowledge of how each idea is calculated.

Exam style questions

1. Describe reliability and validity, using any examples. (6 marks)
2. Describe two types of experimental design, using any examples. (6 marks)

Application question worked examples

Here are three examples of candidate responses (one per series of application questions). There is a detailed commentary related to each of the responses given by the candidates.

Worked example

Example 1: 10 out of 12 marks are awarded

1. Karolina is conducting a laboratory experiment to investigate whether the colour a room is painted has an effect on our personal space. She plans to use a group of candidates from her university as participants.

    (a) Suggest **one** way that Karolina can measure personal space in her study. (2 marks)

Candidate response:

She could measure personal space by using different rooms with different paint colours (such as one white, one beige, and one dark grey) with checkered-coloured tiles on the floor in each room. She would be able to measure the distance in the number of tiles between where the participants are standing in each coloured room.

2 marks
This would earn both marks as it provides a clear suggestion leading to quantitative data.

51

Research Methods — AS

(b) Suggest **one** way that the independent variable can be operationalised by Karolina. (1 mark)

Candidate response:

The IV is the colour of the room that the participants are standing in, either white (control), beige, or dark grey.

> **1 mark**
> This would earn the mark as a clear, detailed description is provided.

(c) (i) Explain **one** ethical problem with Karolina's study. (2 marks)

Candidate response:

One ethical drawback is the use of deception in her study. This would be needed though to limit demand characteristics from participants by not knowing the true aim of the study.

> **2 marks**
> This response identifies deception as an ethical issue and provides a valid reason for the deception.

(ii) Suggest **one** way that Karolina can overcome the ethical problem explained in part (c) (i). (2 marks)

Candidate response:

At the end of the study, participants could be debriefed and told the true aim of the study (a potential correlation between personal space and room paint colour). She could also offer participants the chance to ask questions about the study.

> **2 marks**
> This response clearly identifies debriefing as an answer to an ethical problem and provides two clear ways to debrief the participants.

(d) Karolina wanted to use random sampling to recruit her participants. However, she thinks it might be too time consuming.

Suggest *one* other technique that Karolina could use to recruit her participants. (3 marks)

Candidate response:

Another way to recruit participants would be by using a self-selecting sample. She would go to different classrooms, stand in the corner, and see where the candidates are sitting.

> **1 mark**
> This response identifies a volunteer sample as an alternative, but the following details do not support this type of sample noted. The candidate needs to describe how the process would be completed for up to 2 more marks for this type of question.

(e) Suggest **one** reason why Karolina should use a repeated measures design rather than an independent measures design in her study. (2 marks)

Candidate response:

If she uses a repeated measures design, she would need less participants (as they act as their own control) and this could also limit participant variables.

> **2 marks**
> This response provides a strength of a repeated measures design and details a clear strength of using this design.

Example 2: 3 out of 12 marks awarded

2. Matteo is planning to investigate the toy choices of boys and girls when playing in a nursery. He is thinking about using a structured observation.

   (a) Explain **one** reason why Matteo should use a structured observation for his study. (2 marks)

Candidate response:

A structured observation is where the researcher has a pre-set checklist of behaviour to 'check-off' each time it happens.

> **0 marks**
> This response makes a classic error where the candidate defines the topic rather than discussing a strength of the topic.

   (b) Matteo also wants to be a participant observer. Suggest how Matteo could be a participant observer in his study. (2 marks)

Candidate response:
He could ask the participants to collect the data for him since the participants are already there, making it easier for the data collection.

0 marks
This demonstrates a common misunderstanding of what a participant observation is.

(c) Suggest **two** behaviour categories that Matteo could use in his observation. (4 marks)

Candidate response:
He could use the categories of 'throwing' and 'punching' during the observation of the kids.

2 marks
The response would earn 2 marks for identifying two types of behaviours that he could witness.

(d) Explain how Matteo could test the reliability of his observations. (3 marks)

Candidate response:
He could ask the kids why they played with the toys that they did.

0 marks
The response would not be awarded marks as it does not address reliability.

(e) Explain **one** ethical guideline that Matteo should ensure is **not** broken during his observations. (2 marks)

Candidate response:
He should make sure that no one is harmed in the study.

1 mark
This response identifies 'harm' as the ethical guideline not to be broken, but the response does not elaborate on this idea.

Activity or revision strategy

Activity: Example 2 earned low marks (3 of 12). Answer each of the questions in example 2 with answers that would earn higher marks. Refer to the previous commentary about how to achieve full marks.

Example 3: 9 out of 12 marks awarded

3. Andrie is planning a study to investigate people's attitudes towards healthy eating. He plans to use a questionnaire.

    (a) Suggest **one** question that Andrie could use to collect quantitative data. (1 mark)

Candidate response:
"How many days a week would you say that you eat healthy?"

1 mark
This response provides a relevant question on the topic that can be quantified.

(b) Andrie wants to use a series of questions that generate quantitative data so every participant can be given a total score.

   (i) Explain how Andrie would calculate the median total score for his sample of participants. (2 marks)

Candidate response:
He could take all the data from the participants and rank them in order. If it is an odd number of scores he would use the middle score and if it is an even number of scores, he would use the average of the two scores that are most in the middle.

2 marks
This is a great response. It identifies how to calculate the median, both with an odd and even number of scores.

   (ii) Andrie wants to compare the attitudes of people from different countries. Draw a bar chart to show how Andrie could compare the total questionnaire scores of people from different countries. (4 marks)

Research Methods AS

Candidate response:

Number of times per week participants eat healthy meals

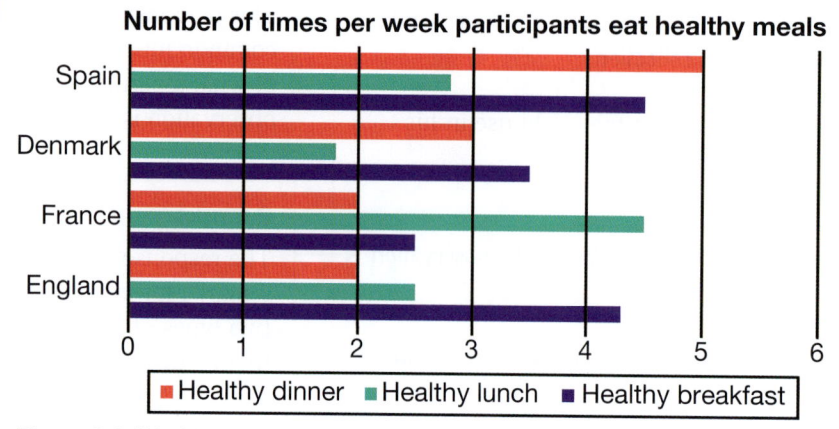

Spain	Healthy dinner ~5, Healthy lunch ~3, Healthy breakfast ~4.5
Denmark	Healthy dinner ~3, Healthy lunch ~2, Healthy breakfast ~3.5
France	Healthy dinner ~2, Healthy lunch ~4.5, Healthy breakfast ~2.5
England	Healthy dinner ~2, Healthy lunch ~2.5, Healthy breakfast ~4.5

■ Healthy dinner ■ Healthy lunch ■ Healthy breakfast

Figure 2.1: Weekly healthy eating during the day, by country

4 marks
The bar chart in Figure 2.1 identifies how many times per week participants from different countries eat a healthy breakfast, lunch, and dinner.

(c) Andrie decides to use an online questionnaire for his study.

(i) Suggest **one** sampling technique Andrie can use to recruit participants to his study. (1 mark)

Candidate response:
One technique would be to use a magazine advert asking for participants to show up at his office for the interview.

1 mark
The notion of a volunteer sample being recruited via the magazine advert earns a mark here.

(ii) Explain **one** strength of using the sampling technique you suggested in question part (c)(i). (2 marks)

Candidate response:
A strength is he can obtain a sample quickly based on who is already in the area.

0 marks
The response does not relate to a strength of a volunteer sample mentioned in part (c)(i)

(iii) Explain **one** way that Andrie can debrief the participants of this online questionnaire study. (2 marks)

Candidate response:
After they complete it, he can give them a summary sheet of what the study was about and what they found.

1 mark
Although this response is not specific, it demonstrates knowledge of the debriefing procedure overall.

Activity or revision strategy

Revision strategy: Example 3 earned many of the available marks (9 of 12). For the questions that did not earn full marks, 3(c) (i–iii), think of how you would approach these questions to earn full marks instead.

Activity or revision strategy

Revision strategy: The bar chart displayed is one technique used to plot data. Think of how you could apply the use of a scattergraph or a histogram if prompted in the exam. You can refer to Chapter 1 of the textbook for additional details on how to plot data.

AS Research Methods

Activity or revision strategy

Activity: Copy the following table and add in your explanations of when each is best to be used and your own example of these visual representations of plotting data from the syllabus. Try to complete this first without notes or the use of the text. If needed, go back and add to the chart using these resources.

Term	Best to use when…	Your own visual example
Bar chart		
Histogram		
Scattergraph		

Application question raise your grade examples

Here are two examples of application questions for this paper, with candidate responses. The candidate responses have check marks (✔) showing where the marks were awarded. There is also a brief commentary related to each of the responses given.

↑ Raise your grade

Example 1

1. Samuel is conducting a study to investigate whether there is a correlation between how many monkeys are in a family troop and the time in which they can solve a new puzzle with a food reward. He has access to monkeys living in a zoo.

   (a) Suggest **one** new puzzle with a food reward that Samuel could use in this study. (2 marks)

   One could be where the monkeys have to work together to hold open two sides of a box at the same time ✔ *(instead of one like other puzzles) in order to receive the reward.* ✔

   Both marks awarded with a clear hypothetical puzzle being identified, including how it would work.

Activity or revision strategy

Revision strategy: Think about a different puzzle that you could suggest to answer question 1(a). Remember your suggestion must be clear and relevant to earn marks.

   (b) Samuel believes that he will find a negative correlation. Explain what the results would be if Samuel found a negative correlation. (2 marks)

   Results would indicate a difference in the number of monkeys in a troop and the speed to solve the puzzle. One example is that the more monkeys there are in a troop, the less time is needed. ✔

   This earns 1 mark (a 'benefit of the doubt' (BOD) mark) with the notion of the variables going in opposite directions.

(c) Samuel wants to make sure that he is following ethical guidelines in relation to animals.

For each of the ethical guidelines in relation to the animals below, explain how Samuel can make sure he follows each one:

(i) Housing (2 marks)

He can make sure that the housing is proper for the monkeys.

This is a generic response that would not earn any marks.

(ii) Minimising harm (2 marks)

He can make sure that the monkeys could not be hurt from the puzzle ✔ *(such as not having sharp pieces) and that they can solve it so they do not become upset and stressed.* ✔

The response earns the 2 marks with the implication of avoiding physical harm and psychological distress.

Activity or revision strategy

Activity: Similar to question 1(c) on housing and harm, try answering for the animal guidelines of: (a) replacement, (b) numbers, and (c) rewards.

2. Dr. Boag is interested in how friendship groups change over time. She wants to conduct a longitudinal study to investigate this and plans for it to last for 10 years.

(a) Suggest **one** way in which Dr. Boag can recruit participants for her study. (3 marks)

Dr. Boag could use a sample by placing an advert around campuses and via candidate email from local universities. ✔ *She could specify that the friendship would have to have a minimum of two years* ✔ *already and that the friendship group would have to be part of a university organisation (like the medical club, fraternity, or sports club).* ✔ *She could also offer a monetary incentive for being part of the study.*

This response would be awarded 3 marks. Great detail is provided with the use of how/where to place an advert and identifying parameters of ideal participants and example organisations.

(b) Suggest **two** ways in which information/data can be collected during her study. (4 marks)

One way to collect data would be to use a survey ✔ *that can be based on quantitative data, such as how many times per week you talk to a friend or how many times a year you see them after graduation.* ✔ *This would enable faster data collection and easier numerical values to compare over time. Another way to collect data would be to use interviews* ✔ *with questions about their friendship.*

This would be awarded 3 marks. Two ways to collect data are suggested; survey with a sample question provides details, but the interview suggestion does not provide further material for the additional mark.

(c) Suggest **one** factor that might affect the validity of the findings over this study. (2 marks)

If she were to use surveys or interviews, the participants may not tell the truth ✔ *in their responses.*

This would be awarded 1 mark. A general mention of not telling the truth in self-reports is noted but does not provide additional details of examples to gain full marks.

AS Research Methods

> **Activity or revision strategy**
>
> **Revision strategy:** For questions 2(b) and 2(c), think of two data collection techniques you would suggest and how the validity may be impacted using such techniques.

Example 2

1. Marek is planning a questionnaire study to investigate people's attitudes to recycling glass. He also wants to measure how often people actually recycle glass. He wants to conduct the study online.

   (a) Suggest **one** closed question that Marek could use in his questionnaire. (2 marks)

   Do you think that recycling glass helps to lower prices of good? ✔✔ Yes or No

   This would be awarded 2 marks. The question is closed-ended (with response categories) and relevant to the named topic.

   (b) Suggest **one** open-ended question that Marek could use in this questionnaire. (1 mark)

   What are your thoughts on recycling and the environment? ✔

   The question is open-ended and relevant to the named topic. This response is therefore awarded 1 mark.

   > **Activity or revision strategy**
   >
   > **Activity:** For exam questions that require you to suggest open and/or closed questions for interviews and questionnaires, your response must be relevant to the situation to earn marks. Using the example of Marek's questionnaire on people's attitudes to recycling glass, write down three of your own closed questions and three of your own open-ended questions as good practice in developing your own questions.

   (c) Suggest **two** disadvantages of using an online questionnaire for his study, rather than a paper and pencil questionnaire. (4 marks)

   One issue could be the online edition of the survey may not allow the participant to go back to a question. Also, the researcher is not present, so if the participant has a question, they could not receive clarification at that time. ✔ This could lead to the misunderstanding of a question and the data from the individual could be inaccurate as a result. ✔

   The first part of this response is unclear by what is meant by being able to go back to a question, earning 0 marks. The second part clearly identifies a possible problem and then further details a potential disadvantage of the data collection. Total 2 marks.

   (d) Suggest **one** way that Marek can test the reliability of his questionnaire. (2 marks)

   He could have two similar questions on the same topic and see if the response is the same. ✔

   A basic knowledge of a way of testing for reliability is noted for the 1 mark earned.

Research Methods   AS

2. Andy is conducting a study to investigate whether having a fragrance/smell in a room makes workers cope better while completing a difficult task. He wants to use a laboratory experiment as his research method.

   (a) Identify the control group in this study. (1 mark)

   The group that does not have a smell in the room ✔ during the study.

   This response properly identifies the control group that does not receive a condition of the IV, earning 1 mark.

   (b) Explain **one** reason why a control group is useful in this study. (2 marks)

   A control group would be needed as a comparison point between those who receive a manipulation of the IV and those who do not. ✔

   One mark is awarded for a general description for the purpose of the control group (it does not relate back to the study for the second mark).

   (c) Suggest **one** way that Andy can operationalise the independent variable in this study. (2 marks)

   The IV can be defined if the room has a smell or not.

   The response identifies the IV rather than operationalising the IV with details that are specific to the prompt; the candidate does not provide sample fragrances, so no marks are awarded.

   ### Activity or revision strategy

   Activity: Questions that require the operationalisation of the IV or DV can be quite challenging for some candidates. Using the scenario in question 2 – Andy conducting an investigation into fragrance and completing tasks – write down how you would operationalise (a) the IV and (b) the DV of the study. Refer to Chapter 1 of the textbook for additional details.

   (d) Andy decides to use a repeated measures experimental design in his study. Explain **one** advantage of using a repeated measures experimental design, rather than independent measures in this study. (2 marks)

   In this design, a participant is exposed to more than one condition of the IV, such as completing the task with the smell of flowers and then the smell of a zoo.

   The response would not earn any marks. A common error is made where the candidate defines the topic of a repeated measures design instead of providing a strength of the design as noted in the question.

   > ★ **Exam tip**
   > Circle key words of the question/prompt to make sure you answer what the question is asking you to answer.

3. Explain **one** way that Andy can get informed consent from his participants. (2 marks)

   He could have them sign a document ✔ that says they are participating in quality control tests on the object of the difficult task (like completing a 3D puzzle) before they begin ✔ – this would be necessary deception to avoid demand characteristics – and that they could leave any time they want.

   This response earns both marks with a way to obtain informed consent and additional sample details.

AS Research Methods

Activity or revision strategy

Activity: A key to performing well on Section A of Paper 2 is having a sound knowledge of the research topics from the syllabus. This activity focuses on the research topics that are often more challenging for learners. Try copying and completing this chart, filling in the non-shaded spaces for the definition, strength, or weakness of the provided research topics. To challenge yourself, you can also complete the last category of 'best used when', such as a field experiment is best used when 'the researcher(s) want to have a study high in ecological validity'. You can create your own chart with the research topics that you find to be more challenging as an extension activity.

Term	Definition	Strength	Weakness	Best used when...
Natural study				
Matched-pairs design				
Counterbalancing				
Random allocation				
Order effects				
Likert scale				
Rating scale				
Participant observation				
Control				
Criterion validity				
Construct validity				
Inter-rater reliability				
Test–retest reliability				
Time sampling				
Event sampling				
Practice effects				

Section B

Section B will focus on you having to apply your knowledge of research methodology by describing how a research study can be conducted. You will be provided with a topic to investigate and a technique to carry out the investigation. For example, you could be asked how a researcher could conduct a field study to see if there is a difference in candidates' grades in morning or afternoon classes. You will be asked follow-up questions regarding a practical/methodological strength or weakness of your suggested study. Question marks will range from 2 to 10 marks.

★ **Exam tip**

Make sure that your suggestions to conduct the study are not replications of a core study, even if the topics are similar.

Activity or revision strategy

Activity: When using the '4P' approach, you can address four main aspects of the design-a-study question in noting the 'purpose, participants, place, and procedure'. When getting ready to address the prompt, a short time to briefly outline the '4Ps' can be used to help you prepare and organise your answer. This can also be used as a revision activity where you can create scenarios and complete the '4Ps' in various techniques as well, focusing on experiments, observation, self-reports, or correlational studies.

★ **Exam tip**

Your proposed study must be ethical even if the question asks you not to mention ethical guidelines. You must plan the study as if you are a psychologist.

Research Methods — AS

Design-a-study worked examples

Here are three examples of design-a-study responses, with two sample candidate responses for each, one scoring in the high range and one in the low range. There is also a detailed commentary related to each of the responses given by the candidates.

Worked example

Example 1

Charles has noticed that younger children at his school play with different toys compared to older children at play time. He thinks that the younger children play with more colourful toys and that the older children play with a wider range of toys.

(a) Describe how Charles can conduct a structured observation to investigate age differences in toy choice using school children as his participants. Do not refer to ethical issues/guidelines in your answer. (10 marks)

Candidate A:

One way Charles can investigate <u>to see if there is a correlation between the age of children and the colour of toys played with</u> during play time would be to <u>use a structured observation</u>. Charles could use <u>two groups of children from an opportunity sample</u>, with one group of five participants being younger than the other group of five participants with a total of 10 children. The younger age would be 3–5 years and an older age group of 7–10 years. Charles could set up the playroom ahead of time, which would consist of different types of toys and different colours of toys. For example, he could have toys such as tea sets, plastic cars/trucks, stuffed animals, and drawing sets. These different toys would all be in the same school playroom where the different classes of students (based on their age) would go to during their assigned play time. Charles could have this take place for <u>one week's time</u> where the children are observed during their regular play time at school. Charles should also ask for permission from the school to conduct such a study as this includes child participants.

For Charles to collect data on if the colour of the toy played with is correlated to the age of the child, he would have two other teachers also be part of the study and be in the playroom at the same time. This is for supervision and to be able to collect data with three people rather than only Charles. This can help inter-rater reliability from the observations. The children in the playroom would play with the available toys as they normally would in a regular setting as they have before, with the ability to play with all the toys in the room. Before he begins, Charles would develop a <u>checklist</u> of the toys available to play with in the room and the age-group of children in the room at that time (younger or older). Each time a toy is played with, this checklist with the toy and colour of the toy would be recorded. Data would be collected each time that each group is in the playroom for the 30 minutes of play for one week with the three observers taking notes on a clipboard in each event. The data from the checklists can then be compared and would give quantitative data that can be reviewed afterwards. This would help to see if Charles was correct about his idea about younger children favouring colourful toys.

Level 4 response (8 marks)

The candidate provides an ethical study that properly uses the given technique of a structured observation. It includes key points in conducting a study, placing this in the Level 4 marking band. The candidate starts with the purpose of the study and potential participants of the study through the use of an opportunity sample and identifying ages of the two given groups. The description of conducting this study with available toys (samples provided for clarity) for a week's time during regularly scheduled play time adds to the credibility of the study. The inclusion of two additional observers helps to improve the data collection and reliability in the study. Noting the use of a checklist and the collection of quantitative data also helps. Terminology and details are mostly evident throughout.

Candidate B:

Charles can investigate if there is a connection between the age of a kid and the toys that they play with by having an observation at school. He can take kids and see what toys they play with during play time by using an observation. He can look to see if different kids play with different toys. He can write down which toy each kid plays with and then review his observations. This would help him find his data.

> **Level 1 response (1 mark)**
>
> The candidate provides a very basic description of conducting an observational study. This lacks clarity, research terminology, and descriptions throughout that limits the carrying out of the study and also the replicability. However, it does follow the given technique of an observation (the structured portion is only implied), enabling this to be placed in the Level 1 marking band.

Activity or revision strategy

Activity: The use of a brief outline before fully writing the design-a-study question can help organise your thoughts. Now that you have read through question 1 with Charles conducting a structured observation, complete a '4P' outline with the content presented for Candidate A and Candidate B. You can use the template provided. Afterwards, for Candidate B, go back and add brief content to the '4P' outline that you think would help make the answer stronger. You can repeat this activity for question 2 (Dr. Garcia's study) and question 3 (Isabelle's study) afterwards.

Candidate _____ example '4P' outline

Purpose	
Participants	
Place	
Procedure	

(b) Identify **one** practical weakness/limitation with the procedure you have described in your answer to part (a) and suggest how your study might be done differently to overcome the problem. Do **not** refer to ethics or sampling in your answer. (4 marks)

Candidate A:

One issue with the proposed study would be the three observers in the room. This may cause the children to behave differently if the observers are near them with a clipboard and a paper they are writing on. It would be good to have the observers away from them to limit this.

Candidate B:

One weakness is that interviews were not used to find out why the kids played with the certain toys. Next time, Charles should do this instead.

> **0 marks**
>
> The candidate's response would earn 0 marks as it does not relate to part (a).

★ **Exam tip**

To ensure you include the 'key parts' of your study, underline the main details concerning how the study would take place.

★ **Exam tip**

Complete a brief outline of '4Ps' (purpose, participants, place, procedure) to organise your thoughts before you start writing your answer.

★ **Exam tip**

Make sure to include descriptions of conducting a study to make it replicable.

> **2 marks**
>
> This response would earn 1 mark as it identifies a potential problem where the children may behave differently if the observers are near them in the room. However, it lacks psychological terminology (such as demand characteristics) and does not clearly explain the 'different behaviour' that is suggested. The candidate would then earn another 1 mark for the possible way to overcome the issue, but it does not identify a clear, appropriate solution to this problem.

Research Methods AS

Activity or revision strategy

Activity: The follow-up question to the design-a-study question will require you to note a strength or a weakness of the study you just described. Your knowledge of strengths and weaknesses of research methodology will be helpful for this question. It can be helpful to review the terminology notecards (a prior suggested activity) and to create a chart of this content before sitting for Paper 2. Part of an example chart is shown here:

Research term	Strength	Weakness
Laboratory study	Increased control of variables	Lowered ecological validity
Questionnaire	Often faster data collection	Answers may not be truthful

Worked example

Example 2

Dr. Garcia is interested in what affects the personal space an individual requires in an office when they are the only person in it. He believes that a person will still want some level of personal space even if no other person is in the office with them to interact with. Dr. Garcia will be following appropriate ethical guidelines.

Describe how Dr. Garcia could conduct a case study to investigate what affects the personal space needed by one person who works in an office by themselves. Do not refer to ethical issues/guidelines in your answer. (10 marks)

Candidate A:

The <u>purpose</u> of Dr. Garcia's investigation is to examine why 'personal space' is established for those who work in an office by themselves, and this is best accomplished via the <u>case study methodology</u>. This in-depth study would investigate a unique situation through the mixed-methods data collection pertaining to the participants involved. To secure participants for the study, Dr. Garcia can <u>send out emails to staff/faculty at a local University</u> in search of <u>five participants</u> who meet the criteria of working at least 6 hours a day individually in an office or laboratory setting at the University. For example, the email to solicit participants could read 'In search of faculty members who work by themselves in an office or laboratory for at least 6 hours a day who are willing to participate in a brief interview to discuss their room layout... you will be compensated for your participation in the study... if interested, please respond to this email to make arrangements.' In using a <u>volunteer sample</u>, this enables Dr. Garcia to select the participants who best fit the criteria of establishing personal space in the setup of office furniture and/or lab equipment. Dr. Garcia could also select the respondents based on how long the setting has been in place, such as for 3-6 months, as this would ensure that all participants have had the chance to work in an environment where personal space has been established. It would also be a good idea for Dr. Garcia to select one or two extra participants on standby in case a participant drops from the study moving forward.

Level 5 response (10 marks)

The candidate provides an ethical and replicable study that properly establishes the given technique of a case study. It includes detailed key points in conducting the study, placing this in the Level 5 marking band. The content clearly demonstrates the candidate's knowledge of what a case study is (an in-depth investigation of a single person or a small group of people who share the same experience) and how data can be collected for such a study. The content provides terminology with examples throughout, ranging from the use of a volunteer sample (including a sample recruitment ad) to the use of a semi-structured interview with sample questions. The description of conducting the study with two data collection techniques (interviews and pictures) is clear and detailed with examples – this demonstrates the candidate's understanding of not just how to collect data, but why to collect certain types of data. The candidate clearly notes what the participants will be doing during the study, when the study will be taking place, how data will be collected, and how it will be analysed (though not necessary, but helps show understanding of the content).

AS Research Methods

After finalising the participants for the study, Dr. Garcia could first ask participants to email <u>pictures of the office/lab setting</u> to see if there is a commonality among how personal space is created, such as if one's primary location in the office/lab is a certain distance away from other tables/chairs that are in the room. Furthermore, such pictures could allow for a better overall understanding of the 'personal space' setup, as it may extend into having pictures of friends/family on the desk, certain awards on the wall, and/or interests (such as Mickey Mouse toys) throughout the space as well. In addition to the participants taking and submitting images of their office/lab, they would also partake in <u>semi-structured interviews.</u> The use of semi-structured interviews would allow Dr. Garcia to ask general questions to all participants and questions unique to each participant depending on how the interview progresses, collecting both <u>quantitative and qualitative data</u> in the process. Such interviews could be conducted <u>face-to-face or via the internet</u> (such as with Zoom) individually with each participant either in the participant's office/lab or in the lobby area of the building at the University (participant's choice). Each interview would last approximately 30-60 minutes and would be conducted during the month of March during the Spring semester (based on the availability of the faculty member). Each interview would be comprised of both <u>closed-ended questions</u> (such as 'Was the room already setup like this or did you have the ability to move things around?') and <u>open-ended questions</u> (such as 'Why is there a yellow line on the floor between the chairs and the workbench in your lab?'). After data collection, Dr. Garcia would then use categorical analysis to look for themes in the participants' responses from the interviews, in conjunction with the pictures, to explain why offices/labs are setup in a certain manner to maintain personal space and to what extent (if any) personal space plays a factor in job satisfaction among those who work in an office/lab alone.

Candidate B:

Dr. Garcia can use the case study methodology to see why personal space is important for people who work by themselves in an office. This could be done by going to a place where people work in an office all day and ask for volunteers, 10 in total. This would be an opportunity sample because the participants are the ones who happened to be working at that time. Dr. Garcia would have to make sure that the participants are employees of the company. Dr. Garcia could then ask the participants why they created personal space in their offices through questionnaires. They can complete the questionnaires about why they created personal space in their office and if they think that it helps them. In addition to the questions, Dr. Garcia could also look at how their offices are setup and maybe ask questions while doing so. This would better help the data collection. After collecting the data from the questionnaires and looking at their offices, Dr. Garcia could then analyse the data from this and conclude why personal space when working alone is wanted.

(b) (i) Describe **one** practical/methodological strength of the procedure you have described in your answer to part (a). Do not refer to ethical issues/guidelines in your answer. (2 marks)

Candidate A:

One practical strength of the study is the use of two ways to collect data – one through the use of pictures that demonstrate the setup of the office/lab for the participants of the study and the second through the use of semi-structured interviews with both open-ended and closed-ended questions.

> ★ **Exam tip**
>
> Include sample questions when discussing a survey or interview.

> **Level 2 response (4 marks)**
>
> The candidate has a limited description of how the case study could be conducted, placing this in the Level 2 marking band. There are attempts at including aspects of research studies, but these are limited to an opportunity sample (not detailed) and the use of questionnaires (only providing a vague focus of the use of them). The inclusion of looking at the office space is not fully developed as an additional data collection of the use of observations but does show an attempt at using different data collection techniques as are often used in case studies. Descriptions, details, and the inclusion of research terminology are lacking throughout.

> **2 marks**
>
> This response would earn both marks as a strength is identified (1 mark) and further detailed (1 mark).

63

Research Methods AS

Candidate B:

The study uses a questionnaire where participants can explain their thoughts on the topic.

> **1 mark**
> This would earn 1 mark as a strength is identified.

(b) (ii) Explain why the feature of the procedure you have identified in (i) is a strength. Do not refer to ethical issues/guidelines in your answer. (2 marks)

Candidate A:

Using two different ways to collect the data by the pictures and interviews allows for a better understanding of the situation overall.

> **1 mark**
> This response would earn 1 mark for a simple explanation, but fails to provide additional details for the second mark.

Candidate B:

It allows for data collection that is better.

> **0 marks**
> This would not earn any marks as the response is too vague.

Worked example

Example 3

Isabelle believes that people's dreams contain images based on the surroundings of where they live. For example, people who live in a city will have dreams about being in a city. Isabelle plans to use a sample of people aged under 25 years.

(a) Describe how Isabelle could conduct an interview study to investigate whether people's dreams contain images based on the surroundings of where they live. Do not refer to sample/sampling technique in your answer. (10 marks)

Candidate A:

The <u>purpose</u> of Isabelle's study is to investigate if people's dreams contain images from where they locally live. For example, if someone who lives in Paris has dreams that have images of the Eiffel Tower, the Louvre Museum, or local bistros during lunch. In order to have a sample aged under 25 years, she could place an <u>advertisement</u> at the local university's psychology department for those who are willing to discuss their dreams and are 18–24 years of age. To collect data on this topic, <u>10 participants</u> would be selected who would respond to interviews. These interviews would take place during the <u>middle of the university term</u> to avoid potential conflicts with end-of-term examinations.

The participants in the study would first be required to keep a sleep journal of their dreams for 6 weeks before conducting the interviews. This can help the participants remember what they dreamed about and could also be referenced during the interviews if someone wants to remember something. Isabelle would use <u>semi-structured interviews</u> to obtain her data and would record the interviews. This will allow for the same questions to be asked to all participants and would allow each participant to expand on topics and responses that they want to. Within these interviews, she would use questions that only have <u>preset responses</u> and ones that allow the participant to expand on an idea. For example, she could ask a question such as "How many times did you dream with places near where you live?" These interviews would take place at the <u>library</u> of the university and would last from

> **Level 4 response (8 marks)**
> The candidate provides an ethical study that correctly uses the given technique of interviews and includes key points in conducting a study, placing this in the Level 4 marking band. The candidate starts with the purpose of the study and provides examples of what the study would investigate, referencing places in Paris as an example. The inclusion of the sampling was simply overlooked for marking purposes as it was not required in the question. The notion of using a sleep journal as a self-report helps to demonstrate that the candidate understands that dreaming is often not remembered and could prove to be useful in the interviews. The candidate further provides when, where, and how the interviews would be conducted (with reasoning for each). However, the lack of specific terminology (such as open-ended and closed-ended questions) and details (such as how the interviews would be recorded) limit this response from moving to a Level 5.

30 to 90 minutes depending on how much the participants have to say about their dreams. After Isabelle collects her data from the interviews, she would then go through and look to see if there is a relationship between where someone lives and if their dreams include surrounding areas.

Candidate B:

Isabelle can use questionnaires for the study about where people live and dreaming. She could send out flyers or email her 25 participants questions about what they dream about and then see how they respond. For example, she could ask her participants if they recall being in dreams that take place where they live. She could collect data on this dreaming for 6 months. Afterwards, she could see if people are where they dream, like living and dreaming by the river.

> **Level 1 response (1 mark)**
> The candidate provides a response that attempts to address the prompt but mainly fails in doing so. Notably, the presented study uses a questionnaire instead and is very general in collecting data. However, the inclusion of a sample question topic does provide a limited attempt in collecting data on the topic, providing enough content to earn a Level 1.

(b) (i) Describe **one** practical/methodological strength of the procedure you have described in your answer to part (a). Do not refer to sample/sampling technique in your answer. (2 marks)

Candidate A:

One strength would be the use of a sleep journal to help the people remember their dreams and for reference during the interviews.

> **2 marks**
> This response would earn 2 marks as a strength is identified with some detail.

Candidate B:

One strength is that the data should be easier to obtain as questionnaires are often easy for participants to complete and often will spend the time to do so.

> **1 mark**
> A generic strength of using a questionnaire is provided.

(b) (ii) Explain why the feature of the procedure you have identified in (b) (i) is a strength. Do not refer to sample/sampling technique in your answer. (2 marks)

Candidate A:

A strength of the sleep journal is that it helps add to the validity of the data collection as participants would record their dreams at that time period (after waking up) so they have better recall then compared to trying to recall it at a later time during an interview. This also reduces the possible issues such as false memories when trying to recall their dreams, adding to the validity of their dreams.

> **2 marks**
> The answer clearly demonstrates how the use of a sleep journal can increase the validity of the data collected.

Candidate B:

Since questionnaires are usually easier to complete, she would be more likely to gather enough data from the responses in order to analyze a correlation between dreaming and where you live.

> **1 mark**
> The notion of gathering enough data to complete the study earns the mark here.

Research Methods AS

> **Activity or revision strategy**
>
> **Activity:** Go through the different aspects of research and collecting data (e.g. lab study, participant observation) from Chapter 1 of the textbook and write down 'key words' that would be helpful to include if you are asked to conduct a study using such techniques.

> **Activity or revision strategy**
>
> **Activity:** Using the three worked examples presented here, have a go at changing the data collection technique and outlining how you would conduct the new study. For example, you could change example 2 from a case study to a field experiment.

Design-a-study questions raise your grade example

Here is an example of a design-a-study response. There is an example candidate response with suggestions for how the candidate can improve their response to move up to the next level.

↑ Raise your grade

Carole believes that there are age differences in people's beliefs about what toys should be played with by boys and girls. She has decided that young people below the age of 20 years will have different beliefs compared to people who are over 80 years.

(a) Describe how Carole could conduct a questionnaire study about age differences in people's beliefs about what toys should be played with by boys and girls. Do not refer to sample/sampling technique in your answer. (10 marks)

Carole can use a questionnaire to conduct a study about age differences in people's beliefs about what toys should be played with by boys and girls. After Carole obtains her sample, she would then go to where they are (e.g. the local university for the younger participants and the nursing home for the older participants) and have them complete the questionnaire. Both age groups of participants would be asked questions that are open-ended and closed-ended ones that ask about beliefs of children playing with toys by gender. Each participant would then be able to explain their ideas and answer questions that all other participants complete as well. This could include which toys they played with when they were a child or possible reasons why they mention that certain toys are aimed at boys or girls. Each participant would have a scheduled time for Carole to come and administer the questionnaire, and this could take 3 months of collecting data due to scheduling with each participant. In total, the questionnaire could be 15 questions that ask about this information and should take a little time to complete. Once Carole obtains her data, she could then see if there is a difference among age groups and beliefs about what toys boys and girls should play with.

Overall, a basic understanding is demonstrated placing this response at Level 3, earning 6 marks. Some of the features of the study are covered but could be expanded upon to move to the next level. In particular, it would help to include a sample of open-ended and closed-ended questions, in addition to the inclusion of Likert or rating questions with examples. It would be helpful to include categories of questions pertaining to toys, such as colour of toy, purpose of toy, and so on. Details on how the questionnaire is administered would help, such as (a) if it is through paper/pencil or an electronic collection and (b) the timing required to complete it.

(b) (i) Describe **one** practical/methodological strength of the procedure you have described in your answer to part (a). Do not refer to sample/sampling technique in your answer. (2 marks)

A strength of the study is that the questionnaire can save time. ✔

The response is awarded 1 mark. A supporting detail or example in this case would better help explain the notion of 'saving time'.

(b) (ii) Explain why the feature of the procedure you have identified in (b) (i) is a strength. Do not refer to sample/sampling technique in your answer. (2 marks)

This is a strength because participants are likely to complete it. ✔

As in (b) (i), a supporting detail or example would help explain the response better to allow for both marks. The response is therefore awarded 1 mark.

This candidate may earn a total of 8 marks out of 14.

Activity or revision strategy

Activity: Now that you have reviewed design-a-study example responses, complete a brief '4P' outline and fully answer these questions in under 30 minutes. Refer to the previous commentary about how to achieve full marks.

1. Dr. Gupta believes that students achieve higher marks on their examinations when they complete them in their everyday classroom compared to a special examination room. Dr. Gupta plans to use the most recent examination series scores from students at her school to investigate this possible difference. Dr. Gupta will be following appropriate ethical guidelines.

   (a) Describe how Dr. Gupta could conduct a correlational study to see if where students complete their examinations influences their scores. Do not refer to ethical issues/guidelines in your answer. (10 marks)

   (b) (i) Describe **one** practical/methodological strength of the procedure you have described in your answer to part (a). Do not refer to sample/sampling technique in your answer. (2 marks)

   (ii) Explain why the feature of the procedure you have identified in part (b) (i) is a strength. Do not refer to sample/sampling technique in your answer. (2 marks)

3 Specialist Options: Approaches, Issues, and Debates

Introduction to the paper

For Paper 3 the structure is as follows:

- There will be four sections in the paper with a total of 16 questions.

- You will be required to choose **two options/sections** and **answer all four questions in one option** and **another four questions in the second option**. The options you choose will have been covered in your classes. The options are clinical, consumer, health, and organisational psychology. For example, if you have studied clinical and health you would answer all four questions in each of these options (eight questions in total).

- Paper 3 has a total of 60 marks. Each question has the total marks indicated in [ ] brackets. The total amount of time to complete Paper 3 is 90 minutes.

- There is a mixture of short and longer questions. Usually, the short questions use command words like 'identify', 'outline', 'explain', 'describe', and 'suggest'. The short questions may range between 2 and 4 marks.

- The last question in the option will be a 'describe' question (6 marks) and an 'evaluate' question (10 marks). The questions will be drawn from topics covered in each option and some 'novel' questions where you need to apply your knowledge.

To excel in this paper, you should have the knowledge and understanding of the psychological issues and debates, the psychological theories, approaches, and the research done including the key studies.

Activity or revision strategy

Revision strategy: Use five minutes to plan for each of the 'describe' and 'evaluate' questions. These two questions together carry 32 marks which is a big factor in your grades. Divide your time evenly to help you complete the paper; 40 minutes for each option.

Knowledge check

Use the following knowledge checklists to ensure that you have studied everything you need to know for the examination. For each of the rows, to tick **green** you must be able to:

- describe the idea
- evaluate the idea.

Also, do not forget that you only need to complete knowledge checklists for two of the four available options.

■ **Red:** I do not understand.　　■ **Amber:** I somewhat understand.
■ **Green:** I do understand.

Option 1: Clinical psychology

Topic: Schizophrenia

Syllabus area	Red	Amber	Green
Diagnostic criteria for schizophrenia			
ICD-11 criteria for schizophrenia including positive and negative symptoms			
A case study of schizophrenia			
Types of delusions			
Using virtual reality: key study – Freeman *et al.* (2003)			
At least three issues and debates linked to diagnostic criteria for schizophrenia			
Explanations of schizophrenia			
Biological: genetic			
Biological: dopamine (biochemical)			
Psychological: cognitive			
At least three issues and debates linked to explanations of schizophrenia			
Treatment and management of schizophrenia			
Biological: typical and atypical antipsychotics			
Electro-convulsive therapy			
Psychological therapy: cognitive-behavioural therapy			
A study about cognitive-behavioural therapy			
At least three issues and debates linked to treatment and management of schizophrenia			

Topic: Mood (affective) disorders

Syllabus area	Red	Amber	Green
Diagnostic criteria for mood (affective) disorders			
ICD-11 criteria for depressive disorder (unipolar) and bipolar disorders			
Beck Depression Inventory			
At least three issues and debates linked to diagnostic criteria for mood (affective) disorders			
Explanations of mood (affective) disorders: unipolar			
Biological: biochemical			
Biological: genetic			
Key study: Oruč *et al.* (1997) – genetics			
Psychological: Beck's cognitive theory			
Psychological: learned helplessness/attributional style, plus a study			
At least three issues and debates linked to explanations of mood (affective) disorders			
Treatment and management of mood (affective) disorders			
Biological: antidepressants (tricyclics, MAOIs, SSRIs)			
Psychological: Beck's cognitive restructuring			
Psychological: Ellis' REBT			
At least three issues and debates linked to treatment and management of mood (affective) disorders			

Topic: Impulse control disorder

Syllabus area	Red	Amber	Green
Diagnostic criteria for impulse control disorder			
ICD-11 criteria for kleptomania, pyromania, gambling disorder			
Kleptomania Symptom Assessment Scale (K-SAS)			
At least three issues and debates linked to diagnostic criteria for impulse control disorder			
Explanations of impulse control disorder			
Biological: dopamine			
Psychological: behavioural – positive reinforcement			
Psychological: cognitive – Miller's feeling-state theory			
At least three issues and debates linked to explanations of impulse control disorder			
Treatment and management of impulse control disorder			
Biological: drugs			
Key study: Grant *et al.* (2008) – drug therapy			
Psychological: covert sensitisation, plus a study			
Psychological: imaginal desensitisation, plus a study			
At least three issues and debates linked to treatment and management of impulse control disorder			

Topic: Anxiety and fear-related disorders

Syllabus area	Red	Amber	Green
Diagnostic criteria for anxiety and fear-related disorders			
ICD-11 criteria for generalised anxiety disorder, agoraphobia, blood–injection–injury phobia			
Generalised Anxiety Disorder (GAD-7) assessment			
BIPI, plus a study			
At least three issues and debates linked to diagnostic criteria for anxiety and fear-related disorders			
Explanations of anxiety and fear-related disorders			
Biological: genetic, plus a study			
Psychological: classical conditioning, plus a study			
Psychological: psychodynamic, plus a study			
At least three issues and debates linked to explanations of anxiety and fear-related disorders			
Treatment and management of anxiety and fear-related disorders			
Behavioural: systematic desensitisation, plus a study			
Psychological: cognitive-behavioural therapy			
Key study: Chapman and DeLapp (2013) – CBT			
Psychological: applied tension with blood phobia			

Syllabus area	Red	Amber	Green
At least three issues and debates linked to treatment and management of anxiety and fear-related disorders			

Topic: Obsessive-compulsive disorder (OCD)

Syllabus area	Red	Amber	Green
Diagnostic criteria for obsessive-compulsive disorder (OCD)			
ICD-11 criteria for obsessive-compulsive disorder (OCD), types of obsessions and compulsions			
A study about OCD			
Maudsley Obsessive-Compulsive Inventory (MOCI)			
Yale–Brown Obsessive-Compulsive Scale (Y–BOCS)			
At least three issues and debates linked to diagnostic criteria for obsessive-compulsive disorder (OCD)			
Explanations of obsessive-compulsive disorder (OCD)			
Biological: biochemical			
Biological: genetic			
Psychological: cognitive (thinking error)			
Psychological: behavioural (operant conditioning)			
Psychological: psychodynamic			
At least three issues and debates linked to explanations of obsessive-compulsive disorder (OCD)			
Treatment and management of obsessive-compulsive disorder (OCD)			
Biological: use of SSRIs			
Psychological: Exposure and Response Prevention (ERP), plus a study			
Psychological: cognitive-behavioural therapy (CBT)			
Key study: Lovell *et al.* (2006) – CBT			
At least three issues and debates linked to treatment and management of obsessive-compulsive disorder (OCD)			

Option 2: Consumer psychology

Topic: The physical environment

Syllabus area	Red	Amber	Green
Retail store design			
Types of store exterior design including landscaping, window displays, and storefront, plus a study			
Types of store interior design including grid, freeform, and racetrack layouts, plus a study			
At least three issues and debates linked to retail store design			
Sound and consumer behaviour			
Music in restaurants: how it influences the amount spent in a restaurant			

Syllabus area	Red	Amber	Green
Key study: music in restaurants – North *et al.* (2003)			
Background noise focusing on how sound and noise affects perception of taste, plus a study			
At least three issues and debates linked to sound and consumer behaviour			
Retail atmospherics			
Pleasure–Arousal–Dominance (PAD) model			
Effects of odour on shopper PAD, plus a study			
Effects of crowding on shopper PAD, plus a study			
At least three issues and debates linked to retail atmospherics			

Topic: **The psychological environment**

Syllabus area	Red	Amber	Green
Environmental influences on consumers			
Wayfinding in shopping malls: factors affecting wayfinding like signs and maps, plus a study			
Shopper behaviour: spatial movement patterns and use of CCTV tracking, plus a study			
At least three issues and debates linked to environmental influences on consumers			
Menu design psychology			
Features of menu design that have a positive/negative impact, plus use of eye tracking, plus a study			
Primacy-recency and menu item position on choice, plus a study			
Effect of food name on choice, plus a study			
At least three issues and debates linked to menu design psychology			
Consumer behaviour and personal space			
Personal space at restaurant tables: Hall's four zones			
Functions of personal space: overload, arousal, behavioural constraint			
Key study: table spacing – Robson *et al.* (2011)			
Defending a place in a queue, including nature of intrusion, social structure, and responses, plus a study			
At least three issues and debates linked to consumer behaviour and personal space			

Topic: **Consumer decision-making**

Syllabus area	Red	Amber	Green
Consumer decision-making			
Models: utility, satisficing, prospect			
Strategies: non-compensatory, compensatory, partially compensatory, including examples for each			
Applied to internet shopping: website design, plus a study			

Syllabus area	Red	Amber	Green
At least three issues and debates linked to consumer decision-making			
Choice heuristics			
Types: availability, representativeness, recognition, take-the-best, anchoring, examples of each			
Point of purchase: multiple unit pricing and suggestive selling, plus a study			
Applying heuristics to styles of decision-making, plus a study			
At least three issues and debates linked to choice heuristics			
Mistakes in decision-making			
Thinking fast thinking slow/System 1 and 2, examples for each			
Choice blindness, preference, and defending choice			
Key study: choice blindness – Hall *et al.* (2010)			
Consumer memory and advertising: retroactive and proactive interference, plus a study			
At least three issues and debates linked to mistakes in decision-making			

Topic: The product

Syllabus area	Red	Amber	Green
Packaging and positioning of a product			
Gift-wrapping: beliefs of giver and recipient – why gifts are wrapped, types of wrapping			
Key study: food package design – Becker *et al.* (2011)			
Attention and shelf position: planograms, central gaze cascade effect, use of eye-tracking, plus a study			
At least three issues and debates linked to packaging and positioning of a product			
Selling the product			
Sales techniques: customer-focused, competitor-focused, product-focused, effect of each on buyer–seller relationship			
Interpersonal influences: disrupt-then-reframe, need to cognitive closure, factors affecting these, plus a study			
Cialdini's six ways to close a sale			
At least three issues and debates linked to selling the product			
Buying the product			
Engel–Kollat–Blackwell model			
Deciding where to buy, reasons for store choice, and demographic, plus a study			
Post-purchase cognitive dissonance, factors that increase it and ways to reduce it, plus a study			
At least three issues and debates linked to buying the product			

Specialist Options: Approaches, Issues, and Debates — AL

Topic: Advertising

Syllabus area	Red	Amber	Green
Types of advertising and advertising techniques			
Yale Model of Communication (five features)			
Advertising media: internet, television, printed, smartphone, eye-tracking, and EEGs, plus a study			
Lauterborn's 4Cs Marketing Mix			
At least three issues and debates linked to types of advertising and advertising techniques			
Advertising–consumer interaction			
Advertising and consumer personality, including self-monitoring			
Key study: consumer personality and advertising – Snyder and DeBono (1985), focus on Study 3			
Product placement in films affecting choice, mere exposure, reminders, plus a study			
At least three issues and debates linked to advertising–consumer interaction			
Brand awareness and recognition			
In children: acquisition of understanding of advertising logos, plus a study			
Brand awareness, brand image, effective slogans, types/functions of slogans, creating effective slogans			
At least three issues and debates linked to brand awareness and recognition			

Option 3: Health psychology

Topic: The patient–practitioner relationship

Syllabus area	Red	Amber	Green
Practitioner and patient interpersonal skills			
Non-verbal communication: practitioner clothing, plus a study			
Verbal communication: understanding medical terminology, plus a study			
At least three issues and debates linked to practitioner and patient interpersonal skills			
Patient and practitioner diagnosis and style			
Making a diagnosis: disclosure of information, false positive and false negative diagnosis, presenting a diagnosis			
Practitioner style: doctor-centred (directed), patient-centred (sharing)			
Key study: practitioner style – Savage and Armstrong (1990)			
At least three issues and debates linked to patient and practitioner diagnosis and style			
Misusing health services			
Delay in seeking treatment: reasons, plus a study			

Syllabus area	Red	Amber	Green
Delay in seeking treatment: alternative explanations, plus a study			
Munchausen syndrome and malingering			
Diagnostic features of Munchausen syndrome: essential and supporting features, plus a study			
At least three issues and debates linked to misusing health services			

Topic: Adherence to medical advice

Syllabus area	Red	Amber	Green
Types of non-adherence and reasons why patients do not adhere			
Types of non-adherence: failure to follow-up, failure to attend, problems caused			
Rational non-adherence, plus a study			
Health Belief Model			
At least three issues and debates linked to types of non-adherence and reasons why patients do not adhere			
Measuring non-adherence			
Subjective measures: clinical interview, semi-structured interview, including a study			
Objective measures: pill counting, medication dispensers, plus a study			
Biological measures: blood test, urine sample			
At least three issues and debates linked to measuring non-adherence			
Improving adherence			
In children, plus a study			
Individual behavioural techniques: contracts, prompts, customisation			
Key study: community intervention – Yokley and Glenwick (1984)			
At least three issues and debates linked to improving adherence			

Topic: Pain

Syllabus area	Red	Amber	Green
Types and theories of pain			
Functions of pain, types of pain: acute and chronic			
Phantom limb pain and mirror treatment, plus a study			
At least three issues and debates linked to types and theories of pain			
Specificity theory			
Gate control theory			
Measuring pain			
Subjective measures: clinical interview and one other			
Psychometric: McGill pain questionnaire			
Visual rating scales and visual analogue scales			
Key study: pain assessment – Brudvik et al. (2016)			

Specialist Options: Approaches, Issues, and Debates

Syllabus area	Red	Amber	Green
At least three issues and debates linked to measuring pain			
Managing and controlling pain			
Biological treatment: biochemical			
Psychological treatment: cognitive strategies, attention diversion, non-pain imagery, cognitive redefinition			
Alternative treatments: acupuncture, TENS			
At least three issues and debates linked to managing and controlling pain			

Topic: Stress

Syllabus area	Red	Amber	Green
Sources of stress			
Physiology: GAS, effects of stress on health			
Causes: Holmes and Rahe life events			
Causes: work, plus a study			
Causes: Friedman and Rosenman Type A personality			
At least three issues and debates linked to sources of stress			
Measures of stress			
Biological: recording devices, heart rate, brain function (fMRI), plus a study			
Sample tests: salivary cortisol, plus a study			
Psychological: self-report, including Friedman and Rosenman's Type A personality and Holmes and Rahe life events			
At least three issues and debates linked to measures of stress			
Managing stress			
Psychological therapy: biofeedback, plus a study			
Key study: Use of imagery – Bridge *et al.* (1988)			
Preventing stress: stress inoculation training (three phases)			
At least three issues and debates linked to managing stress			

Topic: Health promotion

Syllabus area	Red	Amber	Green
Strategies for promoting health			
Fear arousal, plus a study			
Providing information, plus a study			
At least three issues and debates linked to strategies for promoting health			
Health promotion in schools and worksites			
Schools: healthy eating, plus a study			
Worksites: health and safety, plus a study			
At least three issues and debates linked to health promotion in schools and worksites			

Individual factors in changing health beliefs			
Unrealistic optimism, plus a study			
Positive psychology: pleasant life, good life, meaningful life plus a study			
Key study: application of positive psychology – Shoshani and Steinmetz (2014)			
At least three issues and debates linked to individual factors in changing health beliefs			

Option 4: Organisational psychology

Topic: Motivation to work

Syllabus area	Red	Amber	Green
Need theories			
Maslow's hierarchy of needs, plus a study			
McClelland: need for achievement, affiliation, power			
At least three issues and debates linked to need theories			
Cognitive theories			
Latham and Locke: goal setting, principles, and SMART goals			
Vroom (VIE) expectancy theory			
At least three issues and debates linked to cognitive theories			
Motivators to work			
Extrinsic: reward systems, pay, bonuses, profit-sharing			
Intrinsic: non-monetary, praise, respect, recognition, empowerment, sense of belonging			
Deci and Ryan: Self-determination theory: autonomy, relatedness			
Key study: applying self-determination – Landry et al. (2019)			
At least three issues and debates linked to motivators to work			

Topic: Leadership and management

Syllabus area	Red	Amber	Green
Traditional and modern theories of leadership			
Universalist: great person, charismatic, transformational			
Behavioural: Ohio University, Michigan University			
Heifetz: Six principles of meeting adaptive challenges, responsibilities of adaptive leaders			
At least three issues and debates linked to traditional and modern theories of leadership			
Leadership style			
Muczky and Reimann: four styles of leader behaviour			
Scouller: public, private, personal levels			
Key study: leadership style and gender – Cuadrado et al. (2008)			

Specialist Options: Approaches, Issues, and Debates

At least three issues and debates linked to leadership style			
Leaders and followers			
Kouzes and Posner: Leadership Practices Inventory, five practices			
Kelly: followership, two dimensions, five styles			
At least three issues and debates linked to leaders and followers			

Topic: Group behaviour in organisations

Syllabus area	Red	Amber	Green
Group development and decision-making			
Stages of group development (e.g. Tuckman)			
Belbin's nine team roles			
Faulty decision-making: groupthink – features and examples			
Faulty decision-making: Forsyth's cognitive limitations and errors			
At least three issues and debates linked to group development and decision-making			
Individual and group performance			
Social facilitation			
Social loafing, including definitions			
Drive theory and evaluation apprehension			
Social impact theory			
Group performance across cultures (social loafing in individualistic and collectivist cultures)			
Key study: performance monitoring of employee productivity – Claypool and Szalma (2019), experiment 1 only			
At least three issues and debates linked to individual and group performance			
Conflict at work			
Levels of group conflict: intra-individual, inter-individual, intra-group, inter-group			
Causes of organisational and interpersonal group conflict			
Thomas-Kilmann: five conflict-handling modes			
Bullying: types, phases, and causes, plus study			
At least three issues and debates linked to conflict at work			

Topic: Organisational work conditions

Syllabus area	Red	Amber	Green
Physical work conditions			
Impact of physical work conditions on productivity via Hawthorne Effect, plus a study			
Impact of design: open-plan offices, plus a study			
At least three issues and debates linked to physical work conditions			

Temporal conditions of work environments	Red	Amber	Green
Design: shiftwork – rapid rotation, slow-rotation; on-call; flexitime			
Effect of shiftwork on health and accidents, plus a study			
At least three issues and debates linked to temporal conditions of work environments			
Health and safety			
Accidents and work: human errors – errors of omission, commission, sequencing, timing			
Reducing accidents at work: token economy, plus a study			
Key study: monitoring accidents at work – Swat (1997)			
At least three issues and debates linked to health and safety			

Topic: Satisfaction at work

Syllabus area	Red	Amber	Green
Theories of job satisfaction			
Herzberg: two factors (hygiene, motivation)			
Hackmand and Oldham: job characteristics theory			
Techniques of job design: enrichment, rotation, enlargement			
At least three issues and debates linked to theories of job satisfaction			
Measuring job satisfaction			
Job Descriptive Index (JDI): rating scales and questionnaires			
Walton's Quality of Working Life (QWL) scale: eight conditions and evaluation scale			
At least three issues and debates linked to measuring job satisfaction			
Attitudes to work			
Key study: workplace sabotage – Giacolone and Rosenfeld (1987)			
Blau and Boal: absenteeism and organisational commitment, types of absence, categories of commitment			
At least three issues and debates linked to attitudes to work			

A-level issues and debates

Syllabus area	Red	Amber	Green
Issues and debates			
Cultural differences			
Reductionism versus holism			
Determinism versus free-will			
Idiographic versus nomothetic			

Specialist Options: Approaches, Issues, and Debates

Clinical psychology

Short answer questions worked examples

Worked example

1. Celia believes that she has generalised anxiety disorder, but she has never had a diagnosis. She has been referred to a therapist for help. In her first session, the therapist wants to measure Celia's symptoms for generalised anxiety disorder. The therapist uses the Generalised Anxiety Disorder (GAD-7). Explain how the therapist can use the GAD-7 to diagnose whether Celia has generalised anxiety disorder. (4 marks)

Candidate A:

The therapist can give the GAD-7 questionnaire to Celia to fill in when she comes in for therapy to see if she has an anxiety disorder where she will rate her worrying on the seven items.

1 mark

The response is missing how the GAD-7 is completed – examples of symptoms the GAD-7 assesses, the rating scale used, and what the final score would mean. How high would Celia have to score to be assessed as having generalised anxiety?

Candidate B:

The therapist will give her the GAD-7 questionnaire to fill in about how she has felt in the past two weeks. The therapist will explain to her how to assign scores of 0, 1, 2, and 3, to the responses of 'not at all' to 'nearly every day'. She will answer questions such as 'not being able to control worrying' and 'trouble relaxing'. When she is done the therapist will add together the scores for the seven questions and determine if Celia has mild, moderate, or severe anxiety. If the score is 15 or more there is a likelihood of GAD diagnosis being made.

4 marks

This is an excellent response that earns full marks as it shows how the process of filling out the questionnaire will take place and how the GAD-7 will be used to make the diagnosis.

(a) Outline what is meant by the idiographic versus nomothetic debate. (2 marks)

Candidate A:

It is a debate that looks at either the group or individuals and what makes them unique from each other.

1 mark

The candidate has given a correct outline of idiographic but only hinted at nomothetic with the use of the word 'group'.

Candidate B:

The nomothetic side refers to the study of people as a whole, to make conclusions about common characteristics in their behaviour and emotions, while the idiographic side looks at the individual as a unique person and that their behaviour and emotions are experienced by the person and not all.

2 marks

A detailed response that achieves full marks.

(b) Explain **one** strength of an explanation for schizophrenia from the idiographic side of the debate. (2 marks)

Candidate A:

Anyone can get schizophrenia but it depends on how your parents brought you up. This means you may have a parent with schizophrenia and they bring you up differently from another person whose parents do not have the abnormality.

0 marks

This is not written as a strength of the explanation. What is good about taking an idiographic approach to explaining schizophrenia? The student should ideally identify the strength and then give an example.

Candidate B:

It provides a detailed account of an individual with the disorder and avoids labelling people as being the same. The case study of John Nash, the

AL Specialist Options: Approaches, Issues, and Debates

mathematical genius who experienced both persecutory delusions and auditory hallucinations, provides us with lots of qualitative data and helps us to understand his unique experience as a patient with the disorder and also how the disorder was managed with antipsychotics and insulin shocks.

2. (a) Barbara has recently been diagnosed with obsessive–compulsive disorder (OCD). She works in a library. Explain how one obsession and one compulsion might affect Barbara when at work in the library. (4 marks)

Candidate A:

Barbara may have cleaning obsessions and will keep dusting the books all the time, wasting so much time on making the books clean instead of attending to other duties in the library.

Candidate B:

Barbara's OCD can be arranging things. This is where she keeps making sure the books are put in order as soon as they are returned, and she becomes disturbed when people remove books from the shelf.

(b) Explain **one** weakness of diagnostic guidelines for obsessive–compulsive disorders (OCD). (2 marks)

Candidate A:

Obsessions and compulsions such as cleaning, arranging, and checking can be diagnosed incorrectly as they may be similar to each other.

Candidate B:

The diagnostic criteria may be low in reliability as a diagnosis for OCD can be made by one doctor and not another as some of the symptoms may be similar to other disorders. For example, having the fear of germs may be similar to a phobia in anxiety disorders and someone may be wrongly diagnosed as having a specific phobia.

2 marks
An excellent response that states a strength with a clear, well-linked example.

2 marks
The response could earn 2 marks as it identifies a cleaning obsession and briefly outlines the compulsion; however, it is not well developed for a full 4 marks. The candidate needs examples to extend their explanation.

2 marks
The response could earn 2 marks as the candidate understands the obsession and its compulsion. The response needs more detail to earn full marks.

1 mark
The response is partially correct but should show a weakness of diagnosing a person using the ICD-11 for OCD.

2 marks
The response earns full marks as the candidate addresses the lack of consistency in diagnosis, which is correct.

Activity or revision strategy

Revision strategy: To help you answer 'outline what is meant by …' 2-mark questions:

- draw a grid
- list all of the issues and debates
- write definitions for all of these into the grid
- cover up the definitions and quiz yourself.

Activity or revision strategy

Revision strategy: To help remember the features of each measure of abnormality (such as the GAD-7):

- draw a table of measures of abnormality
- list four features of each measure
- including an outline scale of severity of each measure (e.g. a score over 15 on GAD-7 is severe anxiety)
- cover features and quiz yourself.

Specialist Options: Approaches, Issues, and Debates

Short answer questions raise your grade examples

> ## ⬆ Raise your grade
>
> 1. Dominic wants to learn more about a biological explanation for mood (affective) disorders as he believes it could explain why his best friend is depressed. Explain to Dominic **one** biological explanation for mood (affective) disorders. (4 marks)
>
>   *The biological explanation looks at how the neurotransmitter serotonin causes mood disorders.* ✓ *Our brain has serotonin which is released to regulate our mood and make us happy. However, when low levels are produced or too little is made available in the brain we experience symptoms such as sadness, fatigue, and a lack of interest in activities.* ✓ *A study done by Oruc et al. explains how genes such as the 5HT which is a serotonin transporter may be responsible for the low levels of serotonin.* ✓ *Dominic knowing that depression is due to biochemical imbalances could help him understand that his friend's depressive symptoms of low mood could be due to low levels of serotonin.* ✓
>
>   The candidate has applied the question to the scenario correctly. The answer explains the biological explanation and includes a study to support the claim. This answer therefore receives 4 marks.
>
> 2. (a) Outline **one** psychological treatment for impulse control disorder. (2 marks)
>
>   *Covert sensitisation is a therapy based on classical conditioning and involves a person pairing the addictive behaviour such as gambling with an unpleasant stimulus, for example vomiting or an electric shock.* ✓ *Once a person repeatedly associates the two they are able to feel disgusted and avoid the addictive behaviour.* ✓
>
>   Good response as the candidate recognises the theory behind the treatment and explains the association process. This response therefore receives 2 marks.
>
>   (b) Explain why this treatment for impulse control disorder is either reductionist or holistic. (2 marks)
>
>   *The treatment is reductionist because it only provides one treatment based on classical conditioning, which assumes that a person can learn to reduce their impulsive behaviour* ✓ *and does not take into consideration that it could be due to genetics or an imbalance of brain chemicals and not psychological.* ✓
>
>   Good response that earns the full 2 marks as the candidate knows what reductionism is in the first statement they make and also applies the issue to other areas ignored by the treatment.
>
> 3. (a) Lorena is having behavioural therapy to help manage her phobia of frogs. Explain **two** features of behavioural therapy that Lorena will complete as part of the management of her anxiety disorder. (4 marks)
>
>   *Lorena will undergo systematic desensitisation where she is exposed to a frog in stages.* ✓
>
>   The response should have two features clearly stated and explained in detail. The exposure is done through a fear hierarchy and relaxation. This response receives 1 mark.
>
>   (b) Explain **one** advantage of behavioural therapy for anxiety disorders compared to one other therapy. (2 marks)
>
>   *Systematic desensitisation is patient centred as one goes through each stage at their own pace.* ✓
>
>   The response should include a comparison with another therapy to gain full marks. This response therefore receives 1 mark.
>
>   **The full response could earn 10 out of 14 marks.**

Specialist Options: Approaches, Issues, and Debates

Essay questions worked examples

Worked example

Essay question

1. (a) Describe the study by Lovell *et al.* (2006) on the treatment of obsessive–compulsive disorder (OCD) using telephone administered cognitive–behaviour therapy (CBT). (6 marks)

Candidate response:

Patients with OCD were independently treated using telephone CBT and face-to-face CBT. Face-to-face therapy was done in 10 one-hour sessions individually with a therapist and the patient underwent ERP therapy to reduce their anxiety and reactions to the stimuli that they feared. They also created a fear hierarchy which was practised both in therapy and at home for at least one hour a day as part of the homework given to the patient. Patients who received the telephone therapy had two face-to-face sessions with the therapist one in the first session and the other in the last session. They covered the same ERP procedures as in the face-to-face therapy followed by eight weekly telephone calls that were 30 minutes long. They were sent the homework sheets at home. The results collected using the Yale-Brown Scale and the BDI show that there was a significant reduction in symptoms for both groups from baseline and immediately after treatment. Even more, so more improvements were recorded during the three-month follow-up. There were no significant differences between the two therapies on the Y-BOCS or on BDI which shows that both CBT-type therapies are effective in reducing the symptoms of OCD.

(b) Evaluate the study by Lovell *et al.* (2006) on the treatment of obsessive–compulsive disorder (OCD) using telephone administered cognitive–behaviour therapy (CBT), including a discussion about reliability. (10 marks)

Candidate response:

The study is applicable to real-life due to its high ecological validity because these are real patients with OCD who were undergoing actual therapy for the 10 sessions and they were also followed up to see how well they had improved. Therefore, the results help with applications to real-life because we can see that both the telephone and face-to-face therapy CBT is effective for treating people with OCD. This can be used with people who may not have the time to attend therapy sessions and can still get helped by a therapist from the comfort of their home or other location without actually seeing the therapist. The problem with applying this study is that it had a lot of sample attrition as many patients dropped out during the study the results may have been affected as fewer people were able to complete the study as it may be that the people who dropped out of the study had severe OCD and therefore this type of therapy would not be effective for everyone with OCD and reduces its application to everyday life.

The use of quantitative data and standardised measures increases the reliability of the study as we see test-retest being done at baseline, 1, 3, and 6 months later to compare results on the Y-BOCS and BDI. This helps increase the consistency of the measure as the same measure is being used repeatedly and the patient is exposed to the same items. In addition, the data produced is quite objective and less prone to researcher bias. There could be lowered reliability due to the repetition of the Y-BOCS which could have led to practice effects where patients could have become so familiar with what is being measured that they do better

---

Candidate may earn Level 3 (5 marks).

The candidate clearly addresses the requirements of the question in an accurate manner. There is an excellent understanding of the procedures and results of the study. The candidate should consider elaborating more on how the sample was recruited and expand more on the methods used in the study for the full marks to be awarded.

★ **Exam tip**

When answering 'describe' questions that refer to a key study, try as much as possible to lay out the ASMPR (aim, sample, method, procedure, and results).

Candidate may earn Level 4 (7 marks).

The candidate's response is detailed and the evidence has been included in the evaluation. Counter-arguments have been made for each issue and debate with appropriate arguments to support them. The first two paragraphs are fully complete; however, the candidate needs to include more evidence. For the third paragraph, it is better to start this response with the named issue of reliability. The content can be improved if the candidate refers specifically to one or more of the psychometric measures used in the Lovell study.

83

Specialist Options: Approaches, Issues, and Debates

> each time the test is administered. There is also a chance of social desirability bias where they want to look like the therapy has worked and might feel embarrassed to admit if their OCD symptoms have not improved or have worsened.
>
> The use of psychometrics is also an advantage for this study as they produce quantitative data which is objective and easy to analyse. Psychometrics are generalisable to the wider population and can be used to check progress in therapy.

Essay questions raise your grade examples

↑ Raise your grade

1. (a) Describe measures of anxiety and fear-related disorder. (6 marks)

There is the GAD-7 which measures anxiety with seven items and scores between 0 and 3. If the score is high, the patient is referred to a psychiatrist. ✓ The BIPI measures blood and injection anxiety on a 4-point scale of 0–3 and has 18 situations involving blood and injections. ✓ The person with the phobia is supposed to evaluate each situation and how they would react in each situation either mentally or physiologically. ✓ This was tested by Mas *et al.* with a clinical sample comprising 39 patients diagnosed with blood-injection phobia and those without the phobia. ✓ They filled the BIPI with 50 items about diverse situations preferably related to blood, showing that the BIPI can reliably tell the difference between a person with a blood phobia and one without the phobia. ✓

Note: Ticks are useful to annotate the good points made but they are not counted as marks.

Candidate may earn Level 2: 4 marks. The candidate shows very good knowledge of the BIPI. The first part of the response is limited and does not fully provide the labels on each scale range, for example 0 = not at all on the GAD-7. Additionally, examples of some items on the measures are also missing, for example an item on the GAD-7 "being so restless that it is hard to sit still". The example by Mas *et al.* is excellent.

> ★ **Exam tip**
>
> When describing measures, remember to think of FOUR things: What does it measure? How is it scored? What items are in the measure? Who it is used for? (Or evidence of where it has been used.)

(b) Evaluate measures of anxiety and fear-related disorders, including a discussion about psychometrics. (10 marks)

One evaluative issue that applies to measures of anxiety is reliability where the consistency of the measure is checked. A strength of reliable measures is that they are highly standardised, hence the cause and effects of the behaviour are seen. The study by Mas *et al.* found a high ability of the BIPI to discriminate between the non-blood phobic sample and the blood-phobic sample in 92.5% of the participants who were asked similar questions on a fixed scale. ✓ A weakness of reliable measures is that they tend to produce mainly quantitative data which may not provide in-depth explanations of behaviour. For example, the GAD-7 does measure anxiety on a fixed scale with forced choices and does not allow the patients to explain why they have excessive worry or trouble relaxing. ✓

Another issue is low generalisations where the measure cannot be applied to people and situations beyond the study. The use of the BIPI by Mas *et al.* may have ethnocentric bias as the findings are based on a Spanish community and items on the BIPI may apply mostly to the western culture, for example going to the dentist or getting an intravenous injection. ✓

Psychometrics measure the mind in numbers through the use of standardised questionnaires such as the BIPI or the GAD-7. ✓ They are useful because they are quicker for analysis and making comparisons as they produce quantitative data. However, a major problem with this data is that we are not able to get more details about a person's experience with the phobia and we only get a limited amount of information. ✓

Note: Ticks are useful to annotate the good points made but they are not counted as marks.

Candidate may earn Level 3: 6 marks. There is an inclusion of two evaluative issues. The first one is clearly applied with strengths and weaknesses, and examples from the measures to elaborate on the meaning in an accurate manner. There is a limited evaluation of the second issue as the candidate only looked at low generalisability and the analysis of that is limited. The named issue has some details but is limited only to the quantitative data.

This response could earn 10 out of 16 marks.

★ **Exam tip**

For the discussion you should discuss the strengths and weaknesses of psychometric measures while referring to the BIPI and GAD-7 as examples.

★ **Exam tip**

You should include the named issue or debate at the start of your part (b) answer. You should then include two other evaluation issues and/or debates. Within the evaluation you must give specific and detailed examples from part (a) of your answer (the studies, theories, techniques, etc.) to back up your evaluation and discussion points. Analysis should be done for each issue by making counter-points, evaluating strengths and weaknesses, and providing conclusions regarding debates.

Exam style questions

(a) Describe what psychologists have discovered about the treatment and management of impulse control disorders. (6 marks)

(b) Evaluate what psychologists have discovered about the treatment and management of impulse control disorders, including a discussion about idiographic and nomothetic explanations. (10 marks)

Activity 1

Define Reductionism:
Evaluate the five key studies and explain why each study may be considered to be either reductionist or holistic.

Key study 1	Key study 2	Key study 3	Key study 4	Key study 5

Specialist Options: Approaches, Issues, and Debates

Activity 2

Define nature versus nurture:	
Select two explanations of one abnormality (e.g. OCD) and explain why each supports either the nature or the nurture side of the debate.	
Explanation 1	**Explanation 2**
Nature:	Nature:
Nurture:	Nurture:

Activity 3

Define idiographic versus nomothetic:	
Select two treatments of one abnormality (e.g. schizophrenia) and explain why one supports the idiographic and the other the nomothetic side of the debate.	
Treatment 1	Treatment 2

★ **Exam tip**

To help with your evaluation skills in the exam:
- Create more worksheets like this for all of the issues and debates.
- Use the topic areas in clinical psychology to give examples.

Activity 4

ASMPR key study worksheet

Key study:	
Aim	
Sample and sampling method	
Research and data collection methods	
Procedure	
Results and conclusions	

You can copy this worksheet and use it for the different key studies.

Specialist Options: Approaches, Issues, and Debates

> **Activity or revision strategy**
>
> **Revision strategy:** Summarising the key study in 'chunks' will help you better recall the details and also answer specific questions about the study.

> **Activity or revision strategy**
>
> **Activity 5:** It is difficult for students to recall psychologists and their area of study. A **matching game** can be used to aid in recalling. After you have matched the items, give details of each study to test how much you remember. You can alter this for each of the options before the matching game.
>
> ### Impulse control disorders
>
> Use arrows to match the psychologist to the psychology being studied.
>
> | Psychologist | Psychology |
> |---|---|
> | Grant *et al.* | Feeling state |
> | Miller | Imaginal desensitisation |
> | Glover | Dopamine hypothesis |
> | Blaszczynski and Nower | Opiate antagonists |
> | Vroom *et al.* | Covert sensitisation |
>
> **Figure 3.1:** Impulse control disorders matching game
>
> Create more matching games for different topics!

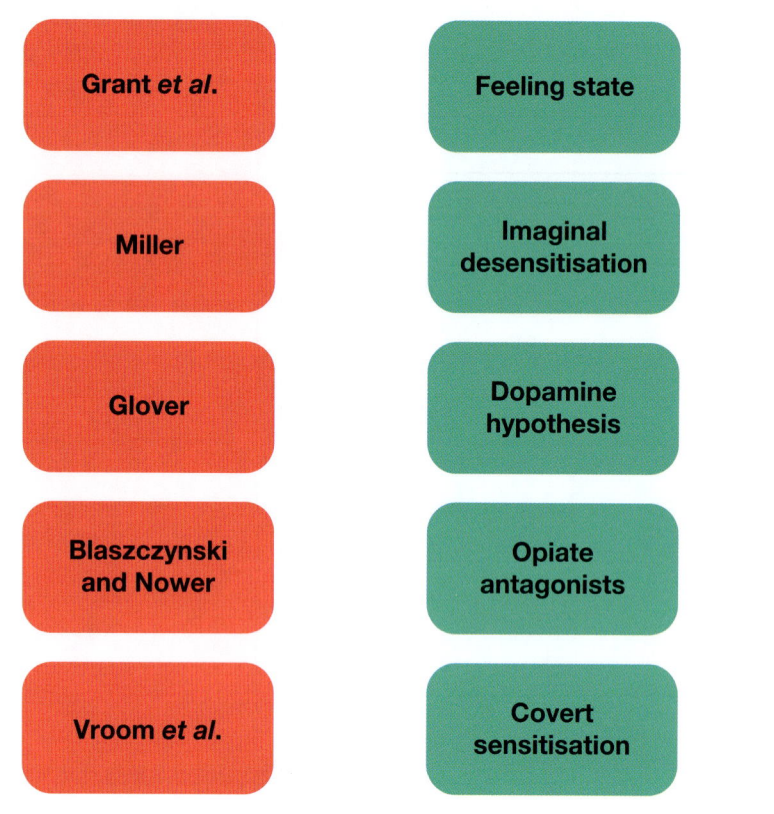

AL Specialist Options: Approaches, Issues, and Debates

Activity or revision strategy

Revision strategy: Make a **mind map** after revising each section. Mind maps are a great way to figure out what you cannot remember after a topic. If some branches are emptier than others, then you will know where to focus your attention and read further.

Here is an example of a mind map.

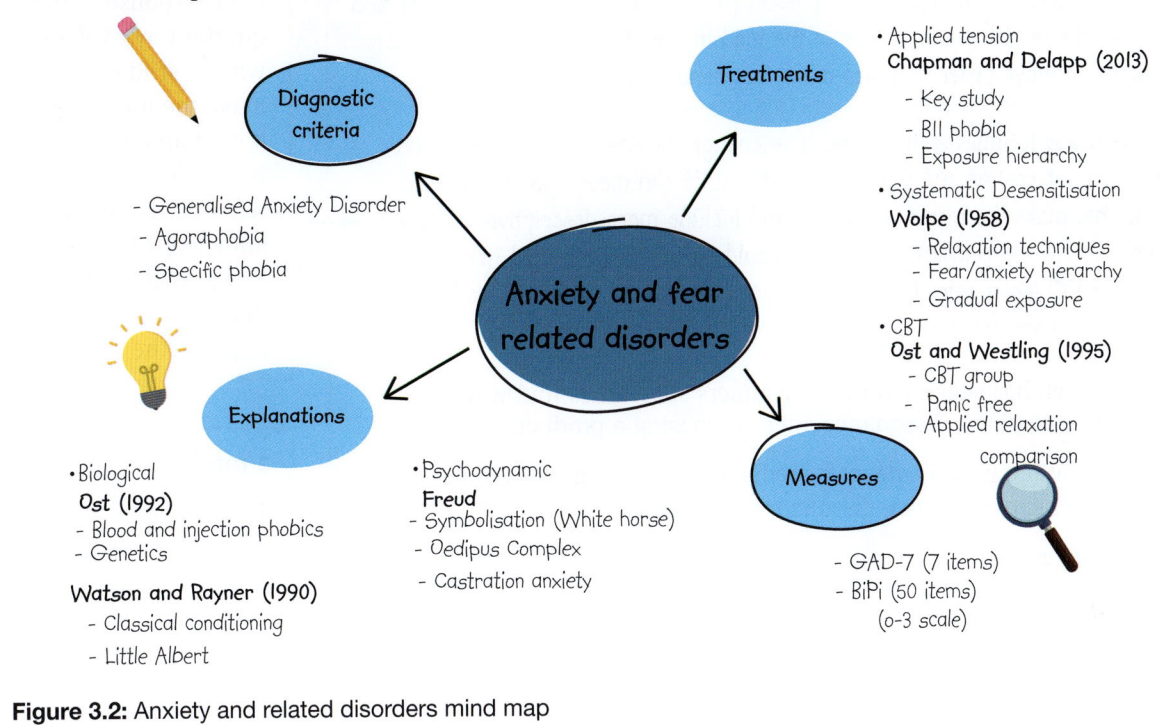

Diagnostic criteria
- Generalised Anxiety Disorder
- Agoraphobia
- Specific phobia

Anxiety and fear related disorders

Treatments
- Applied tension
  Chapman and Delapp (2013)
  - Key study
  - BII phobia
  - Exposure hierarchy
- Systematic Desensitisation
  Wolpe (1958)
  - Relaxation techniques
  - Fear/anxiety hierarchy
  - Gradual exposure
- CBT
  Ost and Westling (1995)
  - CBT group
  - Panic free
  - Applied relaxation comparison

Explanations
- Biological
  Ost (1992)
  - Blood and injection phobics
  - Genetics
  Watson and Rayner (1990)
  - Classical conditioning
  - Little Albert
- Psychodynamic
  Freud
  - Symbolisation (White horse)
  - Oedipus Complex
  - Castration anxiety

Measures
- GAD-7 (7 items)
- BiPi (50 items)
  (0–3 scale)

Figure 3.2: Anxiety and related disorders mind map

Consumer psychology

Short answer questions worked examples

Worked example

1. Tarquin wants to improve the design of the menu used in his restaurant. He believes that the current design is dull and boring. Suggest **two** ways in which Tarquin can improve the design of the menus in his restaurant. (4 marks)

Candidate A:

Tarquin can make sure the menu is arranged in such a way that the items that they need to move fast are placed within eye view of the consumer and using colourful images and vivid pictures of the food that immediately capture the attention of the customers. This was suggested by Pavesic who suggests that some sections of the menu should look different from the rest to catch people's attention. Another way is to ask the waiters to explain the food items on the menu and they can recommend the food that they want to sell the most. This way waiters can be coached to entice customers to buy the popular food items for people who are unable to make a choice.

2 marks

The second suggestion does not address the design of the menu and therefore is not awarded any marks.

89

Candidate B:

Tarquin could ensure that the font and colours on the menus are eye-catching and remove any small fonts that may make the menu difficult to read. The words and prices can be increased in size to attract the consumers' attention and increase the likelihood of ordering the item on the menu. Tarquin can stick to three different font styles as proposed by Pavesic for different food items and increase the brightness or colour of the food images to emphasise on products he wants to move faster and also make the menu quite appealing.

A second way to improve the menu is to change the descriptions of the food into more interesting and richer descriptions. He can move away from basic labels that make the menu look bland and include more descriptive labels. An example from the Wansink *et al.* study would be to change a food item such as 'Grilled Chicken' into 'Tender Grilled Chicken' as the latter will be highly chosen by customers due to the creative use of the food name.

4 marks

The candidate has correctly suggested two ways. They have applied their response to the question by explaining why their ideas would make the menu less boring and dull. The suggestions picked are referenced using previous knowledge learned and provide a clear understanding of how to improve the menu.

2. Research has suggested that consumers sometimes find ways to reduce cognitive dissonance after purchasing a product.

   (a) Outline what is meant by reductionism, using an example about reducing cognitive dissonance. (2 marks)

Candidate A:

Reductionism is where the way to reduce cognitive dissonance in a consumer is explained by breaking it down into simpler parts.

1 mark

The candidate is hinting at a definition of reductionism but not enough to earn the full marks available.

Candidate B:

The study by Nordvall focuses only on cognitive dissonance in post-purchase behaviour of grocery shopping where conflicting feelings and beliefs are solved by increasing or decreasing the desirability of the food.

0 marks

The candidate will earn no marks for this as it is just an outline/definition of cognitive dissonance in post-purchase behaviour.

   (b) Explain **one** weakness of reductionism, using an example about reducing cognitive dissonance. (2 marks)

Candidate A:

A weakness would be overlooking other factors that cause cognitive dissonance; therefore, we do not understand what else caused a person to buy a product.

1 mark

The candidate has suggested a weakness but the response is not fully developed enough to earn the full marks. The weakness should include ignoring how other factors interact together to influence purchasing decisions.

> ★ **Exam tip**
>
> The cognitive dissonance is not causing the person to purchase the product. The customer experiences cognitive dissonance as they have positive attitudes about both products. The customer then reduces the cognitive dissonance in order to purchase one of the products instead of the other.

Candidate B:

A weakness is that it overlooks other factors that could help reduce cognitive dissonance and focuses on only one factor which may not be the only reason consumers experience discomfort when faced with a choice of two products. There could be other factors such as purchasing a product for a family member, a product not being available or difficult to get, or buying the brand you have always purchased.

2 marks

The candidate has provided a correct weakness of the issue and has applied it accurately to the concept of reducing cognitive dissonance.

AL Specialist Options: Approaches, Issues, and Debates

3. (a) Ruth works in advertising. She has been asked to help with the advertising of a new health food product. She wants to use Lauterborn's 4Cs marketing mix model.

   (i) Outline how Ruth can use **one** of the 4Cs to help advertise the new health food product. (2 marks)

Candidate A:

Ruth could use Comprehension where the message is clear and well understood by the audience by making sure the target audience pays attention. For example, if the health food product is for kids she could use TV and include cartoon characters to entice children to eat healthy food.

0 marks

The candidate has not chosen a correct C from the 4Cs and has referred to the Yale Model of Communication instead. As much as it looks like 'Communication' in the 4Cs, the candidate has not chosen the correct C to encourage children to eat healthy food.

> ★ **Exam tip**
> There are a number of abbreviations in this topic. You could create visual aids to help in better recall (e.g. draw a picture to represent each of the 4Cs).

Candidate B:

One of the 4Cs could be communication which involves a dialogue between the company and the consumer. Ruth can use an effective advertising tool such as social media where she could place the information about the healthy food product. Ruth could also include a comments tab where consumers can interact with her, rate the product, and ask questions about the product.

2 marks

The candidate has chosen a correct C from the 4Cs and has shown knowledge of how to apply it in the case of advertising a new health food product in the market.

   (ii) Explain why this would help Ruth advertise the new health food product. (2 marks)

Candidate A:

If the correct audience comprehends the message it means they will pay attention to the product and be interested in the product, and most likely keep it in memory for purchase thereafter.

0 marks

The candidate continues to refer to the Yale Model of Communication which is incorrect.

Candidate B:

Communication via the internet and social media ensure that the message reaches a wider audience from the comfort of their phone. This means that Ruth would be able to reach a larger audience within a short period of time and significantly reduce her costs compared to other advertising methods such as print, billboards, and television. Ruth would also be able to know the response rate and satisfaction of her consumers towards the product straight away due to its interactive nature and instantly make improvements.

2 marks

The candidate's response is correct and explains why the medium chosen would help Ruth advertise the product effectively.

(b) Explain **one** strength of using the way you outlined in part (a)(i) that will help Ruth to advertise the new health food product. (2 marks)

Candidate A:

A strength is that Ruth will sell more if the audience understands what she is selling and if she communicates the benefits of the product in a vivid manner they will be drawn to the product.

1 mark

This response earns a 'benefit of the doubt' (BOD) mark. The candidate should elaborate the strength of communication in advertising. They merely mentioned it.

Specialist Options: Approaches, Issues, and Debates

> ★ **Exam tip**
>
> You should pay more attention to questions that are linked together. When doing revision, write the title of each topic, subtopic, and bullet point at the beginning of each revision note/card or within a mind map and quiz yourself on this to aid recall.

1 mark

The candidate should have talked more about the strength of communication in advertising. This was not clearly elaborated in the response.

Candidate B:

A strength of communication in the 4Cs is that it may encompass all the other Cs as it tells people where to buy the product, select the target audience to communicate to, and highlight the cost in the same communication package.

Short answer questions raise your grade examples

↑ Raise your grade

1. Company Z wants to create a new food package design for potato crisps to improve people's taste perceptions. The potato crisps will remain the same. Company Z wants to base the idea on the key study by Becker *et al.* (2011). Suggest **two** ways that Company Z can create a new food package design to improve people's taste perception, using the key study by Becker as examples. (4 marks)

   Company Z can make the new potato crisp package with colour saturation levels of about 50% as people may rate the price higher for such a colour scheme compared to 100% colour saturation. ✓ The study by Becker supports this as we see that there was a tendency to highly price the 50% colour saturated yoghurt products. This will be effective for consumers who prefer highly priced items and think potato crisps taste better because they are expensive and therefore will find the product more appealing. ✓

   The company could also change the potato crisp packaging so they sell their crisps in a box rather than a soft package as this would emphasise the angles of the packaging better. It would also increase the perception of the potato crisps as being more potent, highly positive, and the taste more intense which could increase purchase rates. ✓ This is supported by Becker's study where people perceived the angular yoghurt as having a higher taste intensity than the rounded one. ✓

   The candidate has referenced Becker correctly while making suggestions about how to improve taste perceptions by improving the packaging. Therefore, this receives 4 marks.

2. (a) Outline the utility theory/model of consumer decision-making. (2 marks)

   This refers to a consumer making a decision based on the best possible outcome or satisfaction they feel. ✓ The amount of satisfaction a consumer perceives they will receive from a product is rationally compared or ranked against a second product. ✓

   The candidate has correctly outlined the theory and used correct psychological terminology. This therefore receives 2 marks.

AL Specialist Options: Approaches, Issues, and Debates

(b) Explain how the utility theory/model of consumer decision-making is idiographic. (2 marks)

Everyone is unique in their preferences therefore what one perceives as the best outcome in a product may not be the same for everyone. ✓

The candidate needs to elaborate the response with an example and apply the debate to the question. Therefore, this receives 1 mark.

3. (a) A new shopping mall/centre wants to use odours (smells) to give shoppers a pleasurable experience whilst in the mall/centre.

(i) Outline **one** way the new shopping mall/centre can use an odour to give shoppers a pleasurable experience. (2 marks)

They could introduce light scents to the mall that are not irritable but pleasant to smell ✓ and this way consumers can enjoy the shopping experience.

The candidate could have elaborated what 'enjoy' means to the shoppers or refer to Chebat and Michon's results about the effect of odour. Therefore, this receives 1 mark.

(ii) Explain why the way you outlined in part (a) (i) would give shoppers a pleasurable experience. (2 marks)

A pleasant odour in the mall as seen in Chebat's study could help increase shoppers' view of the shops in the mall as selling high quality products ✓ and also this can positively alter the mood of consumers in this shopping mall who view the product and shopping experience as more pleasant. This mood elevation could lead to more spending in the shops in the mall. ✓

An excellent reference to Chebat and Michon's findings about the effect of odours. Therefore, this receives 2 marks.

(b) Explain **one** weakness of using odour to give shoppers a pleasurable experience. (2 marks)

Consumers may find an odour pleasant but they may still not buy the product because of price and other factors in the store like colour schemes and the demeanour of the attendants.

The candidate did not understand the question and needed to give a weakness of using odours. The candidate could have discussed individual differences in terms of which odours are found to be pleasant or some customers find shopping unpleasant and odour will not make a difference to how they feel. Therefore, this receives 0 marks.

The candidate's full response could score 10 out of the 14 marks.

> ★ **Exam tip**
>
> You should ensure, when answering this type of question, that you refer to topics learned. This will help you make better suggestions backed up by research, rather than providing your own point of view.

Specialist Options: Approaches, Issues, and Debates

Essay questions worked examples

> **Worked example**
>
> 1. (a) Describe what psychologists have discovered about:
>   - types of store exterior design, including storefront, window displays, and landscaping
>   - types of store interior design. (6 marks)
>
> **Candidate response:**
>
> External designs can attract consumers to your business such as how the signs and displays at the front of the store are placed and how products are displayed on the windows. This can make people come in and even the decorations around your store front.
>
> Interior designs are equally important like the colour schemes of your store can attract people who like a certain colour. The lighting in your business, such as luminous lighting can cause customers to feel positive about your products. Even the scent of a store can cause people to spend more.
>
> (b) Evaluate what psychologists have discovered about:
>   - types of store exterior design, including storefront, window displays, and landscaping
>   - types of store interior design
>
>   Including a discussion about ecological validity. (10 marks)
>
> **Candidate response:**
>
> Studies that look at how interior and exterior designs impact consumers are applicable to real life because they inform other business owners on how to best place certain variables such as shop furniture or displays; and what causes people to spend more and stay longer in their business. There is a study that looks at how supermarkets are arranged for example in grid form compared to a race track design. People found the grid type design easier to navigate for planned shopping. Supermarkets can borrow the easier design if they want customers to find products faster but it may be a disadvantage if they want them to see other products too. The study however may be applicable to online retailers and does have good ecological validity as the participants were doing a virtual shopping task which is similar to how customers shop online. This lacks ecological validity as you would not normally be in a lab sitting at the computer but at home on your computer or phone. Also the participants were given money by the researcher to spend which is different to using your own money. There is also another online study which uses American students only to see if the landscaping and window displays attract a student to buy for example jeans. This may not be applicable and can only work for products that can be displayed and not for the service industry.

Candidate may earn Level 2: 3 marks.

The candidate has provided an overview of the exterior and interior designs but has not fully answered the question. The candidate needs to describe psychological evidence to support their response.

Candidate may earn Level 2: 4 marks.

The candidate made an attempt to provide evidence and it was clear two studies were stated. The candidate should be using the evidence as examples to explain their evaluation/discussion points rather than providing evidence. There is a need to recognise the name and the topic area that this researcher has investigated in order to answer questions.

> ★ **Exam tip**
>
> You should include the named issue or debate at the start of your part (b) answer. You should then include two other evaluation issues and/or debates. Within the evaluation you must give specific and detailed examples from part (a) of your answer (the studies, theories, techniques, etc.) to back up your evaluation and discussion points. Analysis should be done for each issue by making counter-points, evaluating strengths and weaknesses, and providing conclusions regarding debates.

AL **Specialist Options: Approaches, Issues, and Debates**

Essay questions raise your grade examples

⬆ Raise your grade

1. **(a)** Describe the study by North *et al.* (2003) on musical style and restaurant customers' spending. (6 marks)

   The study aimed to investigate the effects of music on the amount of money customers spent in a restaurant. ✓ The restaurant served high-quality food at prices that attracted customers from the upper-middle class. The study was carried out over a period of three weeks. The sample consisted of an equal number of males and females who were not aware that they were being studied. ✓ There were three conditions which were the levels of the IV: pop music, classical music, and the no-music conditions. This was therefore an independent measures design as each participant was exposed to only one of the music conditions through the use of music played on a CD. ✓ The measures were collected by an experimenter who pretended to be working as a waitress in the restaurant. The experimenter collected data on what was spent on different categories of foods like starters, main meals, and desserts and the overall spend amount spent per person or for each party of diners. ✓ The results showed that there was more spending when classical music was played compared to the other two conditions. ✓

   Note: Ticks are useful to annotate the ASMPR (aim, sample, method, procedure, and results) but they are not counted as marks.

   Candidate may earn Level 3: 5–6 marks. The description is accurate and detailed. The use of psychological terminology is accurate and appropriate. This response demonstrates an excellent understanding of the material. The candidate could add more to the results.

   (b) Evaluate the study by North *et al.* (2003) on musical style and restaurant customers' spending, including a discussion about determinism and free-will. (10 marks)

   Named discussion:

   This study can be considered to be deterministic as it is the type of music (classical or pop) that is determining the spending behaviour according to the researchers. The diners spent more when classical music was played and less when no music was played. This external factor of music being played is what affected spending in the restaurant and even specifically ordering specialty items like coffee and desserts. ✓ This is useful for businesses to use classical music as it may determine how much consumers spend. Free-will is not clearly evident but one can argue that the amount spent can also be the personal choice and not determined by the music. ✓ For example, if it was a special day like a birthday one may decide to spend more and is not merely due to the music entertainment. The results also show that in the no-music condition there was high spending on wine which could be the will of a person to spend more rather than because of the environmental factors. ✓

   Generalisations can be made from the findings because the study included over 300 male and female participants which is a large sample. This helped provide detailed quantitative data about their spending habits in the restaurant over the three-week period. ✓ There could be low generalisability because they all came from the UK and in an affluent area which may not apply to less wealthy areas. In addition, countries other than the UK may have different appreciation of classical music. ✓

   The study has good validity as it was conducted in a real-life setting of a restaurant where the diners went to eat on a normal day and they were not aware they were being observed on their spending habits and interacted with the experimenter who acted as a waitress. ✓ This is advantageous as it reduces demand characteristics as the diners will not change to fit with the study aims which makes the findings ecologically valid. ✓ There may be low validity because there could have been other extraneous variables that may have affected spending rather than the music such as the waiting staff who may have been more welcoming to the customers, providing a better service which could have influenced the amount spent. In addition, the collection of quantitative data only does not offer a detailed account of why people may have spent more on food and drinks. ✓ To improve validity the experimenters may have considered asking the diners how they felt about the music on their way out to see if it was indeed the music that caused them to spend more and stay longer to order the different meal courses. ✓

Specialist Options: Approaches, Issues, and Debates AL

> **Note:** Ticks are useful for noting where creditworthy evaluation points are.
>
> Candidate may earn Level 4: 8 marks. This is a detailed evaluation of the research by North *et al*. The analysis was good and the named issue was well discussed. The supporting evidence is thorough and effective. The candidate needs to include more details in the second paragraph and also show the strengths and weaknesses of generalisations.
>
> **This candidate would earn up to 14 marks out of 16.**

Exam style questions

(a) Describe what psychologists have discovered about choice heuristics in consumer psychology. (6 marks)

(b) Evaluate what psychologists have discovered about choice heuristics in consumer psychology, including a discussion about individual and situational explanations. (10 marks)

Activity 1

Define generalisations:

Evaluate the five key studies and explain why each study is generalisable or not generalisable.

Key study 1	Key study 2	Key study 3	Key study 4	Key study 5

Activity 2

Define individual and situational explanations:

Select two areas in one subtopic (e.g. choice heuristics) and explain why each supports either the individual or situational side of the debate.

Topic 1	Topic 2

AL Specialist Options: Approaches, Issues, and Debates

Activity 3

Define idiographic versus nomothetic:	
Select two areas in one subtopic (e.g. personal space) and explain why one supports the idiographic and the other the nomothetic side of the debate.	
Topic 1	Topic 2

★ **Exam tip**

To help with your evaluation skills in the exam:
- create more worksheets like this for all of the issues and debates
- use the topic areas in consumer psychology to give examples.

Activity 4

ASMPR key study worksheet

Key study:	
Aim	
Sample and sampling method	
Research and data collection methods	
Procedure	
Results and conclusions	

97

Specialist Options: Approaches, Issues, and Debates

> **Activity or revision strategy**
>
> **Revision strategy:** You can copy the worksheet and use it for the different key studies.

> **Activity or revision strategy**
>
> **Revision strategy:** Summarising the key study in 'chunks' will help you better recall the details and also answer specific questions about the study.

> **Activity or revision strategy**
>
> **Activity 5:** It is difficult for students to recall psychologists and their area of study. A **matching game** can be used to aid in recall and as students match the items, they can give more details about each study to see if they recall the content learned.
>
> **The physical environment**
>
> Use arrows to match the psychologist to the psychology being studied.
>
> | | |
> |---|---|
> | North *et al.* | Store layouts (grid/freeform/racetrack) |
> | Vrechopoulos *et al.* | Noise on perception of food taste |
> | Mower *et al.* | Classical music on spending behaviour |
> | Woods *et al.* | Perceived crowding on PAD |
> | Machleit *et al.* | Effects of landscaping and window displays |
>
> **Figure 3.5:** The physical environment matching game
>
> Create more matching games for different topics!

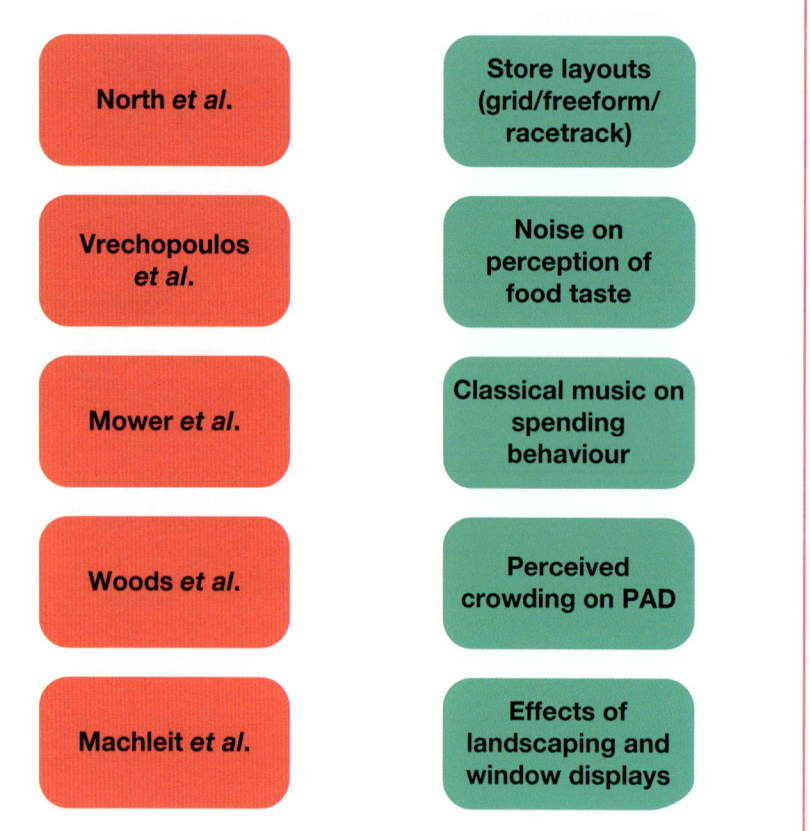

Activity or revision strategy

Revision strategy: Make a **mind map** after revising each section. They are a great way to figure out what you cannot remember after a topic. If some branches are emptier than others, then you will know where to focus your attention and read further.

Here is an example of a mind map.

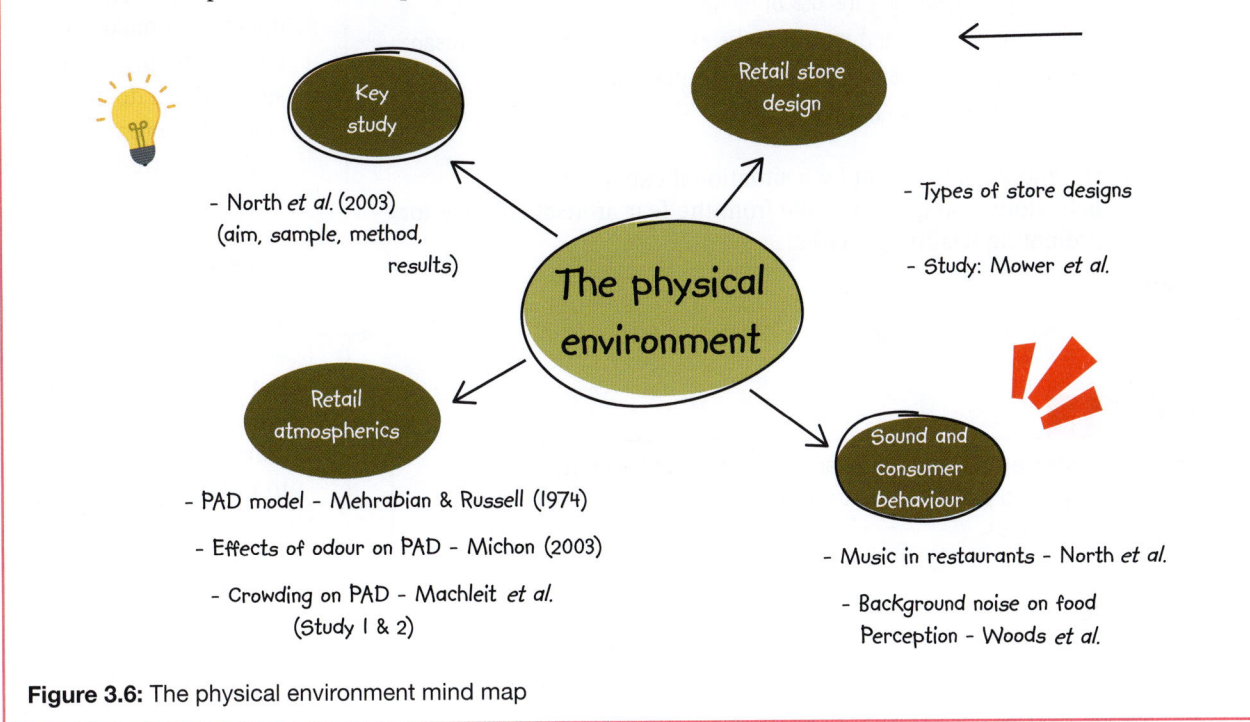

The physical environment
- Key study
  - North *et al.* (2003) (aim, sample, method, results)
- Retail store design
  - Types of store designs
  - Study: Mower *et al.*
- Retail atmospherics
  - PAD model - Mehrabian & Russell (1974)
  - Effects of odour on PAD - Michon (2003)
  - Crowding on PAD - Machleit *et al.* (Study 1 & 2)
- Sound and consumer behaviour
  - Music in restaurants - North *et al.*
  - Background noise on food Perception - Woods *et al.*

Figure 3.6: The physical environment mind map

Health psychology

Short answer questions worked examples

Worked example

1. Dr. Bentley wants to change his practitioner style from a doctor-centred approach to a patient-centred approach. Suggest **two** changes that Dr. Bentley could make to change his practitioner style. (4 marks)

Candidate A:

The doctor should only ask closed questions that require short responses like 'yes' or 'no' and also use a lot of medical language to avoid the patient asking for too much information about their diagnosis.

0 marks

The candidate misread the question. The question was asking about the patient-centred approach.

★ **Exam tip**

Candidates are often rushed when reading a question and provide incorrect responses. Read the question carefully as failing to do so may reduce your marks even when you have knowledge about the alternative terminology.

99

Specialist Options: Approaches, Issues, and Debates

Candidate B:

One change that Dr. Bentley could make is use open questions rather than closed ones that require a 'Yes' or 'No' answer when having a conversation with his patients as this will allow them to openly communicate any concerns they have and ask questions about the diagnosis he has made and medications he prescribes. Another change could be limiting the use of medical terms that may be hard for his patients to understand and make sure he explains what the terms mean and ask the patient if they have understood the diagnosis made and seek any clarification for things they do not understand.

4 marks

The candidate has provided a correct response and understands the two changes the doctor can make to change his practitioner style from a doctor-centred approach to a patient-centred approach.

2. (a) Outline what is meant by a situational explanation for behaviour, using an example from the fear arousal strategy for promoting health. (2 marks)

Candidate A:

This is when behaviour is affected by the situation a person is in.

1 mark

The candidate provides a simple outline for 1 mark but does not elaborate with an example from fear arousal as a strategy to promote health.

> ★ **Exam tip**
>
> **Revision strategy:** Candidates are advised to use synonyms when defining terms to provide a better definition of the term rather than repeat themselves.

Candidate B:

The situational explanation states that our behaviour is influenced by external factors such as the environment and the people around us. The situation of showing fear arousal images, for example brushing your teeth to prevent mouth sores may cause people to change behaviour as soon as possible because they are fearful of the negative consequences.

2 marks

The candidate has provided a correct response and has applied the topic correctly to the debate.

(b) Explain **one** weakness of the situational explanation for behaviour, using an example from the fear arousal strategy for promoting health. (2 marks)

Candidate A:

One weakness is that not all behaviour is influenced by others/the environment we are in. People can decide whether they will allow the situation to influence their behaviour. Even though a message is fearful, some people are not scared as much and they will continue with the bad behaviour because it may not happen to them.

0 marks

The candidate has given a clear explanation of one weakness. However, the example given from fear arousal does not link to this weakness. They are instead outlining a weakness of the fear arousal message and not a weakness of the debate.

Candidate B:

One weakness is that it is difficult to separate the individual from the situational factors that may affect one's behaviour. For example, in the Janis and Feshbach study, it could be situational as oral hygiene improved more in the minimal fear group compared to the strong fear message. However, 64 per cent of the minimal fear group did not change their oral hygiene which could be due to a variety of individual reasons.

2 marks

The candidate has provided a detailed and correct response with an example from the study that highlights why it is difficult to distinguish whether behaviour is due to just one side of the debate.

3. (a) Alessandra has long-term back pain. She has tried biochemical treatments, but these do not work for her. Suggest **two** other treatments that Alessandra could try to treat her long-term back pain. (4 marks)

100

Candidate A:

Alessandra could use acupuncture where needles are inserted at the point of pain. She could also use imagery where she gets an App that could walk her through pleasant images to forget her back pain.

> **2 marks**
>
> The candidate has briefly outlined two correct treatments. The question is worth 4 marks so the response should either explain how each treatment would reduce back pain or explain why the treatment would be effective for chronic/long-term pain to be awarded full marks.

Candidate B:

She could ease her back pain through attention diversion which is a cognitive strategy where Alessandra could be asked to focus on something that is not related to the pain. She can use something that she finds engrossing in the immediate environment, for example looking at family pictures on her phone or watching a happy video to distract herself when the pain becomes unbearable. She could also buy a TENS machine to use at home where she places the electrodes on the pain points on her back.

> **3 marks**
>
> The candidate's first suggestion is fully correct and well applied to the scenario provided. However, more details are required to earn full marks on the second treatment.

(b) For one of the treatments that you suggested in part (a), explain **one** strength of this treatment compared to a biochemical treatment. (2 marks)

Candidate A:

For imagery, a person is trained to create a pleasant image when in pain and this effort by the patient ensures that they are in control of their pain without experiencing any harmful side effects that may come from pain medication. The drugs could pose more risks such as dependency and worsening of symptoms as they may damage other body organs that may not be involved in the pain due to long-term use.

> **2 marks**
>
> The candidate's response is correct. A good comparison is given that explains why the strength of imagery is a weakness of a biological treatment.

Candidate B:

A TENS machine is easy to use as one can comfortably change the electrical current settings depending on the level of their pain. It may be expensive but good for long-term use.

> **1 mark**
>
> The candidate did not understand the question fully and gave a strength of TENS. The question requires a comparison between one treatment (e.g. TENS) and a biochemical treatment to achieve full marks.

Specialist Options: Approaches, Issues, and Debates

Short answer questions raise your grade examples

⬆ Raise your grade

1. Edina is feeling stressed. She has a busy lifestyle which she believes is enjoyable, including her work, so she cannot understand why she feels so stressed. Suggest **two** causes of stress that might explain why Edina is feeling this way. (4 marks)

   A cause of stress could be life events that are not work related. Edina could be going through life changes as exemplified by Holmes and Rahe who list a number of life events on the SRRS to measure how much stress a person experiences as they try to make readjustments. ✓ Edina should evaluate herself on the 43 life events and score the life changing events to see which events in her life could be causing her stress. It could be marriage, death of a loved one, mortgage, and so on. ✓

   Another cause of her stress could be her personality as explained by Friedman and Rosenman. They observed that a Type A personality can lead one to develop high stress that could result in stress related illnesses such as CHD. ✓ Edina seems to find a busy lifestyle and work enjoyable which means she may be highly competitive, aggressive, and always rushed in her work, these attributes in her personality may be causing her the stress. ✓

   The candidate has clearly understood the demands of the question and has suggested two causes of stress that could be causing the stress besides the busy lifestyle. Therefore, this receives 4 marks.

2. (a) Explain what is meant by reductionism, using an example from misusing health services. (2 marks)

   Reductionism is the breaking down of a phenomenon or feature into simpler parts where you study a part of it rather than the whole. ✓ For example, Aleem and Ajarim's case study looks at one patient with Munchausen syndrome and the focus is on the factitious disorder while ignoring other factors that may cause the misuse of health services such as social or cognitive reasons. ✓

   The candidate has correctly defined reductionism and given a study example to explain the issue. Therefore, this receives 2 marks.

   (b) Explain **one** strength of reductionism, using an example from misusing health services. (2 marks)

   By focusing on one explanation a researcher could gain an in-depth understanding of that one level of explanation and clearly see the cause-and-effect relationship. ✓ For example, in the case study of Munchausen syndrome by Aleem and Ajarim, we see that by looking at one perspective of misuse of health services they were able to provide a detailed account of a female with the mental disorder and how she misused the health facilities. ✓

   The candidate understands the strength of reductionism and includes accurate evidence to support the strength. This therefore receives 2 marks.

3. (a) Dr. Dallenbach wants to improve the adherence of his older patients to a new drug to help reduce blood pressure. Suggest **two** ways Dr. Dallenbach could use to help improve the adherence to the new drug. (4 marks)

   Dr. Dallenbach could come up with a verbal contingency contract ✓ where each patient commits to taking the new drug and records on a chart each time they take the medication, as advised by the doctor. This could involve the delivery of positive feedback or reinforcements once the contract guidelines have been adhered to and medication consumed as instructed. He could provide one free clinic check-up or a free refill of some tablets in their next prescription. ✓

   Another way to improve adherence could be customising the treatment ✓ for the older patients by meeting each individual patient and working out a plan of taking medication based on daily lifestyle preferences of the patient.

102

For example taking the new drug during their meal times or as they go about their daily chores or sorting out the medication in easy to open packages so that taking the drug does not cause them to go out of their way which they could find tedious hence not adhere. ✓

The candidate has provided a detailed and correct response. The response is well applied to the scenario provided. This therefore receives 4 marks.

(b) For one of the ways to improve adherence you suggested in part (a), explain **one** weakness.
(2 marks)

A weakness of contingency contracts is that they can be inaccurate because the patients may report following the contract if there is no close monitoring. ✓ They could easily fill in the contract charts even when they have not taken the drug. This is because they are self-administering the drug and not being monitored. ✓ Dr. Dallenbach could use a medication dispenser which measures the number of pills taken out of the bottle rather than relying on a patients' self-report which is highly prone to social desirability.

The candidate has correctly explained one weakness in the context of their suggestion from part (a) – contingency contracts. This part of the response would achieve 2 marks.
The suggestion on how to improve this weakness is not part of the question. This part of the response is not rewarded any marks and it has been ignored.

The candidate's full response could score 14 out of 14 marks.

Essay questions worked examples

Worked example

1. (a) Describe the study by Brudvik *et al.* (2016) on comparing pain assessments by doctors, parents, and children. (6 marks)

Candidate response:
The study measures children's pain using the visual analogue scale to see if they are in pain. The scale ranges from 0 to 100 and you select the number which you think represents your pain.

> ★ **Exam tip**
>
> When answering 'describe' questions that refer to a key study you should outline the ASMPR (aim, sample, method, procedure and results).

(b) Evaluate the study by Brudvik *et al.* (2016) on comparing pain assessments by doctors, parents, and children, including a discussion about generalisations from findings. (10 marks)

Candidate response:
The scale can be generalised to children below 15 years who can use the VAS in an easy and quick manner. The problem is that the children used in the study may be different from other children in their understanding of the scale. This is because they are from the same country and hospital which may be different from other countries where children may not be educated enough or have had experience of how to use a rating scale.

Candidate may earn Level 1: 1 mark.

The candidate provides a brief outline of one of the scales used in the study but fails to describe the study in detail. It should include a summary of ASMPR (aim, sample, method, procedure, and results).

Candidate may earn Level 1: 2 marks.

The candidate has discussed 'generalisability' in relation to the possible education or cultural differences between the participants and children from other countries. They have given a specific example from the study (understanding of the 1–100 scale) which is good and specific to the study. However, the response is very brief and needs to consider two/three more issues and/or debates.

Specialist Options: Approaches, Issues, and Debates   AL

> ★ **Exam tip**
>
> You should include the named issue or debate at the start of your part (b) answer. You should then include two other evaluation issues and/or debates. Within the evaluation you must give specific and detailed examples from part (a) of your answer (the studies, theories, techniques, etc.) to back up your evaluation and discussion points. Analysis should be done for each issue through making counter-points, evaluating strengths and weaknesses, and providing conclusions regarding debates.

Essay questions raise your grade examples

↑ Raise your grade

1 (a) Describe what psychologists have discovered about biofeedback and imagery. *(6 marks)*

Stress can be managed through biofeedback where a person can physiologically reduce their stress through bodily control. ✓ An EMG is attached to the skin surface and this gives feedback about their heart rate and muscle tension. Budzynski et al. measured the effect of biofeedback on patients with tension headaches. They tested this technique on 15 participants divided into three groups; the experimental group was told to keep the tone pitch low with muscle relaxation, the second group was told to relax around the constant tone, and the last group to relax as much as possible in silence. ✓ The experimental group with biofeedback had the greatest reduction in muscle tension over the five sessions provided than the control groups without it. After doing biofeedback the patient will notice they have a biological stress reaction they can use their relaxation strategies to reduce the physiological symptoms and therefore they will then feel less stressed. ✓

Imagery is also used to reduce stress through visualising a pleasant or relaxing image mentally. A patient is helped to imagine something pleasant such as a beautiful scenery and immerse themselves into this scene while using their senses of smell, sound, and feel to help them feel as relaxed as possible. ✓ When the patient experiences stress, they can use imagery to distract them from the stress as well as reduce the physical feelings of stress. Bridge tested this technique on 139 women being treated for breast cancer through radiotherapy for a period of 6 weeks. It was found that the women who had breast cancer diagnosis and taught both imagery and relaxation had lower stress scores. ✓

Note: Ticks are useful to annotate the good points made but they are not counted as marks.

Candidate may earn Level 3: 6 marks. This response clearly describes the two treatments and explains how each of the treatments can lead to a reduction in the symptoms of stress. The results of the relevant studies have been outlined to show that the treatments are effective for reducing stress.

(b) Evaluate what psychologists have discovered about biofeedback and imagery, including a discussion about application to everyday life. *(10 marks)*

The individual-situational explanations are evident in the research conducted on stress management. The individual side of the debate shows the personal factors may contribute to the reduction of stress as different people may conjure up different images that may help them feel less stressed through imagery and this cannot be tailor made for each individual. ✓ The situational side of the debate shows that depending on the situation a person is placed in they can reduce their stress or not. In the study by Budzynski those placed in the biofeedback group had more control of the tone and therefore were more likely to relax more than the two groups placed in a situation where they could not get feedback on their relaxation levels. ✓ The debate is useful in looking at the environmental and personal factors that may help reduce stress but looking at one side of the debate may be reductionist as stress management requires an interaction of both for patients to fully benefit from the treatment techniques. ✓ Both studies are also highly reliable as the psychologists use the independent measures design and a number of controls in the groups under research. This helps to see the clear cause-and-effect relationship of which particular strategy works better to reduce stress in patients with medical conditions. ✓

104

Note: Ticks are useful to annotate the good points made but they are not counted as marks.

Candidate may earn Level 2: 4 marks. This candidate has covered two evaluative issues. Individual versus situational is clearly applied to both stress management techniques outlined in part (a). The candidate has given strengths and weaknesses and examples from the stress management techniques/research. There is a limited evaluation for the second issue as the candidate only looked at reliability and no counter-argument was provided. The named issue was not included which is a major omission and has caused the candidate to lose substantial marks.

This candidate may earn a total of 10 marks out of 16.

★ **Exam tip**

Always cover the named issue or debate first.

Exam style questions

(a) Describe the study by Shoshani and Steinmetz (2014) on using positive psychology in schools to improve mental health. (6 marks)

(b) Evaluate the study by Shoshani and Steinmetz (2014) on using positive psychology in schools to improve mental health, including a discussion about psychometrics. (10 marks)

Activity 1

Define validity:

Extension task: include reference to different types of validity in this table such as ecological and/or temporal validity

Evaluate the five key studies and explain why each study is high in validity or low in validity.

Key study 1	Key study 2	Key study 3	Key study 4	Key study 5
Study:	Study:	Study:	Study:	Study:
High:	High:	High:	High:	High:
Low:	Low:	Low:	Low:	Low:

Specialist Options: Approaches, Issues, and Debates

Activity 2

Define application to real life:	
Select two ways of managing health from one subtopic (e.g. managing and controlling pain) and explain advantages of this application and disadvantages of this application.	
Topic 1	**Topic 2**
Topic:	Topic:
Advantage:	Disadvantage:
Advantage:	Disadvantage:

Activity 3

Define idiographic versus nomothetic:	
Select two areas in one subtopic (e.g. health promotion in school and worksites) and explain why one supports the idiographic and the other the nomothetic side of the debate.	
Topic 1	**Topic 2**

★ **Exam tip**

To help with your evaluation skills in the exam:

- Create more worksheets like this for all of the issues and debates.
- Use the topic areas in organisational psychology to give examples.

AL Specialist Options: Approaches, Issues, and Debates

Activity 4

ASMPR key study worksheet

Key study:	
Aim	
Sample and sampling method	
Research and data collection methods	
Procedure	
Results and conclusions	

You can copy this worksheet and use it for the different key studies.

Specialist Options: Approaches, Issues, and Debates

> **Activity or revision strategy**
>
> **Revision strategy:** Summarising the key study in 'chunks' will help you better recall the details and also answer specific questions about the study.

> **Activity or revision strategy**
>
> **Activity 5:** It is difficult for students to recall psychologists and their area of study. A **matching game** can be used to aid in recall and as students match they can give more items, details about each study to see if they recall the content learned.
>
> ### The patient–practitioner relationship
>
> Use arrows to match the psychologist to the psychology being studied.
>
> | Psychologist | Psychology being studied |
> |---|---|
> | Mckinstry and Wang | Delay in seeking treatment |
> | Mckinlay | Munchausen syndrome as misusing |
> | Savage and Armstrong | Non-verbal communication: doctor clothing |
> | Safer *et al.* | Consulting styles: directing and sharing |
> | Aleem and Ajarim | Medical jargon in verbal communication |
>
> **Figure 3.7:** The patient–practitioner relationship matching game
>
> Create more matching games for different topics!

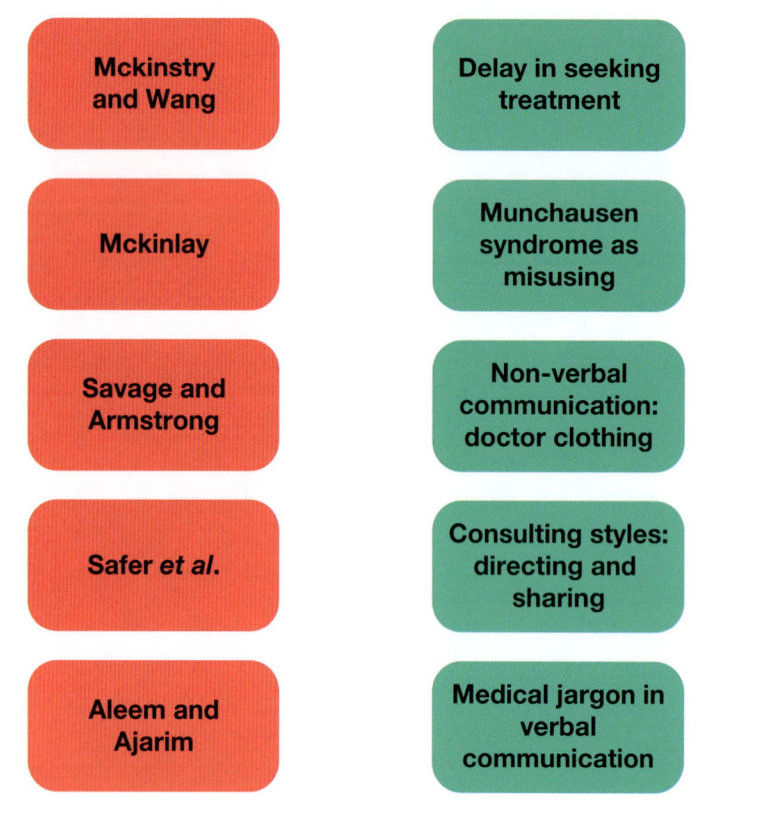

AL Specialist Options: Approaches, Issues, and Debates

> ### Activity or revision strategy
>
> **Revision strategy:** Make a **mind map** after revising each section. They are a great way to figure out what you cannot remember after a topic. If some branches are emptier than others, then you will know where to focus your attention and read further.
>
> Here is an example of a mind map.
>
> **Pain**
> - Key study
>   - Bruduik *et al.* (aim, sample, methods, results)
> - Types & theories of pain
>   - Types of pain
>   - Case study: Machachlan *et al.* (2004)
>   - Specificity and Gate Control theories
> - Managing & controlling pain
>   - Biochemical treatments
>   - Cognitive strategies
>   - Alternative therapies
> - Measuring pain
>   - Clinical interviews
>   - Psychometric measures
>   - Behavioural measures
>
> Figure 3.8: Pain mind map

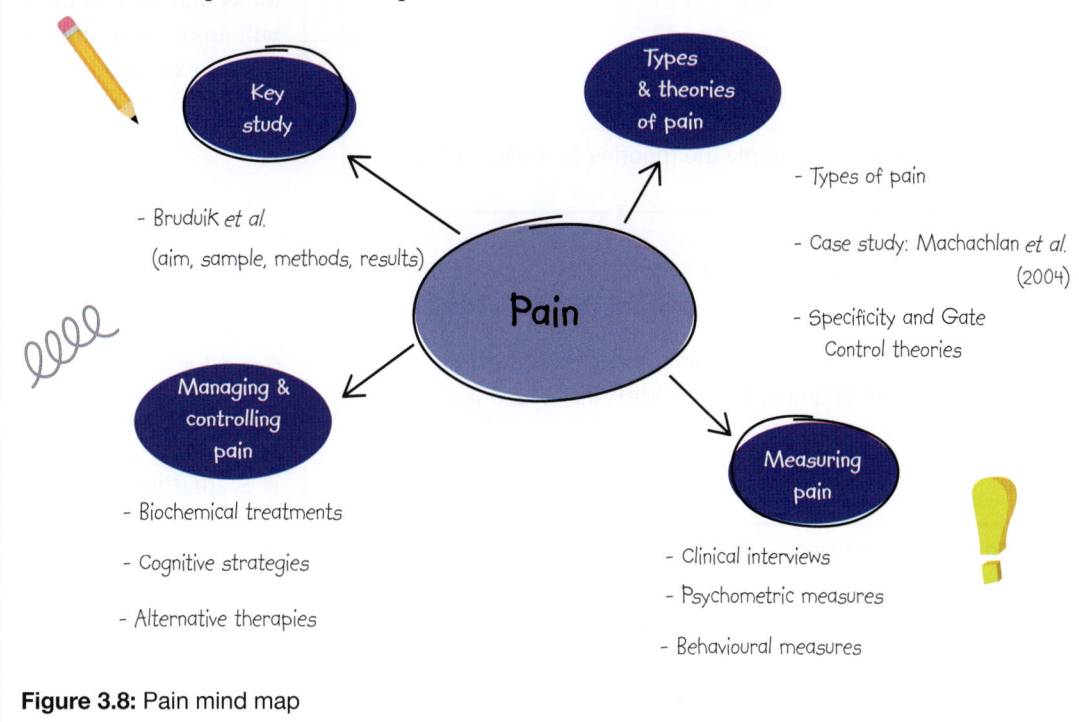

Organisational psychology

Short answer questions worked examples

Worked example

1. Rodion has recently been asked by his company to investigate how satisfied employees who work for the company are. He wants to use a measure called the Job Descriptive Index (JDI). Explain how Rodion can use the JDI to measure job satisfaction in the company. (4 marks)

Candidate A:
They will fill in a questionnaire by indicating Yes or No and he will then count the scores to see satisfaction.

Candidate B:
Rodion can give each individual employee the JDI questionnaire to fill in on their own on a particular day. He will instruct the employees to complete all five sections of the scale which look at salary and promotion among others. He can explain to them how they will fill the scale where they have to write Y for

0 marks

The response does not earn marks as the candidate has little understanding of the JDI. The response should match the amount of marks allocated for the questions. A 4-mark question requires a more in-depth explanation of the measure and application to the scenario to earn the full marks.

109

Specialist Options: Approaches, Issues, and Debates

Yes, N for No and ? if they are undecided about their response, for each word or phrase. For example, for pay they can indicate a Y on the item 'well paid' if they feel well paid or N if they feel underpaid. He can then compare the scores and see which area shows high satisfaction and which areas need improvement. He can discuss with the managers on how to raise job satisfaction, for example if the majority indicate the job is boring then they can help make the work environment more exciting.

4 marks

The candidate has given a very thorough response. The inclusion of a narrative of how the JDI looks and how Rodion will administer and use it is well explained.

> ★ **Exam tip**
>
> The question is testing the ability to apply the theories or measure to a real-life situation.

2. (a) Outline Vroom's VIE (expectancy) theory of motivation. (2 marks)

Candidate A:

It does not account for individual factors like training and the amount of workload that lowers motivations and what happens when the reward is not delivered.

0 marks

The candidate has misread the question and is evaluating the theory. The focus should be on giving a brief general overview of the theory, no evaluation is needed here.

> ★ **Exam tip**
>
> The question is testing the knowledge and understanding of the psychological theory.

Candidate B:

It is about rewards. For an employee to be motivated they must believe that their effort will result in a reward for their work and that the organisation will deliver the reward after they perform as promised, for example giving a bonus.

2 marks

A good response which gives a brief overview of the theory which is well explained for the marks available.

> ★ **Exam tip**
>
> The question is testing AO1 – your knowledge and understanding of the psychological theory. Learn how to define or explain briefly the theories.

(b) Explain how Vroom's VIE (expectancy) theory is either idiographic or nomothetic. (2 marks)

Candidate A:

There may be individual differences as some employees may want a reward so badly and others may not be motivated by it, therefore they won't be motivated.

0 marks

The candidate has not indicated which side of the debate they are discussing. In addition, they are outlining individual differences rather than the actual debate from the question.

Candidate B:

I believe it supports the nomothetic side of the debate as employees are quite similar in that they are motivated at work by money and so expect something in return for their performance. It can be generalised to almost all employees and motivate them to work extra hard when they know they will get a reward such as a bonus.

2 marks

The candidate understands how to apply the debate to the VIE theory accurately with an example.

> ★ **Exam tip**
>
> The question is testing the ability to analyse and evaluate the theory based on the issue provided.

3. (a) Suggest **two** ways in which a manager can adapt to challenges in the workplace. (4 marks)

Candidate A:

On the basis of the six principles by Heifetz *et al.*, I would suggest that an adaptive leader maintains disciplined attention and be open to differing views from the workers. This involves listening to what they have to say and reviewing this information and then act on it by confronting the problem at hand in an amicable way and avoiding covering up issues or ignoring what workers have to say.

2 marks

This is a correct response. The candidate, however, misread the question and has not provided a second way of adapting to challenges. Therefore, a second suggestion is needed to earn the full marks.

> ★ **Exam tip**
>
> Read questions carefully and underline the most important parts of a question to avoid omitting information that is crucial to gain full marks.

Candidate B:

They should not allow their personal feelings and emotions to affect their work.

They should trust their employees and listen to different contributions rather than avoid those who have differing opinions.

1 mark

The second part of the response is correct as it addresses the question on how they can adapt to challenges; however, it needs more elaboration to earn more marks. The first point does not answer the question and requires more elaboration as to how such emotions can affect how they handle challenges in the workplace.

> ★ **Exam tip**
>
> You should refer to two of the six key principles of adaptive leadership by Heifetz *et al.* to be able to answer this question correctly.

(b) For **one** of the ways a manager can adapt to challenges you suggested in part (a), explain one strength of this way of adapting to challenges. (2 marks)

Candidate A:

A strength of disciplined attention is that a manager is able to quell any resistance because the workers feel that their opinions have been taken into consideration. Adaptive leadership is more about teamwork and less about the power a manager can throw around; therefore, if you have a manager who listens and then acts on the recommendations there will be greater motivation to work.

2 marks

This is a good response that supports the claim made in (a) about adaptable leadership.

Candidate B:

A strength of listening to different contributions by employees rather than avoiding them helps a manager change some aspects of the organisation that may not be working. This is because those who are doing the actual job may be the best to identify the solutions needed. The manager may not see solutions as readily as employees do.

2 marks

The candidate provides a plausible strength to the response they gave in part (a).

> ★ **Exam tip**
>
> The question is testing the ability to apply the theories or perspectives to a real-life situation.

Specialist Options: Approaches, Issues, and Debates

Short answer questions raise your grade examples

⬆ Raise your grade

1. A company wants to introduce new designs of work. They currently only use an on-call design but feel that this is not the best design. Suggest **two** other designs of work that the company can introduce. (4 marks)

   One design the company can use is Rapid Rotation where the company has set shifts such as day, afternoon, and night. The worker will be given frequent shift changes. For example: two day, two afternoon, two night, two days off, or semi-continuous shifts where a worker has two or three shifts per day including weekends and have days off. ✓ *Another design could be Slow Rotation with set shifts but a longer time between changing from one shift to the next. For example, the worker will work the day shift for several weeks and then change to the afternoon shift for several weeks.* ✓

   The correct response has been given for one design and is well linked to the question. It is evident that the candidate believes they have discussed two designs when in fact they have discussed one which is shift work. Another design besides on-call design could have been flexitime. This would therefore be awarded 2 marks.

   ★ **Exam tip**

   The question is testing the ability to apply the theories or perspectives to a real-life situation.

2. **(a)** Explain what is meant by cultural differences. (2 marks)

   These are differences between people who come from different cultures and countries.

   The candidate has simply repeated the question and has not provided an understanding of these differences. This therefore does not receive any marks.

   ★ **Exam tip**

   When a question asks for a definition, avoid repeating the same words in the phrase, find other synonyms to use in their place for better elaboration.

   (b) Explain why knowledge of cultural differences is a strength, in relation to job satisfaction. (2 marks)

   Different cultures have different jobs for their people. I would imagine those with low wages, because their countries are poor, may have lower job satisfaction because they are not paid enough money.

   The candidate has misread the question and is giving an example of economic differences rather than explaining why the issue of cultural differences is advantageous to job satisfaction. This therefore does not receive any marks.

   ★ **Exam tip**

   An example of a full mark response: Knowledge of cultural differences is an advantage as we can see differences between which aspects may be unique to a particular group and which aspects are universal to avoid making stereotypical conclusions about behaviour and improving job satisfaction.

3. **(a)** Danilo wants to improve how the managers in his company handle conflict. He wants to use **one** of Thomas-Kilmann's five conflict-handling modes.

Specialist Options: Approaches, Issues, and Debates

(i) Outline how Danilo could use **one** of Thomas-Kilmann's five ways to handle conflict with his managers. (2 marks)

Danilo could use compromise to handle the conflict where each individual has to give up something ✓ he could instruct his managers that if for example they could be facing conflicts about how much time and effort workers are putting on a task, the managers can set a limit of how many task items must be completed by each worker daily. ✓

This is a correct response that identifies one conflict mode and proceeds to apply it to the scenario. This therefore receives 2 marks.

(ii) Outline how this way would help Danilo's managers handle conflict in the company. (2 marks)

It could help the managers focus on other organisational tasks that help grow the company rather than keep managing individual conflicts. ✓ Such inter-individual conflict, once managed, can help increase job satisfaction and the workers will focus their effort on meeting their targets, rather than dwelling on the conflict. ✓

This is a good application to how the mode can be a benefit to the organisation. This would receive 2 marks.

(b) Explain **one** strength of this way to handle conflict in the company. (2 marks)

A strength of compromising is that as much as everyone should enjoy a different working style and pace, the cooperation of workers should be the priority rather than a source of conflict. ✓ This can encourage employees to learn to deal with each other's differences by getting out of their comfort zones and norm, and give up something which will eventually contribute to the success of the entire organisation. ✓

This is a good response on the strength of the mode selected from Thomas-Kilmann, so this has received 2 marks.

The full response could earn 8 out of 14 marks.

Essay questions worked examples

Worked example

1. (a) Describe what psychologists have discovered about motivators at work. (6 marks)

Candidate response:

Psychologists have discovered that motivation at work can be extrinsic, where people get monetary rewards such as bonuses and performance-related payments. Bonuses are usually added to a person's salary while some companies also share a percentage of the company profits among all employees for their work, which gives them a strong sense of belonging to the company and increases their motivation to work hard. Evidence by Hollowell claimed that companies that pay their senior executives performance-related rewards report and maintain a high stock market presence. Motivation at work can also be intrinsic, where employees are encouraged through praise, respect, and empowerment. In a previous study by Landry et al., they cite Google as one of the companies that provide intrinsic rewards such as time off and choice of workload, which has led to high productivity ratings including being one of the best places to work. The self-determination theory (SDT) argues that the impact of rewards is largely attributable to the way they are presented to individuals, which is the meaning these rewards take on. Landry et al. investigated the functional

Candidate may earn Level 3 (6 marks).

This response is detailed and links the description clearly to motivation at work. It has been awarded full marks. The candidate has described the type of motivators at work and has also included a brief outline of self-determination theory as well as a detailed outline of the psychological evidence to support this theory.

113

meaning of rewards both informational and controlling, and propose that organisations should pass a clear message when providing rewards to encourage self-motivation among workers. They propose that the message should be conveyed in a supportive and encouraging way and not in an autonomy-threatening and pressuring way as this conveys a controlling meaning to workers. They found that students who received the informational meaning of the rewards had higher psychological satisfaction and thereby a greater intrinsic motivation to perform than the control condition that received a controlling message.

Activity or revision strategy

Revision strategy: Arrange each paragraph in two parts: one paragraph explaining the concept/theory in general and the second paragraph providing the evidence of how this has been proven through a study. That is why the questions ask '… what psychologists…'

(b) Evaluate what psychologists have discovered about motivators at work, including a discussion about reductionism versus holism. (10 marks)

Candidate response:

Individual and situational factors are relevant to the research done on motivators at work. The individual explanation can be applied to intrinsic/extrinsic rewards as there may be individuals who may thrive better at work when provided with cash rewards while others may be better motivated when provided with non-monetary rewards. A strength of this explanation is that each worker is motivated differently and we cannot apply a blanket approach to motivation at work and companies must look at their individual employees and see what draws them towards higher productivity. Situational factors can be seen in the design of the work environment. According to Landry et al., providing direct and clear information about rewards that will be received increases the effectiveness of the monetary motivator. This way, workers know what to expect in a positive way and therefore aim for higher productivity to receive the rewards.

Determinism versus free-will is also evident in the research on work motivators. The study by Landry et al. clearly states that the type of message, whether informational or controlling, may affect the satisfaction and performance quality of employees. This is deterministic because it is the external message that influences their motivation to work. A strength of determinism is that we can see that certain behaviours come from outside of us and this can help with making predictions about future behaviour. For example motivators being carefully packaged to convey positivity can determine worker performance in many organisations. Free-will also comes from one's personal choice to be motivated by the incentives or not. In Hollowell's study, as much as a monetary reward is being offered, it is really up to the individual executive to want to attain the reward; if they don't feel that the reward is sufficient they are less likely to increase their performance. A weakness of deterministic arguments is that they tend to ignore that we are individuals with the ability to make personal choices no matter what reward is offered by an organisation.

Named debate:

Reductionism is evident in Hollowell as we see that the main focus is on performance-related rewards and there seems to be no explanation about

Candidate may earn Level 5 (9 marks).

The candidate has evaluated the topic using three appropriate debates including the named debate of reductionism versus holism. The only shortcoming was not including the weaknesses of the individual–situational debate which helps provide a complete evaluation. Overall, the response was well structured with a good range of issues including the named issue. The selection of evidence is very thorough and with excellent analysis throughout the majority of the response.

AL Specialist Options: Approaches, Issues, and Debates

the effectiveness of other types of extrinsic rewards such as bonuses and profit-sharing. Reductionist studies make it easier to understand and test one component to show clear cause and effect, for example how performance rewards do help companies thrive in bigger markets like stock exchanges. Deci and Ryan's self-determination approach is holistic as it includes three psychological needs – competence, autonomy, and relatedness – and this approach found that self-determination allows people to feel that they have control over their choices, which has an impact on motivation when promised intrinsic rewards. However, reductionist arguments only provide a limited understanding and holistic viewpoints provide a fuller understanding of how different factors interact to motivate workers to feel in control.

> ★ **Exam tip**
>
> Ensure the named issue/debate is included in your essay as that could lead to achieving a higher mark.

Activity or revision strategy

Revision strategy: Spend about 30 minutes on the 'describe and evaluate' question, 12 minutes on part (a) and 18 minutes on part (b). This will ensure you have ample time to finish all questions.

Essay answer questions raise your grade examples

↑ Raise your grade

1. (a) Describe what psychologists have discovered about conflict at work. (6 marks)

    There is a study done with Finland employees to find out why people bullied each other. Factors such as envy, job status, and one's position in the workplace brought conflicts. ✓ Others felt it was the personality of the person. A worker could be naturally a bully or aggressive and that is why they ill-treat others at work.

    Note: Ticks are useful to annotate the good points made but they are not counted as marks.

    Candidate may earn Level 1: 1–2 marks. There is an attempt to describe Einarsen's (1999) findings but the study is not explained in detail to earn the full marks. The candidate has also described bullying at work and omitted other areas in this topic such as levels of conflict and the causes of this conflict.

    (b) Evaluate what psychologists have discovered about conflict at work, including a discussion about cultural differences. (10 marks)

    Cultural differences can affect how people relate at work depending on their cultural beliefs and behaviour. ✓ People in the west may be more likely to bully due to being in a more competitive environment. Eastern countries that are more collectivist value the group more and there may be more pressure to not bully. ✓ The study has good application as it can help to prevent bullying at work. Finally, ethics are broken as the participants in the study answered questions about bullying and this could be upsetting. ✓

    Note: Ticks are useful to annotate the good points made but they are not counted as marks.

    Candidate may earn Level 2: 3 marks. There is an attempt to respond to the named discussion issue but the counter-argument has not been made on psychologists who have no glaring cultural differences in their research. The candidate seems to have run out of time and should ensure they include two more issues and debates for a comprehensive evaluation.

    The full response would earn up to 5 marks out of a total of 16.

Specialist Options: Approaches, Issues, and Debates

> ★ **Exam tip**
>
> You should include the named issue or debate at the start of your part (b) answer. You should then include two other evaluation issues and/or debates. Within the evaluation you must give specific and detailed examples from the part (a) of your answer (the studies, theories, techniques, etc.) to back up your evaluation and discussion points. Analysis should be done for each issue through making counter-points, evaluating strengths and weaknesses, and providing conclusions regarding debates.

Exam style questions

(a) Describe the study by Swat (1997) on the monitoring of accidents and risk events. (6 marks)

(a) Evaluate the study by Swat (1997) on the monitoring of accidents and risk events, including a discussion about temporal validity. (10 marks)

Key term

Idiographic versus nomothetic: the idiographic side of a debate is where psychologists study what is unique about an individual and investigate this in a detailed manner.

The nomothetic side of a debate is where psychologists study what is similar between humans and establish general laws that can be applied to the wider population.

Activity 1

Define determinism versus free-will:

Evaluate the five key studies and explain why each study supports either the deterministic or free-will side of the debate.

Key study 1	Key study 2	Key study 3	Key study 4	Key study 5

Activity 2

Define individual and situational explanations:

Select two areas in one subtopic (e.g. leadership style) and explain why each supports either the individual or situational explanation.

Topic 1	Topic 2

Specialist Options: Approaches, Issues, and Debates

Activity 3

Define idiographic versus nomothetic:	
Select two areas in one subtopic (e.g. conflict at work) and explain why one supports the idiographic and the other the nomothetic side of the debate.	
Topic 1	Topic 2

★ **Exam tip**

To help with your evaluation skills in the exam:
- create more worksheets like this for all of the issues and debates
- use the topic areas in organisational psychology to give examples.

Activity 4

ASMPR key study worksheet

Key study:	
Aim	
Sample and sampling method	
Research and data collection methods	
Procedure	
Results and conclusion	

Specialist Options: Approaches, Issues, and Debates **AL**

> **Activity or revision strategy**
>
> **Revision strategy:** You can copy this worksheet and use it for the different key studies.

> **Activity or revision strategy**
>
> **Revision strategy:** Summarising the key study in 'chunks' will help you better recall the details and also answer specific questions about the study.

> **Activity or revision strategy**
>
> **Activity 5:** It is difficult for students to recall psychologists and their area of study. A **matching game** can be used to aid in recalling and as students match items, they can give more details about each study to see if they recall the content learned.
>
> **Physical work conditions**
>
> Use arrows to match the psychologist to the psychology being studied.
>
> | Psychologist | Psychology being studied |
> |---|---|
> | Fox et al. | Effects of shiftwork on sleep and accidents |
> | Swat | Monitoring and documenting accidents |
> | Gold et al. | Effects of shiftwork on health |
> | Oldham and Brass | Accidents in operator-machine systems |
> | Knutsson | Open-plan offices and reactions to work environment |
>
> **Figure 3.3:** Physical work conditions matching game
>
> Create more matching games for different topics!

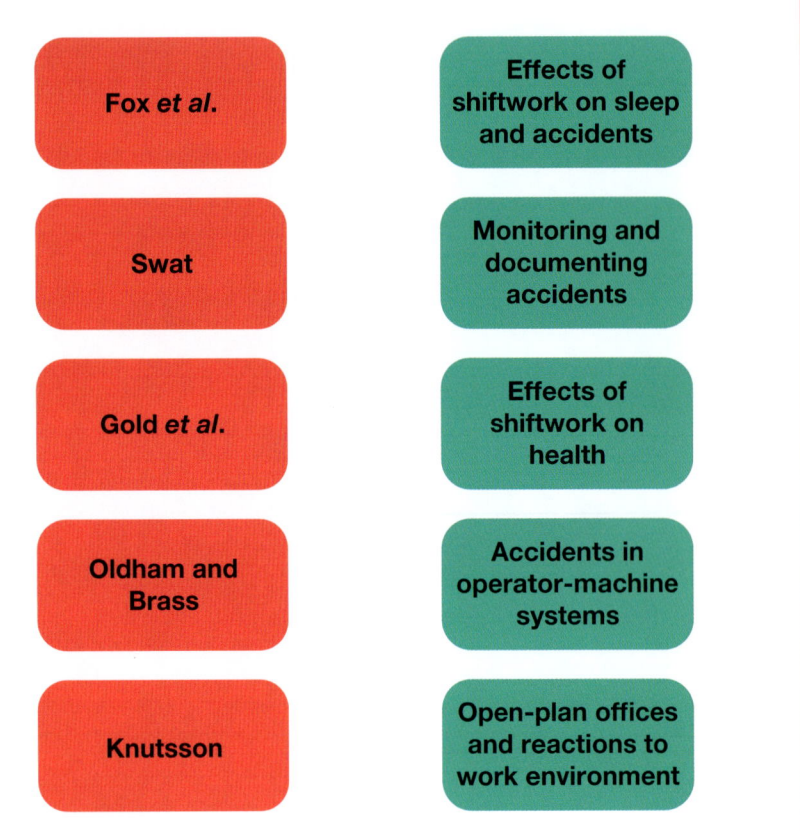

118

AL Specialist Options: Approaches, Issues, and Debates

Activity or revision strategy

Revision strategy: Make a **mind map** after revising each section. They are a great way to figure out what you cannot remember after a topic. If some branches are emptier than others, then you will know where to focus your attention and read further.

Here is an example of a mind map.

Satisfaction at work

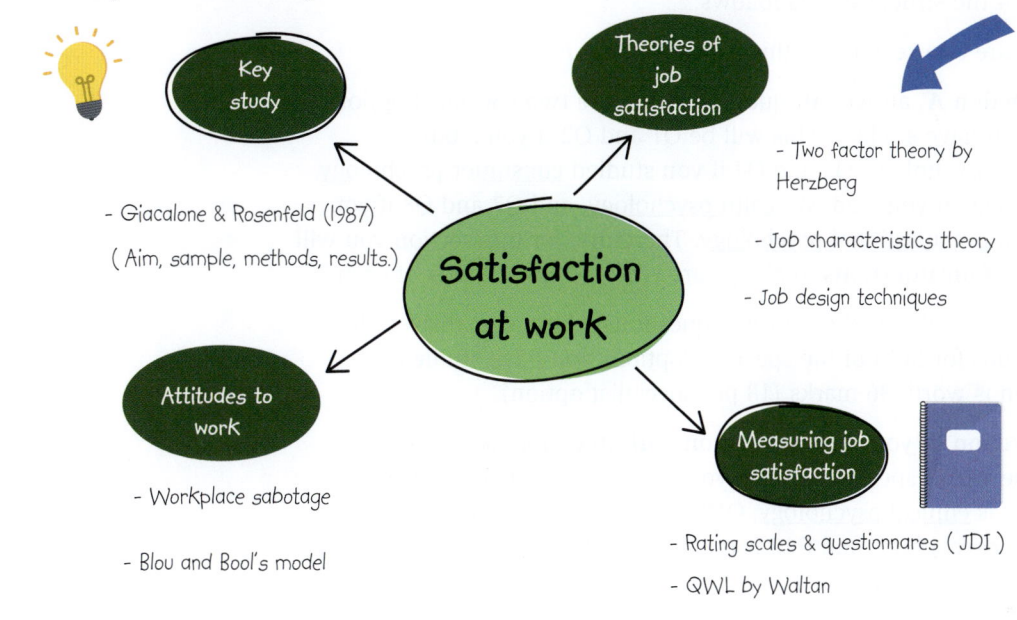

- **Key study**
  - Giacalone & Rosenfeld (1987) (Aim, sample, methods, results.)

- **Theories of job satisfaction**
  - Two factor theory by Herzberg
  - Job characteristics theory
  - Job design techniques

- **Attitudes to work**
  - Workplace sabotage
  - Blou and Bool's model

- **Measuring job satisfaction**
  - Rating scales & questionnares (JDI)
  - QWL by Waltan

Figure 3.4: Satisfaction at work mind map

119

4 Specialist Options: Application and Research Methods

Introduction to the paper

For Paper 4 the structure is as follows:

- There are two sections to this paper: Section A and Section B.

- For **Section A**, answer **all** questions from the **two** specialist options that you have studied. This will be Q1 and Q2 if you studied clinical psychology, Q3 and Q4 if you studied consumer psychology, Q5 and Q6 if you studied health psychology, and Q7 and Q8 if you studied organisational psychology. Therefore, for this section you will answer **four questions**, making sure you attempt all parts of each.

- **Section A** includes short answer questions where you answer <u>all</u> questions for **both** of the specialist options you have studied. This section is worth 36 marks (18 per specialist option).

- For **Section B**, you **only answer one full question**, so you can choose which specialist option you would like to answer questions on. Q9 is clinical psychology, Q10 is consumer psychology, Q11 is health psychology, and Q12 is organisational psychology. For example, if you had studied clinical psychology and health psychology, you would choose **either** clinical **or** health for Section B and answer all questions for that **one option**.

- **Section B** includes a 'design a study' question followed by a series of questions about your design (two questions worth 4 marks each, then three questions worth 2 marks each). You only answer a set of questions for **one** of the specialist options you have studied. This section is worth 24 marks.

- The paper is marked out of a total of 60 marks.

> ★ **Exam tip**
>
> This paper lasts for 90 minutes and there are 60 marks available. This equates to 1 mark every 1.5 minutes. Therefore, the 10-mark question should take you approximately 15 minutes to complete.

Knowledge check

In addition to the checklist for your chosen options from the Paper 3 chapter, you also need to know the following extra research methods for Paper 4.

🟥 Red: I do not understand.   🟨 Amber: I somewhat understand.   🟩 Green: I do understand.

Syllabus area	Red	Amber	Green
Experiments: Be able to describe and evaluate randomised control trials			
Questionnaires: Be able to describe and evaluate the use of postal questionnaires in psychological research			
Questionnaires: Be able to describe and evaluate the use of both ratings scales and fixed/forced choices			
Psychometrics: Be able to describe and evaluate the use of these in psychological research			
Hypotheses: Be able to write a null hypothesis and know why we use this type of hypothesis			
Hypotheses: Be able to write an alternative directional (one-tailed) hypothesis and know when we choose to use this type			
Hypotheses: Be able to write an alternative non-directional (two-tailed) hypothesis and know when we choose to use this type			
Validity: Be able to evaluate any study on its validity, including temporal validity			

Section A

2-mark questions

These will always focus on **one** thing. It can be about a key study, a theory, a concept, a finding, and so on. Anything that is compulsory (e.g. a key study or a named therapy) on the syllabus can feature here. When there is an e.g. in the syllabus, this means that a direct question cannot be asked about that study as it is just a suggestion.

4-mark questions

These will tend to focus on **two** things. It could be about two strengths of a study, two applications of a theory, one strength and one weakness of a study, describing two aspects of a study, and so on. Essentially, these can be seen as two, 2-mark questions! However, sometimes it may be one question worth four marks.

> ★ **Exam tip**
>
> Look at how many marks are assigned to every question that you answer to ensure that you are giving a response that has enough detail to be able to be awarded maximum marks.

Activity or revision strategy

Activity: Using the checklist from the Paper 3 chapter of this book, make sure that you have a study for every example listed. It may <u>not</u> be the study that is listed in the syllabus, but you must <u>make sure</u> that the study you have learned covers the concepts. For example, for menu design psychology in consumer psychology, the effect of food name on menu choice items has, for example, Lockyer (2006). If you have found a different study, <u>make sure</u> it is directly about the effect food name has on menu choice items!

Worked examples

For these, there are two sets of candidate responses for **all four options**. Therefore, locate the two options you have studied and look at those. Each option will have a full Section A set of questions. There is detailed commentary related to each of the responses given by the candidates.

Worked example

Clinical psychology

1. From the study by Chapman and DeLapp (2013) on the treatment of anxiety disorders:

   (a) Outline the context of this study. (2 marks)

Candidate A:

'T' was always fearful of crowds when he was younger and had witnessed people dying on several occasions. He completed several questionnaires like the Beck Depression Inventory, and he did get treated for his phobia.

Candidate B:

People who are phobic of blood and injections tend to faint when they encounter situations that involve either or both. Treatments for this type of anxiety disorder must allow a patient to be conscious when they are exposed to blood and/or injections, otherwise it cannot work.

> **0 marks**
>
> This response is not answering the question. The candidate has believed that context is describing the case history of 'T' and what he did during the therapy. A context question is asking about the reason(s) why the study was conducted.

> **2 marks**
>
> The context is clear, and the candidate understands the study and why the case study and treatment plan was important for blood/injection phobic patients.

   (b) Describe what was reported in the follow-up sessions in this study. (4 marks)

> **Key term**
>
> **Outline** means to provide a brief overview of something.

> **Key term**
>
> **Describe** means to provide an overview of a concept, theory, idea, process, and so on.

121

Specialist Options: Application and Research Methods

Candidate A:

After four months, 'T' said that he felt he had overcome his phobia of blood and injections. This was the same at 10 months.

> **2 marks**
>
> The first mark is awarded for the four-month result as it is correct. The second sentence has to get credit as it is a reported result from the 10-month follow-up session. The candidate needed to add two more follow-up results/findings to be able to earn the other 2 available marks.

Candidate B:

When he was followed up at 4 months, 'T' stated that he had a few doctor appointments coming up. He also stated that he felt he had overcome his phobia. When they met him after 12 months, his anxiety score had dropped significantly. He stated that he could control things like feeling anxious or sweating when exposed to blood/injections.

> **4 marks**
>
> Each sentence is awarded 1 mark as each point is correct. The candidate clearly knows the study and what happened during the follow-up sessions. The candidate noted that the question was out of 4 marks so wrote four different follow-up findings to be awarded all available marks.

(c) Explain **one** strength and **one** weakness of using case studies to study the treatment of anxiety disorders. (4 marks)

Candidate A:

One weakness can be that there is limited generalisability as a case study tends to be focused on just one individual. Therefore, a specific treatment for a case study may not apply to someone else with the same disorder as their experiences are unique. Another weakness is they can lack generalisability as no two cases are the same.

> **2 marks**
>
> The first weakness about limited generalisability is clearly outlined in generic terms. The candidate then explains why this could be a problem with treating anxiety disorders. The second weakness is repetition of the first so cannot gain any credit. Also, the candidate has not read the question carefully – it is asking for one strength and one weakness. Therefore, only the first weakness can be credited.

★ Exam tip

Always read the number of marks available for a question. Usually, a 4-mark question on Paper 4 is a 2+2 question, but this might not always be the case. When it is 'open' like this one, then four different points would need to be written to gain the available marks.

Key term

Explain means to provide reasons why. In this instance, something is a strength, and something is a weakness.

Candidate B:

One strength of a case study is that in-depth valid data can be collected as we are only focusing on one individual. This will allow interviews, questionnaires, and observations to happen to make sure we have the 'full picture' and fully understand the causes and progression of treatment over time for the anxiety disorder. However, one weakness is about generalisability. As it focuses on one individual, they may be unique with their lifestyle and experiences meaning it may only apply to them and no one else.

3 marks

The strength about in-depth valid data is clearly outlined in generic terms by the candidate. The candidate then explains why it is a strength in the context of the treatment of anxiety disorders, so this would be awarded the 2 available marks. The weakness is clearly outlined in generic terms. However, the candidate does not then explain why it is a weakness in the context of treating anxiety disorders so this can only be awarded 1 mark. The candidate needed to apply the weakness to the treatment of anxiety disorders to be awarded the fourth available mark.

2. There are several explanations for impulse control disorder.

    (a) Outline the biological explanation of impulse control disorders.
    (2 marks)

Candidate A:

One biological explanation of impulse control disorders involves the biology of the person like their brain. If we get rewarded, we do the action again, so gamble more.

Candidate B:

The release of dopamine into the body.

0 marks

The first sentence 'hints' at biology in terms of the brain but it is too generic to be awarded any credit. The second sentence is more about positive reinforcement than biology.

1 mark

The response would be awarded 1 mark for identifying a biological explanation. The candidate would need to then outline what the role of dopamine is to be awarded the second available mark.

   (b) Suggest how the biological explanation **cannot** explain individual differences in the development of impulse control disorders. (2 marks)

Candidate A:

All people have dopamine but not everyone has an impulse control disorder.

> **Key term**
>
> **Suggest** means to provide an idea based on knowledge and understanding of a concept.

1 mark

This response is brief but has a creditworthy point. It is a bit implicit but there is enough in the response to show some understanding, and this is why it would gain credit.

Candidate B:

Two people can have the same dopamine pathway in their brain. Both people may like to gamble. However, one person develops an impulse control disorder of gambling, but the other one does not. They have the same biology but not the same outcome, therefore, biology cannot explain this.

> **2 marks**
>
> The argument is clear and is focused on the development of impulse control disorders with a logical progression. The suggestion clearly tells the examiner why biology cannot explain the individual differences shown between the two people.

(c) Explain **two** ethical issues related to the biological **treatment** of impulse control disorders. (4 marks)

Candidate A:

One ethical issue is that it gives people an excuse for their behaviour as they can say 'my ICD is my biology and not my choice!' Another ethical issue is the potential side effects of treatments. Even though the treatment may be effective there could be unwanted side effects to taking drugs to treat ICD like vomiting and blisters.

> **2 marks**
>
> The first issue presented by the candidate is **not** about the treatment, but about the cause. The candidate has not read the question carefully so this cannot be awarded any marks. However, the second issue is well explained and in the context of treatment so it would be awarded the 2 available marks.

Candidate B:

One ethical issue is that people taking naltrexone can experience severe side effects like blistering of the skin and lumps which can be dangerous if not treated. Doctors would have to make sure that the person is aware of these side effects. However, if there is no other alternative, or they cannot have psychological therapy, then they might have no choice. Another ethical issue is about testing the effectiveness of treatments. If a placebo is used it means half the participants do not receive the actual drug. If the drug is seen to work it means that half the participants have been deprived of help, just to test out the effectiveness of the drug. This is not justified.

> **3 marks**
>
> The first issue presented by the candidate is outlined and explained using a drug that is commonly given for the treatment of impulse control disorder (naltrexone). Therefore, it would be awarded the 2 available marks. The second issue is well presented and shows good understanding, but the candidate has not applied it directly to impulse control disorders so the response can only be awarded 1 mark. The candidate needed to apply it to impulse control disorders to be awarded the second available mark.

> **Key term**
>
> An **ethical issue** can be two things. Firstly, it can be about the breaking of ethical guidelines and the impact this may have on a study or treatment, and so on. Secondly, it can be a wider moral issue like side effects, preventing people from accessing treatment, or restricting the free-will of people, for example. If a question asks about ethical guidelines, then your answer must focus on aspects like deception, lack of the right to withdraw, valid informed consent, and so on.

AL Specialist Options: Application and Research Methods

Worked example

Consumer psychology

1. From the study by Hall *et al.* (2010) on choice blindness:

   (a) (i) Explain the sampling technique used to recruit participants in this study. (2 marks)

Candidate A:

It was opportunity sampling as the shoppers happened to be passing by the stall and were asked if they would like to take part. They were 'chosen' from whoever happened to be shopping that day.

> **2 marks**
>
> This candidate response correctly identifies opportunity sampling and then explains how this was used to recruit the participants for the study by Hall *et al.*

Candidate B:

The shoppers volunteered to try the jam or the tea as they chose themselves to do it and were in the supermarket.

> **0 marks**
>
> The candidate has given the incorrect sampling technique so cannot gain credit.

   (ii) Explain **one** weakness of using this sampling technique in this study. (2 marks)

Candidate A:

It can be difficult to generalise as they are from a supermarket.

Candidate B:

Some people may have ignored the stall.

> **0 marks**
>
> This response is not answering the question. It is not clear that they are referring to opportunity sampling and the question asks the candidates to 'explain' so they would need to provide an argument as to why some people ignoring the stall could be a weakness.

   (b) After a participant had tasted a jam or smelled a tea, they had to rate it.

   (i) Outline the rating scale used in this part of the study. (2 marks)

Candidate A:

They rated on a 10-point scale.

> **1 mark**
>
> There is one element correct here: the 10-point scale.

Candidate B:

It was a 10-point scale from not very good at all up to very good.

> **2 marks**
>
> There are two correct elements here: the 10-point scale and then an outline of what the two ends of the scale were.

   (ii) Explain **one** strength and **one** weakness of this rating scale used in the study. (4 marks)

> **1 mark**
>
> This response would be awarded 1 mark as it correctly outlines one weakness of using opportunity sampling. However, there is no 'context' from the study (simply stating supermarket is not enough), so the second available mark cannot be awarded. The candidate needed to explain why only using participants at one particular supermarket who happened to be around when the study was being conducted could make generalisability difficult (e.g. one region, one type of customer visits that type of supermarket, etc.).

125

Specialist Options: Application and Research Methods

Candidate A:
One strength is that the scale is standardised for use in the study, and we know the rating is on a 10-point scale so then we can use the same scale to test for reliability by replicating the study. One weakness is that the scale is subjective, and it makes some comparisons difficult. For example, how one participant feels a '5' is will not be the same as another participant. This can reduce the validity of comparisons.

Candidate B:
Everyone gave the jam a score, so it obviously worked. However, the rating scale is subjective even though it is producing a number score. One person might rate a '10' as being the best jam they have ever tasted but for someone else, a '10' might be a jam they would eat every day and is not that special. Comparisons can be limited by this scale and reduce validity.

> **4 marks**
> The first strength is clearly identified and outlined in terms of a standardised scale. The candidate then explains why this is a strength in terms of reliability and replication so this would be awarded the 2 available marks. The weakness is also clearly identified and described in terms of potential subjectivity and comparisons. The candidate then also explains why this is a weakness using an example from the rating scale. Therefore, this would be awarded the 2 available marks.

> **2 marks**
> The first sentence is not a creditworthy strength about the scale 'working'. This is not a response based on psychology. However, the weakness is clearly identified and described in terms of subjectivity and then the candidate uses an example from the rating scale to explain what the weakness actually is.

2. Research into store exterior design has used questionnaires (surveys) to measure what people think about them.

   (a) Outline **one** finding from a study that has researched what people think about store exterior designs. (2 marks)

Candidate A:
In the study by Mower, the window displays and landscaping both had a positive impact on liking the exterior of a store.

Candidate B:
Landscaping had a positive effect on the store.

> **2 marks**
> This is a clear, well written finding from the study by Mower.

> **1 mark**
> This is a correct finding but it is brief and only tells us about landscaping. The Mower study also found window displays have the same effect so this would be awarded 1 mark. This candidate needed to add something similar to Candidate A to be awarded the second available mark.

   (b) Suggest **one** way in which store exterior design can be researched, other than using questionnaires. (2 marks)

Candidate A:
A field experiment could be used. Two stores in different shopping centres/malls could be set up in different ways and then see how many people look at the store displays.

> **2 marks**
> This candidate has identified a suitable alternative in terms of a field experiment. They have then added their suggestion of how this type of study could be run with explicit reference to store exterior design.

Key terms

Result: This refers to the data that was collected and analysed within the study. You can see it as the 'facts of the study' in terms of what the data is telling us about the study.

Conclusion: This refers to a generic 'summing up' of a study's results. You can see it as 'what we can take away from the study'. Conclusions do not refer to specific data or results.

Findings: This refers to either the results and/or the conclusion(s) of a study.

Candidate B:

An online questionnaire. They could fill in questionnaires about different stores they visit in a shopping centre/mall asking them to rate how much the landscaping and window displays affect if they would go into the store.

(c) Explain **two** weaknesses of using questionnaires (surveys) to measure the effectiveness of store exterior design. (4 marks)

Candidate A:

One weakness is that if there are many closed questions with various choices for the participant to choose from, they might not be able to give an honest opinion. For example, the choices might be 'really like the window display', 'no opinion', and 'do not like the window display.' How would a participant who likes the display but does not 'really like it' rate their response? Another weakness is that people can give socially desirable results as they want to look good for the experimenter.

0 marks

This candidate looks like they have not read the question carefully. The question asks for an alternative to questionnaires. However, this candidate has chosen online questionnaires with a suggestion of how the study could be conducted. Therefore, it is not answering the question.

3 marks

The first weakness is clearly identified and described by the candidate in terms of closed questions maybe not having the actual way someone feels as an option. The candidate then uses a clear example from store exterior design to explain why this is a weakness. This would be awarded the 2 available marks. The second weakness is also clearly identified and described by the candidate. However, there is no explanation as to why this could be a weakness for store exterior design research so this would be awarded 1 mark. The candidate needed to give an explanation using store exterior design as an example to be awarded the second available mark, like they did with their first weakness.

Candidate B:

One strength is that people are more likely to be truthful as they are not interacting with someone else. One weakness is that some participants might give socially desirable answers. So, some participants might rate the window display higher than they actually feel as they do not want to offend the people who set up the display.

2 marks

This candidate looks like they have not read the question carefully. The question is asking for two weaknesses. Their first point is a strength and even though it is correct, it cannot be awarded any marks as it is not answering the question. However, the weakness about socially desirable answers is clearly identified and described with an example from store exterior design research, so this would be awarded the 2 available marks.

Activity or revision strategy

Activity: For all 10 key studies you need to learn (five for each option you have chosen), write out each part of the procedure onto a different index card. Shuffle them and then attempt to put them in the correct order. Once you have become confident that you know the procedures, mix up all of the cards from <u>all five</u> key studies from one option you have studied and then try to sort them by key study and then in the correct order! Then repeat this process for the second option you have studied.

★ Exam tip

Always read the question carefully, underlining what is being asked for. For example, the question may be asking for two weaknesses, so make sure that you write about two weaknesses!

Specialist Options: Application and Research Methods AL

Worked example

Health psychology

1. From the study by Shoshani and Steinmetz (2014) on positive psychology in schools:

    (a) (i) Outline how the intervention group was set up in the study. (2 marks)

Candidate A:

This group was the PPIP (Positive Psychology Intervention Programme). The teachers were trained to deliver the PPIP in the school and then the teachers delivered the PPIP in age-appropriate groupings using a textbook. Aspects included letter writing to be grateful and also poetry.

Candidate B:

This group completed questionnaires like the Brief Symptoms Inventory, and they were all female, and they went to school.

> **2 marks**
>
> The first sentence identifies the intervention group but cannot gain credit as the question is about how it was set up. However, the second sentence has two valid points about teachers being trained **and** that it was age-appropriate with a textbook and these would be awarded 1 mark each.

> **0 marks**
>
> This response is not answering the question. The candidate has written about who the participants were and what they had to complete as part of the intervention programme.

(ii) Outline what the control group had to do in the study. (2 marks)

Candidate A:

The control group was half male and half female with average household income and most lived in a two-parent household. They all went to the same school.

Candidate B:

The control group followed the same curricula as the PPIP group with social science lessons. They simply did not participate in any PPIP lessons or activities.

> **0 marks**
>
> This candidate has written about the sample of participants used as the control group. Therefore, it is not answering the question, as the question is asking about what the control group did.

> **2 marks**
>
> One mark would be awarded for them following the same curricula and the second mark would be awarded for them not participating in the activities of the intervention group.

(b) (i) Outline what is meant by a baseline measure. (2 marks)

Candidate A:

These are measures taken at the beginning of a study. Before any intervention.

Candidate B:

This is a measure taken before any intervention or experimental aspect of a study is started. It gives a 'base' for any changes over time to be compared to, to see if any changes have happened.

> **1 mark**
>
> This is a creditworthy response for 1 mark as it only briefly outlines what a baseline measure is. However, the candidate needed to elaborate on this to be awarded the second available mark.

> **2 marks**
>
> Each sentence would be awarded 1 mark. The first sentence clearly outlines when the measure is taken. The second sentence then outlines what that measure is used for in a study.

128

(ii) Explain **one** strength and **one** weakness of using a baseline measure in this study. (4 marks)

Candidate A:

One strength is that there are a range of measures of psychological welfare before the PPIP started. This means that any changes in mental health can be tracked throughout the study as it can be directly compared to this initial score. Any changes add to the validity of the PPIP. One weakness is that the baseline measure is how each participant felt on that day when they filled it in. As this is transient it may not truly reflect how each candidate felt and this means that it could be a false reading as they were having a bad day. Therefore, any changes in scores over time might not be a valid reflection of change from the PPIP.

Candidate B:

One strength is that it gives a valid starting point to compare any changes in a longitudinal study. Without it you would not know how much any behaviours have changed. One weakness is that the initial measure may not be valid as it is taken at one single time point.

> **4 marks**
>
> The strength is well explained here using examples from the study itself. The question requires this as it states, 'in this study'. It is evident that the candidate knows when baselines measures are a strength. The weakness is also well explained using examples from the study and, again, it is evident that the candidate knows a weakness of baseline measure.

> **2 marks**
>
> Both the strength and weakness are valid evaluation points in relation to baseline measures. However, neither of them is applied to the study so they can only be awarded partial credit, in this case, 1 mark for the strength and 1 mark for the weakness. The candidate needed to provide examples from the study to be awarded the second available mark for each evaluation point.

2. Pain can be managed and controlled in many different ways. There are biological treatments, psychological treatments, and alternative treatments.

   (a) Outline **one** alternative treatment for the management of pain.
   (2 marks)

Candidate A:

One treatment is using a TENS machine. Electrodes are placed either side of where the pain is, and a very mild electrical current is passed through.

Candidate B:

People have used acupuncture.

> **2 marks**
>
> One mark would be awarded for identifying a correct alternative treatment (TENS). A second mark would be awarded for the description of how this alternative technique is administered.

> **1 mark**
>
> Only 1 mark would be awarded here for identifying acupuncture as an alternative treatment. To be awarded the second available mark, the candidate would need to describe what is involved in acupuncture.

Worked example

(b) Outline **one** other treatment for the control of pain, other than an alternative treatment. (2 marks)

Candidate A:

People can take drugs to combat pain. One example is the use of peripherally active analgesics that inhibit neurochemicals produced by damage.

2 marks

One mark would be awarded for identifying an 'other' treatment, in this case, drugs. A second mark would be awarded for an outline of what drugs do to help control pain.

Candidate B:

Acupuncture is an alternative treatment. Fine metal needles are placed slightly under the skin in areas near the pain. They are then 'twirled'.

0 marks

Whilst all of this is correct in terms of a way of controlling pain, the response is not answering the actual question. The question states that it has to be a treatment 'other than an alternative treatment'. It looks like the candidate has not read the question carefully.

(c) Explain **one** strength and **one** weakness of the treatment you outlined in part **(b)**. (4 marks)

Candidate A:

One strength is that the treatment is objective as we know the biological pathways that allow them to be able to reduce physical pain. This means that the pain can be targeted with the best type of drug. One weakness is that some people experience side effects.

3 marks

The strength would be awarded 2 marks. The response clearly outlines a strength of using drugs and then explains why. However, the weakness would only be awarded 1 mark as even though it is correct, it is brief. The candidate would need to explain what side effects might happen from taking drugs to control pain.

Candidate B:

One strength of acupuncture is that there are virtually no side effects which can happen with drugs. Therefore, it is a more ethical way of treating pain as it can be combined with other treatments for maximum effect. One weakness is that the place in which the needles are inserted can remain sore after treatment in the short term.

0 marks

This response is correct about acupuncture, but it is not answering the question. The candidate has correctly evaluated acupuncture, but the evaluation had to be about an 'other' treatment for pain that is not an alternative one. This candidate did not read the question carefully for both parts **(b)** and **(c)**. This is a good example of why reading the question carefully is essential for success.

AL Specialist Options: Application and Research Methods

Worked example

Organisational psychology

1. From the study by Swat (1997) on the monitoring of accidents and risk events:

    (a) Explain how an accident and an incident were defined in this study. (4 marks)

Candidate A:
An accident was one that is formally reported to a supervisor in the company. An incident was one that was not formally logged, but just talked out.

Candidate B:
An accident was something not pleasant that was reported directly to a safety supervisor in the Polish plant. An incident included personal injury.

> **2 marks**
>
> The response for 'accident' is correct and in some detail (formal and to supervisor) so would be awarded 2 marks. However, the definition of 'incident' is not one used in the study so could not be awarded credit.

> **3 marks**
>
> The response for 'accident' is correct and has some detail from the study (reported to supervisor) so would be awarded 2 marks. Look back at Candidate A's response and see how two different ways of answering both scored 2 marks. The definition for 'incident' is very brief but has one correct element about it being a personal injury so would be awarded 1 mark. To get the final available mark, the candidate needed to have a more detailed definition based on the study by Swat (e.g. it being a sudden event).

    (b) Suggest **one** reason why accidents happen in factories. (2 marks)

Candidate A:
Accidents happen when they are formally reported to a supervisor in a company.

Candidate B:
There may not be any safety procedures written up for using a piece of machinery and someone uses it incorrectly or without being trained on safety.

> **0 marks**
>
> The candidate has not answered the question here. They have attempted to use the definition from the study by Swat, but this is not what the question is asking!

> **2 marks**
>
> This response is a clear suggestion with some elaboration (no procedures, machinery, no training) so shows good understanding.

Activity or revision strategy

Revision strategy: On index cards write out the features and characteristics of the sample of participants used in all <u>10 key studies</u> you have learned for A-level on index cards – one for each key study. Write the name of the key study on the reverse of the card. Get someone to test you by showing you either the sample or the name of the study. Then you have to say what is on the other side of the index card.

131

Specialist Options: Application and Research Methods

(c) Explain **two** weaknesses of using a longitudinal study to investigate accidents in the workplace. (4 marks)

Candidate A:

People may leave the study or move away. A longitudinal study looks at a group of people over a certain time period and measures the same things at different timepoints to look for changes.

Candidate B:

As they take place over a period of time, some workers may have left the company before the end of the study. This means that you will not know if a certain new safety policy did work in the long-term or that the 'unsafe' workers simply left the company. Also, researchers can lose objectivity over time as they may become attached to the participants and may judge their behaviours subjectively and overlook certain behaviours that do not fit into the aim of the study.

> **1 mark**
>
> The first sentence is a generic weakness of using longitudinal studies but there is no context of the workplace so can only be awarded 1 mark. The second sentence is a description of what a longitudinal study is. It is correct, but the question is asking about weaknesses of using a longitudinal study. Therefore, it cannot gain credit. The candidate needed to write about a second weakness.

> **3 marks**
>
> The first weakness is thorough, clearly explains a weakness generically, and then uses an example 'in the workplace' with the safety policy example. The second weakness is also thorough, but it is all generic without any context of the 'workplace'. Therefore, the first weakness would be awarded 2 marks and the second 1 mark. The second weakness needed an example from the 'workplace' to be awarded the final available mark.

> ★ **Exam tip**
>
> When the question states 'in this study', or for this example, 'in the workplace', make sure that your response has something explicitly about the study (or workplace in this example) to be able to access all marks. Generic responses can only receive half the available marks.

2. Kelley (1988) proposed the idea of followership in relation to leaders and followers in the workplace. Kelley proposed five followership styles.

   (a) Outline **one** followership style proposed by Kelley. (2 marks)

Candidate A:

One style is called passive. This is when a follower is not critical in how they think, and they lack any initiative at work.

Candidate B:

One style is called forming. This is when a worker is critical in how they think and being active at work.

> **2 marks**
>
> The candidate has clearly named a correct followership style for the first mark and then outlined what that style is for the second mark.

> **1 mark**
>
> The style is not named correctly and is from group development. However, the description is correct for one of the followership styles proposed by Kelley so it must be awarded some credit.

132

Specialist Options: Application and Research Methods

(b) Each followership style is said to be based around an individual. Suggest why situational factors might also affect the followership style that a worker has. (2 marks)

Candidate A:

The job itself can affect how much a person is willing to follow rather than a particular personality style. A person might believe that their job is fine and follows a leader as their situation means they do not need to challenge.

Candidate B:

The personality of a worker can easily affect whether they follow a leader or not. People who are outgoing might be more critical, but even workers who are quiet can be critical, just to their best friend at work.

> **0 marks**
>
> The candidate has not answered the question. This is because their whole response is about why individual factors may affect workers, but the question is about situational factors.

(c) Explain **one** strength and **one** weakness in relation to how followership style can be applied to everyday life. (4 marks)

Candidate A:

It means that a person can choose whether to believe other people without questioning them so you might be able to look at your friends and see which type of follower they are and tell them.

Candidate B:

One strength of followership style is that if workers are assessed for their specific style, then an organisation can 'best place' them in certain roles within the company that requires, say, an effective follower or a conformist depending on the demands of the job and whether the company wants worker input into a project. One weakness is that it labels workers with one label. People may change their followership style in different roles and jobs they have within a company so having one label may mean that some workers are not working to the best of their ability within a company as they may be labelled passive but can be 'effective' in certain work-based situations. It means an organisation might not be getting the best out of their workers.

> **4 marks**
>
> The strength clearly outlines a way in which followership style can be used in the workplace to improve productivity and the potential wellbeing of an employee by placing them in a job that uses their skills more efficiently. The weakness also clearly outlines a potential problem of using a 'one label' system by not allowing a worker to show their best abilities at work.

---

1 mark

The first sentence is creditworthy as it shows knowledge of a potential situational factor. However, the second sentence is not clearly explaining why situational factors might affect followership. It would need clarity to be awarded the second available mark and is quite tautological (using the word situation to explain what situation is). An example from the workplace showing how the situation a worker finds themselves in affects who they choose to follow would have been awarded the second available mark.

0 marks

This response does not answer the question as it is attempting to relate followership style to everyday life, but it is anecdotal and not really clear how it would be useful to know about your friends.

★ Exam tip

For questions that ask about everyday life, make sure that your suggestions are not anecdotal but based on something that is useful in everyday life (e.g. improving the quality of life of someone, or a practical idea that will help a certain group of people). Also, ensure that all suggestions are ethical.

Specialist Options: Application and Research Methods **AL**

Raise your grade examples

> ## ⬆ Raise your grade
>
> ### Clinical psychology
>
> 1. One psychological therapy for the treatment and management of schizophrenia is cognitive-behavioural therapy (CBT).
>
>   **(a)** Outline the sample of **one** study that has tested the effectiveness of *CBT* for the treatment of schizophrenia. (4 marks)
>
>   In the Sensky study, participants had to be between 16 and 60 years of age. ✔ They had to be diagnosed with schizophrenia using DSM and ICD manuals. ✔ The had to be clear of alcohol or drug abuse and use. ✔ They also had to have tried medication for treatment, but it had not worked. ✔
>
>   This candidate has seen that the question is out of 4 marks and has outlined four different features of the sample – 4 marks.
>
>   **(b)** Outline **one** result from the study you outlined in part **(a)**. (2 marks)
>
>   At a nine-month follow-up, those patients in the CBT group had continued to improve with their symptoms of schizophrenia compared to the befriending group (both groups had initially shown improvements though). ✔✔
>
>   Correct response (with a comparison between the two groups) – 2 marks.
>
>   **(c)** Explain **one** strength and **one** weakness of using a longitudinal study to investigate the effectiveness of using CBT for the treatment of schizophrenia. (4 marks)
>
>   One strength is that you can investigate the longer-term effects of CBT rather than it being a 'one-off' assessment. ✔ It would allow the psychologist to know exactly when the CBT helps to show improvement in schizophrenia symptoms and if this continues well after a treatment programme has officially ended. ✔ One weakness is that there is a risk of only a small number of participants being left in the study by the end, reducing the validity of findings. ✔
>
>   Strength is very thorough so 2 marks are awarded. Weakness is only generic with no application to CBT so only 1 mark would be awarded.
>
> 2. There are several explanations of fear-related disorders.
>
>   **(a)** Outline the behavioural explanation for fear-related disorders. (2 marks)
>
>   One behavioural explanation for fear-related disorders is classical conditioning. ✔ Repeated associations of a neutral stimulus with 'fear' can mean that the neutral stimulus becomes a phobic stimulus and produced fear in the person. ✔
>
>   Correct response – 2 marks.
>
>   **(b)** Explain **one** reason why the behavioural explanation for fear-related disorders can be generalised. (2 marks)
>
>   It can be generalised as everyone has a phobia.
>
>   This is not true so cannot be awarded any credit – 0 marks.
>
>   **(c)** Explain **two** strengths of using case studies to investigate the causes of fear-related disorders. (4 marks)
>
>   As it is focused on one person, the researchers can gather a great deal of in-depth data about factors that could have caused the phobia, therefore ensuring that there is validity in findings. ✔✔ Another strength is that it gives an opportunity to follow the participant over time to see if anything else can be remembered or if a further event happens that can elaborate on why the phobia developed in the first place (and this could be first-hand rather than relying on memory). ✔✔
>
>   Both strengths are well argued, logical, and related to the causes of phobias – 4 marks.
>
>   **The full response could earn 15 out of 18 marks.**

AL Specialist Options: Application and Research Methods

⬆ Raise your grade

Consumer psychology

1. The effect of food name on menu item choice has been studied by consumer psychologists.

   (a) Outline the procedure of **one** study that has investigated the effect of food name on menu item choice. (4 marks)

   Wansink wanted to investigate whether 'rich' descriptions of food on a menu affected whether someone would buy/eat the food. The descriptions of six commonly chosen foods were manipulated. Anyone who selected one of these chosen foods (e.g. chicken or chocolate pudding) was given a questionnaire to complete. ✔ They had to rate the food on three main nine-point scales. ✔ There was also space on the questionnaire where participants were encouraged to add a comment about the name of the food/how it tasted. ✔

   This response could earn 3 marks. The first two sentences are not about the procedure so could not receive credit.

   (b) Outline **one** conclusion from the study you outlined in part **(a)**. (2 marks)

   It was concluded that adding a few descriptive words (like succulent, or Grandma's) to food on a menu positively affects how a consumer perceives the quality of the food. ✔✔

   Full, correct conclusion – 2 marks.

   (c) Explain **one** strength and **one** weakness in relation to how research into the effect of food name on menu item choice can be applied to everyday life. (4 marks)

   One strength is that is can be used by restaurants to improve sales and perception of quality of food. ✔ One weakness is that the choice of descriptive words is subjective so it may appeal to the people who own the restaurant but not the diners! ✔

   This could earn 2 marks. The strength is too brief to be awarded a second mark as it does not tell us how this could be achieved. The weakness is also brief with a lack of elaboration/examples.

2. Research has sometimes used an electroencephalograph (EEG) to study the effectiveness of different types of advertising media.

   (a) Describe **one** finding from research that has used an EEG to study the effectiveness of different types of advertising media. (2 marks)

   Ciceri reported that when EEG data was analysed when looking at a series of advertisements in different types of media, those who were viewing it on a tablet had the highest 'frustration EEG' score of any of the conditions. ✔✔

   One clear correct finding is evident here and could earn 2 marks.

   (b) Suggest **one** way in which the effectiveness of different types of advertising media can be studied, other than using an EEG. (2 marks)

   One other way could be to interview people about their experiences. ✔ There could be a structured interview that asks people about how much they like viewing advertising on different types of media like TV or a magazine. ✔

   A valid suggestion that could earn 2 marks.

   (c) Explain **one** strength and **one** weakness of using an EEG to measure the effectiveness of different types of advertising media. (4 marks)

   One strength is that EEG measurements are objective and require minimal interpretation. ✔ Therefore, it can make comparisons across different conditions meaningful as a different EEG pattern whilst watching adverts on a TV might be seen compared to watching it on a tablet. The comparison is a valid one. ✔ One weakness is that it lacks ecological validity and probably mundane realism. ✔ Watching advertisements whilst wearing an EEG and rating advertisements is not an everyday task so people's brain activity might be different whilst viewing at home rather than in a laboratory, lowering overall ecological validity. ✔

   This is a thorough response – 4 marks.

   The full response could earn 15 out of 18 marks.

Specialist Options: Application and Research Methods   **AL**

↑ Raise your grade

Health psychology

1. Health psychologists are interested in improving adherence to medical advice in children.

    (a) Outline the procedure of **one** study that has investigated improving adherence to medical advice in children. (4 marks)

    Children aged 1–6 years were recruited to take part. It was in Australia. They got half to use a Funhaler and complete questions about how they adhered to the medical advice. ✔ *The children who used the Funhaler were much more likely to take the recommended dosage, compared to those in the Breath-Tech group.*

    This could earn 1 mark. Only one sentence here is the actual procedure of the study. The candidate writes about the sample and then a result but this is not answering the question.

    (b) Explain **one** ethical issue in relation to using children in research about improving adherence to medical advice. (2 marks)

    Children would be forced by their parents to participate in the study as they are never given the right to withdraw. ✗

    This would not gain any credit. The A-level is all about learning how a psychologist would research in the real world and this would simply not happen!

    (c) Explain **one** strength and **one** weakness in relation to using children in research regarding improving adherence to medical advice. You **cannot** refer to ethics in your answer. (4 marks)

    It can be argued that younger children are much less likely to show demand characteristics in a study as they would probably not work out the aim. ✔ *One weakness is the ethics of using children as they may not understand that they have the right to withdraw from treatment if they feel uncomfortable or do not like whatever is being used (e.g. a Funhaler).*

    The strength is generic with no context so is only awarded 1 mark. The weakness is a good response, <u>but</u> the question specifically states that you cannot use ethics in the answer, so this would not be awarded any marks.

2. Holmes and Rahe constructed a Social Readjustment Rating Scale (SRRS) to measure the impact of life events on stress.

    (a) Describe how this scale is used to measure the impact of life events on stress. (2 marks)

    Participants are asked to read a list of 43 Life Events ✔ *and indicate which have happened to them in the last year.* ✔ *Each life event has a stress score (LCU) out of 100 and these are added up across all of the events that have happened.* ✔

    Correct response. This could earn 2 marks.

    (b) Suggest **one** other way in which the impact of life events on stress can be measured, other than the SRRS. (2 marks)

    People can be interviewed about what has happened to them recently. ✔ *Questions could be asked about certain life events and then they can be asked about stress. They can also be asked about their perception of how these life events have affected their stress levels.* ✔

    Well explained suggestions that could earn 2 marks.

    (c) Explain **two** weaknesses of using the SRRS to measure the impact of life events on stress. (4 marks)

    One weakness is that the LCUs are subjective. ✔ *Just because the original scale rates divorce as 73, does not mean every person feels it is that stressful. Some might be happy to be divorced!* ✔ *Another weakness is that it is unethical to ask people about this.*

    This response could earn 2 marks. The first weakness is well argued. The second weakness is too brief so could not be awarded any marks. What is unethical?

    The full response could earn 8 out of 18 marks.

Raise your grade

Organisational psychology

1. Shiftwork can affect the health and wellbeing of employees.

   (a) Outline the aim of **one** study that has investigated the effect of shiftwork on the health and wellbeing of employees. (2 marks)

   Gold investigated the effect that shiftwork had on nurses on their sleep and accidents at work. ✔✔

   Full, correct aim that could earn full marks.

   (b) Explain **two** findings from the study you outlined in part **(a)**. (4 marks)

   Those with a rotating work shift pattern and those on nights reported less sleep during the study. ✔✔ They had to complete a range of questionnaires to measure sleep patterns, amount of alcohol consumed, and medication taken. ✘

   The first finding is clear and correct and could earn 2 marks. The second sentence is not a finding, but how variables were measured.

   (c) Explain **two** ethical issues in relation to investigating the effect shiftwork has on the health and wellbeing of employees. (4 marks)

   Invasion of privacy as people might feel under pressure to reveal behaviours that they might not usually talk about. ✔ Participants may drop out and then it could be difficult to debrief them about the study. ✔

   Each sentence correctly identifies a potential ethical issue, but neither are applied to shiftwork by the candidate. This response would be limited to 2 marks.

2. Hackman and Oldham proposed a Job Characteristics Theory.

   (a) Outline **one** of the five critical decisions of their Job Characteristics Theory. (2 marks)

   Autonomy. ✔ This is about whether a job allows the worker to have some freedom in terms of organising a project and planning. ✔

   Correct response that could earn 2 marks.

   (b) Suggest **one** reason why this theory is based around an individual explanation. (2 marks)

   Every worker can be different and each one will have a different job in an organisation. This means that the decisions are already made by the management and so any 'critical' decision has already been made. ✔

   The argument provided here reads more like the situation of how a hierarchy of a manager affects a worker, rather than it being an individual explanation. This could earn 1 mark only.

   (c) Explain **one** way in which this theory **can** be applied to everyday life and **one** way in which this theory **cannot** be applied to everyday life. (4 marks)

   One clear application is that a management board can use the five critical decisions to create jobs that workers will want to apply for. It can also make current positions more appealing by maybe giving workers more autonomy or allowing workers to feed back to improve aspects of a job. ✔✔ One way it cannot be applied is that all jobs are different so it cannot be applied to every single job. ✘

   The reason why it can be applied is very thorough and logically written. It is explained well using terms from Hackman and Oldham. The reason why it cannot be applied is not correct as the whole idea of Job Characteristics Theory is that it can be applied to any job in any organisation (or at least they can test the five crucial decisions). This response could earn 2 marks.

   Overall, this candidate would have been awarded 11 marks out of a total 18.

Specialist Options: Application and Research Methods

Section B

For this section of Paper 4, you need to answer **one** full question from just **one** of the options you have studied. This section is comprised of the following:

- Question (a) will be a 10-mark question asking you to plan a study. Sometimes the research method is already chosen for you, but there will be some questions where you get to choose the research method. There will be **two** elements of the plan that will be listed in the question that you **must** cover in your response.

- Question (b) will be in two parts. The first part will ask you to describe psychological knowledge that your plan is based on. The second part will ask you how **two** features of this knowledge helped you to plan your study.

- Question (c) will be in three parts. The first part will ask you to state **two** reasons for choosing a particular technique/format, and so on. The technique/format, and so on will be one of the two elements of the plan that were listed in question (a). The second part will ask you to explain **one** strength or weakness of the technique/format you chose. The third part will ask you to explain **one** reason for your choice of technique/format, from the other element listed in question (a).

The syllabus lists the general features and specific features that need to be covered in your plan for question (a) which is very useful. There are eight research methods that could feature in question (a): laboratory experiment, field experiment, questionnaires, interviews, case studies, observations, correlations, and longitudinal studies. Table 4.1 summarises the general and specific features needed for each of the research methods:

General	These are expected for **all** research methods Aim/hypotheses Procedure Sample and sampling technique Ethical guidelines adhered to How the plan is valid How the plan is reliable Data collection and how it will be analysed

Specific *if applicable	**Experiments** Type IV DV Controls/standardisation Experimental design Counterbalancing* Random allocation* Field: location	**Self-reports** Open/closed questions Examples of questions Scoring of questions Interpretation of question responses Questionnaires: Paper/pencil, online, postal (technique) Interviews: Structured, semi-structured, unstructured (format) Face-to-face, telephone (technique)	**Case study** Detail about sample What information will be collected Two + techniques for collecting data Analysis, interpretation, triangulation
	Observations Overt/covert Participant/non-participant Naturalistic/controlled Structured/unstructured Number of observers	**Correlations** Two measured variables (co-variables) How first variable will be measured How second variable will be measured Type of correlation Scatter graph	**Longitudinal** Tasks being used How the task will be scored The frequency and interval of follow-ups How re-contacting of participants will happen Controls Standardisation

Table 4.1

Specialist Options: Application and Research Methods

In order to be awarded a mark in the top level, all of Table 4.1, both general and specific, must be included in your response.

Worked examples

Here are two sets of candidate responses for **all four options**. Locate the two options you have studied and take a good look at them. Each option has a full Section B set of questions. There is detailed commentary related to each of the responses given by the candidates. For the 'plan a study' question, the commentary is in a useful box that you can use for revision purposes. It lists all general and specific features that are expected in an answer to be awarded Level 5.

Worked example

Clinical psychology

1. Mood (affective) disorders can be treated biologically with antidepressants.

   (a) Plan an experiment to investigate the effectiveness of two different types of antidepressants. Your plan must include the following details:
   - sampling technique
   - how you would implement a randomised control trial. (10 marks)

Candidate A:

I would recruit a random sample of people who are about to begin treatment for depression. I would get a local health centre to use a list of all people eligible for antidepressants and then use a random name selector to choose the 40 people I want for the study. 20 would take a course of SSRIs and the other 20 would take a course of MAOIs. Therefore, it would be an independent measures design. The independent variable would be the type of antidepressant (SSRI or MAOI) and the dependent variable would be their score on a depression scale. I would probably use the Beck Depression Inventory. Each participant would have an equal chance of being in the SSRI group or the MAOI group, but no participant would be told which group they are in. Also, I would make sure that the people giving out the drug also do not know which group a participant is in. After they have taken the course of antidepressants, which for this study is four months, I would use the Beck Depression Inventory to measure how severe the depression is and take an average for both groups to see which one is the most effective. The group with the lower score would be the one that is most effective. All participants would then be debriefed and told which antidepressant they had taken, and any questions asked would be answered.

Experiments				
General	**Covered?**	**Specific**	**Covered?**
Aim/hypothesis	No	Type	N/A
Procedure	There is a general idea of how the study would be run	Independent variable	Clearly operationalised
Sample/ sampling technique	Yes, good coverage of random sample	Dependent variable	Clearly operationalised (maybe needed range of scores)
Ethics	There is a mention of debriefing	Controls, standardisation	There is mention of a four-month protocol
Validity	Nothing explicit	Experimental design	Clearly identified
Reliability	Could be replicated	Counterbalancing, random allocation	Random allocation is clearly covered as one of the bullet points
Data analysis	Analysis between groups is mentioned	Field only: location	N/A

This answer would be awarded Level 4 (7 marks). There is a range of both generic and specific features covered but, as can be seen in the commentary table, some are brief and there are gaps. The response covers the Level 4 response criteria.

Candidate B:

The aim is to test the role of antidepressants in treating depression. There would be two types of antidepressants used: MAOIs and the selective serotonin one. I would have 10 people in each group, and they would not know which group they are in – only I would know that. They would be volunteers. My independent variable would be the type of drug and the dependent variable would be the reduction of depression. I would ask for informed consent by telling them that they would be getting an antidepressant and would they like to take part. If the person cannot give their own consent, then I would ask a family member. All of this would be confidential. All people in the same group would get the same level of antidepressant over the same time period. At the end, the group with the largest reduction in depression would be the most effective.

Experiments			
General	**Covered?**	**Specific**	**Covered?**
Aim/hypothesis	One is presented	Type	N/A
Procedure	Lacks some detail about how the study would be conducted	Independent variable	Identified and operationalised implicitly
Sample/sampling technique	Only mentions volunteer but do not know how	Dependent variable	Not clear what measure will be just 'reduction in depression'
Ethics	Consent is covered	Controls, standardisation	Not fully clear how the study is standardised, just that both groups will be taking it for the same amount of time
Validity	Nothing explicit	Experimental design	Not mentioned
Reliability	Could partially replicate	Counterbalancing, random allocation	Allocation to groups mentioned but not random
Data analysis	Not clear as to how data will be analysed	Field only: location	N/A

This would be awarded Level 3 (5 marks). There is a range of both generic and specific features covered but, as can be seen in the commentary table, there are quite a few gaps, and some are brief or implicit. The response covers the Level 3 response criteria as it lacks detail but there is some coherence.

(b) For **one** piece of psychological knowledge on which your plan is based:

(i) Describe this psychological knowledge. (4 marks)

Candidate A:

The first type of antidepressant is the SSRI. This prevents the re-uptake of serotonin so that it will then be absorbed by the post synaptic neuron and not back into the neuron that released it. The MAOIs stops a chemical that breaks down serotonin.

3 marks

The description of SSRIs is good here and shows clear understanding. The MAOI description is brief and basic. Elaboration on MAOIs would allow the candidate to access the final available mark.

Candidate B:

The MAOIs prevent the breakdown of serotonin so more is available to use. A way to measure depression is to get a person to fill in a questionnaire such as the one that Beck created.

1 mark

The first sentence is a brief description of how an MAOI works so this would get credit. However, the second sentence is a second piece of knowledge that is also brief. The question asks for one piece of knowledge and the candidate has presented two. Both would receive 1 mark each. However, only one piece of evidence can be awarded overall.

(ii) Explain how you used **two** features of this psychological knowledge to plan your experiment. (4 marks)

Candidate A:

One feature was SSRIs which are common antidepressants. As the study would be about the effectiveness of antidepressants this type had to be included. We already know they can be very effective, so inclusion was definitely needed. This is the same for MAOIs as the second drug – they are readily available, and they work.

3 marks

This may not be a conventional response, but it is answering the question set about using both types of antidepressants as they are readily available and have been shown to work in previous studies and everyday life. However, the MAOI part is a little repetitive so this would be awarded 3 marks. The answer is logical based on the demands of the question.

Candidate B:

It would be better than using ECT which can have very negative side effects and is only used when no other treatment appears to work. Also, they could have CBT to help them with depressive thoughts.

0 marks

This response is not answering the question. The candidate is writing about alternative treatments that could have been part of the study, but the plan question asked for it to be about antidepressants. It is crucial to read questions carefully.

(c) (i) State **two** reasons for your choice of sampling technique. (2 marks)

Candidate A:

Everyone has an equal chance of being chosen for the study so it is more likely to be representative. As I will not be choosing the participants as they are from a health centre, a random sample means I will not be biased towards choosing a particular type of patient. I will not be involved so this improves generalisability too.

2 marks

The candidate clearly states (and explains) two correct reasons for using a random sample.

Candidate B:

They would want to take part as they are looking for treatment for depression and it would be easy to find them in a health centre.

0 marks

The argument from the candidate is difficult to follow here. Who is looking for treatment as it does not really match their plan in question (a)? As it is a volunteer sample, we do not know if it would be easy to find them as this could also refer to opportunity sampling. The answer is quite confused.

Specialist Options: Application and Research Methods

(ii) Explain **one** weakness of your choice of sampling technique. (2 marks)

Candidate A:

A weakness of opportunity sampling is that the representativeness is low as I would be choosing the participants and I might not ask a certain type of person.

Candidate B:

One weakness of using volunteers is that only a certain type of person would come forward to take part in studies which could hinder generalisability. In this case, there might only be a certain type of person with depression who is willing to take part in a trial to test out the effectiveness of an antidepressant. My findings might not generalise to people who would not voluntarily take drugs for their depression.

> **0 marks**
>
> The candidate clearly stated that they would use a random sample in their plan, but they have written about opportunity sampling here. Therefore, this is not answering the question.

> **2 marks**
>
> This is quite a long answer, but it does clearly explain one weakness of using volunteer sampling and it is directly linked to their plan. Although it would be awarded full marks, the candidate may have 'over-answered' and written too much. This can become a problem if a candidate does this for every question as it is likely that they will run out of time.

(iii) Explain **one** reason for using a randomised control trial.

(2 marks)

Candidate A:

As the whole randomised control trial is double-blind, it decreases any effects of experimenter bias. As patients and researchers do not know which drug each participant is being given, there can be the effect of people knowing that they are taking a certain drug and expecting it to work. It increases the credibility of the study.

> **2 marks**
>
> A very clear response that shows excellent understanding of why randomised control trials are a good research design decision. The candidate has also linked it directly to their plan.

Candidate B:

One weakness of a random sample is that people can still refuse to participate which can affect overall generalisability.

> **0 marks**
>
> It looks like the candidate has mis-read the question. They have written about a <u>random sample</u>, but the question is about randomised control trials! This response is not answering the question.

★ **Exam tip**

Ensure that when you are completing these short answer questions after you have planned your study that the techniques/formats, and so on are the same as the ones in your plan!

★ **Exam tip**

Look at how many marks are given for every question. Many questions in this paper are worth 2 marks and so two sentences can be enough to be able to be awarded both available marks.

Worked example

Consumer psychology

1. Gifts are an important part of some people's lives. There could be many reasons why people gift-wrap presents. There could also be many beliefs about what a gift-wrapped present should look like.

    (a) Plan a study using a questionnaire to investigate the beliefs/reasons people have about gift-wrapping as a giver and as a recipient. Your plan must include the following details:
    - sampling technique
    - questionnaire technique. (10 marks)

Candidate A:

I would use a sample of at least 20 people. They would be given a questionnaire asking them to tell me about what they believe a wrapped gift should look like and whether it is okay to simply give a gift in a bag. I would also get them to draw what they think a perfect boxed gift should look like. I would tell them that their responses would be confidential and that nothing they say or draw would be identifiable as them when the findings were published.

Self-reports				
General	**Covered?**	**Specific**	**Covered?**
Aim/hypothesis	Not covered	Open/closed questions	Only generic ideas about questions being asked
Procedure	This is not fully clear	Examples of questions	None presented
Sample/sampling technique	Only covers the sample size, not technique	Scoring of questions	Not covered
Ethics	Covers confidentiality	Interpretation of question responses	Not covered
Validity	Nothing explicit	Questionnaires only: Paper/pencil, online, postal (technique)	Nothing explicit
Reliability	Nothing explicit	Interviews only: Structured, semi-structured, unstructured (format)	N/A
Data analysis	Nothing explicit	Interviews only: Face-to-face, telephone (technique)	N/A

This would be awarded Level 2 (3 marks). There is a plan presented but a lot of it is basic and lacks detail. It would be very difficult to fully replicate as crucial features like what questions would be asked, or where the sample is from are missing. The response fulfils the criteria for Level 2 as it is a limited range of features and replication would be very difficult.

Candidate B:

The aim of my study would be to investigate what people believe a gift-wrapped present should look like and reasons for and against gift-wrapping presents for friends and family. I would advertise for participants at a variety of locations like local colleges, local stores, and local businesses. The advertisement would direct them to an online questionnaire (web-link) so that they can complete the questionnaire when they are ready. I would want to have 100 participants, so after 100 questionnaires had been completed, the link would no longer work. This is a volunteer sample. The questions would be a variety of open and closed questions. For example:

- On a scale of 0–10, how important is it that a gift is wrapped when you receive it?
- Please explain the rating you have just given.
- On a scale of 0–10, how important is it for you to gift-wrap a present you are giving to a friend?
- Please explain the rating you have just given.

All responses would be anonymous, and participants would be told this before they are allowed to access any question online. There would be a description of the aims of the study so I can get informed consent. They would have to tick a box to say they give consent before being able to access the questionnaire. They would also be told that they can withdraw at any time and that their responses would be deleted and not used in the data analysis. I would collate the findings and publish a report.

Self-reports			
General	**Covered?**	**Specific**	**Covered?**
Aim/hypothesis	Clearly presented	Open/closed questions	This is covered
Procedure	There is a logical procedure presented	Examples of questions	Examples presented that are logical
Sample/sampling technique	Clearly covers both	Scoring of questions	A scale is presented but without parameters (e.g. what does a 0 and a 10 mean?)
Ethics	Consent and right to withdraw covered	Interpretation of question responses	Nothing about how the open questions will be analysed
Validity	Nothing explicit	Questionnaires only: Paper/pencil, online, postal (technique)	Online chosen
Reliability	The procedure allows for this	Interviews only: Structured, semi-structured, unstructured (format)	N/A
Data analysis	Nothing is covered	Interviews only: Face-to-face, telephone (technique)	N/A

This would be awarded Level 4 (8 marks). There is a range of both generic and specific features covered but, as can be seen in the commentary table, there are a couple of gaps about how some of the question data will be analysed. The response covers the Level 4 response criteria as it covers a good range of general and specific features, and the plan is coherent. However, it lacks 'accurate detail' to get into Level 5 with the omission of how the overall data will be analysed.

(b) For **one** piece of psychological knowledge on which your plan is based:

(i) Describe this psychological knowledge. (4 marks)

Candidate A:

The study by Porublev looked at people's perceptions of gift-wrapping. They looked at several things. These included observing people gift-wrapping at a Christmas stall and then getting two people to wrap presents for a friend and then someone they know less well. The majority of participants liked to receive a present that had been wrapped carefully.

> **3 marks**
>
> The response has enough detail to be awarded a top band mark (3–4 marks). This would need slightly more detail about the Porublev study (e.g. how they analysed the discussions to be able to conclude the study) to be awarded maximum marks.

Candidate B:

One study did find that people really did like to receive gifts that had been wrapped based on what they expected a gift to look like.

> **1 mark**
>
> The response lacks some detail about the procedure of the study by Porublev.

(ii) Explain how you used **two** features of this psychological knowledge to plan your questionnaire study. (4 marks)

Candidate A:

The Porublev study did report on past studies where a gift should look like a gift and that one that was not wrapped was sometimes called a naked gift. They wanted to see if this was still true.

> **0 marks**
>
> This response is not answering the question as it is simply describing more of the Porublev study. The candidate needed to pick two features of the Porublev study and then explain how both of these features helped them to plan their own questionnaire study.

Candidate B:

The Porublev study did analyse the discussions people had when wrapping their gifts for friends in the workshop. I also asked my participants to explain why they would or would not want a gift wrapped so I could analyse the reasons why people do or do not like wrapped gifts, just like Porublev – that study let the participants speak whereas my study got them to type their answers.

> **2 marks**
>
> The response here is very thorough but it only focuses on one feature and the question requires two. The candidate needed to choose a second feature and then explain how it helped them make decisions about their own plan. This could be how the sample was recruited, or any theory behind the study.

(c) (i) State **two** reasons for your choice of sampling technique. (2 marks)

Candidate A:

The opportunity sample would be convenient to be able to recruit.

> **1 mark**
>
> The candidate states one valid reason for using opportunity sampling. However, the question requires two reasons. A second reason would need to be stated to be awarded the second available mark.

Candidate B:

As they are volunteers, they could be less likely to drop out or not complete the survey, meaning generalisations might be better.

> **1 mark**
>
> The candidate fully explains one reason why volunteer sample was chosen. However, the question requires two reasons. A second reason would need to be stated to be awarded the second available mark.

(ii) Explain **one** strength of your choice of sampling technique.

(2 marks)

Candidate A:

As the sample can be collected relatively quickly (might get all the people in a day), it is less likely that any external factors are affecting their responses, so extraneous variables are limited which should increase the validity of findings. So, people's ideas about gift-wrapping should be their true feelings and ideas.

> **2 marks**
>
> This response fully explains one strength of using opportunity sampling and it directly applies to the candidate's plan.

Candidate B:

The advertisements would be placed in various locations so that many people would see them.

> **0 marks**
>
> The response does not make it clear why this is a strength. If the candidate had mentioned something about increasing potential generalisations as different locations means different types of people then they may have been awarded some credit.

(iii) Explain **one** reason for your choice of questionnaire technique.

(2 marks)

Candidate A:

Having a questionnaire that is paper and pencil does mean that people are probably more likely to give honest answers as they are perceived as being more anonymous than other forms. This means that the responses given by participants about gift-wrapping and reasons why they do/do not like it would be more valid.

> **2 marks**
>
> This is a correct, and well explained reason why the candidate chose a paper and pencil questionnaire for their plan.

Candidate B:

The use of closed questions would give easy-to-compare data across participants as it is numerical. The open questions would give some data in detail to see the actual reasons why people like gift-wrapping. This should give valid results.

> **0 marks**
>
> The syllabus states that 'technique' is whether the candidate has chosen paper/pencil, online, or postal. Therefore, this response is not answering the question as 'type of question' is not a technique according to the syllabus. It would be a very good response if the question was about type of question used in their plan!

Worked example

Health psychology

1. (a) Plan a field experiment to investigate whether a technique can be used to prevent stress from affecting people in the community. Your plan must include details about the following:
   - sampling technique
   - how the dependent variable will be measured. (10 marks)

Candidate A:

The aim of my study would be to investigate the effectiveness of using stress inoculation training in the community to help prevent and manage stress. My sample would be recruited from local GP surgeries. I would place advertisements in 20 local surgeries with an email address for them to show their interest. I would aim to have 50 people volunteering for the study. Half would be given stress inoculation training whilst the other half would be a self-help group. I would gain consent from the participants by asking them if they would like to take part in a study that looked at helping reducing stress in the community. I would tell them that they would remain anonymous, any measures would be confidential and that they had the right to withdraw at any point. I would also assure them that their GP would not know the outcome of the study in terms of their personal data. The participants would be randomly allocated to one of two groups, so overall it is a field experiment using an independent measures design:

- Stress inoculation training. This would take place in a local community hall once per week for 8 weeks. It would cover the three main stages of training: education about the nature of stress, acquiring skills to cope and prevent feelings of stress, and people applying what they know in everyday situations

- Self-help group. This would mean the group met once in a local community hall where they would be given a self-help pack (not stress inoculation) that they would read at their own pace. It would give useful suggestions on how to cope with stress.

I would take a measure of stress using a rating scale where the participant would have to rate how stressful they found certain situations. For example, all on a scale of 0-10 (0 = not stressful; 10 = very stressful), how stressful does it feel to lose your house/car keys? There would be 25 situations and a total score could be calculated at four time points: baseline, two weeks into the study, end of study, three months after the end of the study. Therefore, my IV would be the stress training a participant has and the DV would be their total scores from the 25-situation checklist (overall 0–250 points). I can compare the two groups at each time point with the median score being calculated per group and I could also analyse changes from baseline to see if either group is reducing stress scores faster. At the end of the study, all participants will be debriefed fully about which group they were in and what we intended to find. The self-help group would then be offered the full stress inoculation training if they wanted it.

Specialist Options: Application and Research Methods

Experiments			
General	**Covered?**	**Specific**	**Covered?**
Aim/hypothesis	A clear aim is presented	Type	Field
Procedure	There is a logical progression that makes replication easy	Independent variable	Correctly operationalised
Sample/sampling technique	Clear who the sample will be and how they would get recruited (volunteer)	Dependent variable	Clearly operationalised and very clear as to what data would be collected
Ethics	Consent and confidentiality covered correctly	Controls, standardisation	Easy to follow procedure
Validity	Implicit	Experimental design	Correctly identified
Reliability	Easy to replicate	Counterbalancing, random allocation	N/A
Data analysis	Clear as to how the collected data would be analysed	Field only: location	Health centre and own home

This would be awarded Level 5 (10 marks). It covers all of the criteria for a Level 5 response with excellent coverage of general and specific features and it could easily be replicated. Data analysis and collection is covered well and the DV is thoroughly explained.

Candidate B:

I would get a sample of 20 people from a health centre to take part in the study. They would be asked to come to the health centre once a week for three weeks. There would be one week for the three stages of stress inoculation training. I would measure stress levels each week with a questionnaire asking them how they feel. I would allow people the right to withdraw.

Experiments			
General	**Covered?**	**Specific**	**Covered?**
Aim/hypothesis	Nothing presented	Type	Field
Procedure	Quite difficult to follow how the study would be conducted	Independent variable	Nothing presented
Sample/sampling technique	Sample size covered but not technique	Dependent variable	Stress measured but nothing is explicit
Ethics	Mentions right to withdraw	Controls, standardisation	One phase per week is mentioned
Validity	Nothing explicit	Experimental design	Not presented
Reliability	Nothing explicit	Counterbalancing, random allocation	N/A
Data analysis	Only hints at a questionnaire asking them something	Field only: location	Health centre but not 100% clear

This would probably be awarded Level 1 (2 marks). Most of the response is brief and it mainly covers the amount of people and that they would be engaging in some form of stress inoculation. Measurements are not clear, and it would be extremely difficult to replicate.

AL Specialist Options: Application and Research Methods

(b) For **one** piece of psychological knowledge on which your plan is based:

(i) Describe this psychological knowledge. (4 marks)

Candidate A:

I have based my idea on stress inoculation training. This is a three-phase approach to preventing stress and stressful feelings. The conceptualisation stage is when a trainer and client establish a relationship and may educate a client on stress in their lives. The skills acquisition stage is when the client is taught ways to cope with stress and prevent stressful feelings happening in the first place. This might be relaxation training. The final stage is application where the client then tries the new skills at home especially when faced with stress.

> **4 marks**
>
> This response is thorough and covers the main elements of stress inoculation training in detail.

Candidate B:

There are three parts to inoculation. The client meets the trainer, they teach them some ways to cope then the client tries them at home/ work and evaluates them.

> **2 marks**
>
> This response lacks detail about each stage with brief descriptions/ identifications of all three stages.

(ii) Explain how you used **two** features of this psychological knowledge to plan your experiment. (4 marks)

Candidate A:

One feature is the three stages. It was important for my plan to use the three stages of inoculation (concept, skills, apply) in order to properly test if the training works overall. The whole training has to happen, otherwise we are not testing it with validity.

Candidate B:

Using the three stages is necessary to test stress inoculation.

> **2 marks**
>
> The candidate clearly explains how one feature of the knowledge (the three stages) helped them to plan their field experiment. However, the question asks for two features. The candidate needed to choose a second feature and explain how that also informed their plan.

(c) (i) State **two** reasons for your choice of measurement of the dependent variable. (2 marks)

Candidate A:

Allows for direct comparison from one time point to another as the same person is completing the 25-situation scale each time. Meaningful statistical analyses, like calculating a median for each group at each time point, means comparisons are valid.

> **1 mark**
>
> This is a basic response that identifies a feature that helped inform their plan. In this case, three stages.

> **2 marks**
>
> Both of the reasons provided by the candidate are correct and linked to their own plan.

Candidate B:

Measuring stress is objective which is needed for validity.

> **0 marks**
>
> The candidate did not use an objective measure of stress so they cannot be awarded any credit here. The response must match the measure that they wrote about in their plan.

> ★ **Exam tip**
>
> Ensure that any reason is directly linked to <u>your plan</u> and not concepts in general. The examiner will check that what you have written here matches what you provided in your plan!

Specialist Options: Application and Research Methods

(ii) Explain **one** weakness of your choice of measurement of the dependent variable. (2 marks)

Candidate A:

Subjectivity could be a problem as not everyone rates stress in the same way.

Candidate B:

Participants may lie.

> **0 marks**
>
> This is not creditworthy as it is unclear how this is directly linked to the dependent variable in their plan. As the question asks to 'explain', the candidate needs to provide an explanation as to why lying could be a problem, for instance, affecting validity.

> **1 mark**
>
> This is a weakness that is brief and there is an attempt to link it back to the plan, but it is not clear. An example of how two individuals could rate stress in different ways using the same scale would mean that the second mark could be awarded.

(iii) Explain **one** reason for your choice of sampling technique. (2 marks)

Candidate A:

As they are volunteers, they are more motivated and less likely to drop out. Since this study is being conducted over a time period as participants have to come back to the local community hall several times, there will be less drop out meaning results should be more valid.

Candidate B:

Relatively easy to recruit participants compared to having to advertise.

> **2 marks**
>
> This response is clear, provides a valid reason why volunteer sampling was chosen for the plan and then applies it directly to the plan; therefore justifying why it is a solid choice of sampling technique.

> **1 mark**
>
> A reason is provided here for the use of opportunity sampling; however, it is not <u>fully</u> justified. The candidate attempts a comparison, but it is not explicitly explained or justified.

Worked example

Organisational psychology

(a) Plan a study using an interview to investigate the experiences of female and male leaders in the workplace. Your plan must include details about:

- interview format
- sampling technique. (10 marks)

Candidate A:

I would visit a local factory and ask if I can interview any leaders who are available. I would ask them questions about how they felt, why they were a leader and other questions about style of leadership and if it works. There would be as many participants as I could recruit. If there is not enough, I would go to a second factory and ask the same. I would look at the reasons and then see if there are any differences between the males and the females. I would report the findings to the factory.

Self-reports			
General	**Covered?**	**Specific**	**Covered?**
Aim/hypothesis	Nothing presented	Open/closed questions	Nothing presented
Procedure	Brief and difficult to follow and replicate	Examples of questions	Nothing presented
Sample/sampling technique	Nothing presented clearly	Scoring of questions	Nothing presented
Ethics	Nothing presented	Interpretation of question responses	States would look at 'reasons'
Validity	Nothing explicit	Questionnaires only: Paper/pencil, online, postal (technique)	N/A
Reliability	Nothing explicit	Interviews only: Structured, semi-structured, unstructured (format)	Nothing presented
Data analysis	Nothing presented	Interviews only: Face-to-face, telephone (technique)	Nothing presented

This would probably be awarded Level 1 (2 marks). Most of the response is brief and it mainly covers a generic idea about asking questions and looking at responses. Measurements are not clear, the sample is virtually unknown, and it would be extremely difficult to replicate.

Candidate B:

The aim would be to see if there are any differences in the leadership experience of female leaders and male leaders. I would use an opportunity sample of leaders from a range of organisations. I would first telephone organisations and ask if anyone would be willing to take part in my interview. I would assure them confidentiality and privacy. Once I had five females and five males to take part, I would interview them individually. The questions I would ask could include:

- On a scale of 0–10, how happy are you being a leader in your organisation?
- Can you please explain the rating you have just given me?
- What do you think makes a good leader?
- Please describe one good experience of being a leader in this organisation.
- Please describe one bad experience of being a leader in this organisation.

After I have interviewed all 10 participants, I would look for differences in ratings and the examples given to see if any gender differences are happening. I could calculate the mean happiness rating for instance. I could also see if the good and bad experiences are similar or different between males and females. I could even look at whether any answers are stereotypically linked to male or female leaders in organisations.

Self-reports			
General	**Covered?**	**Specific**	**Covered?**
Aim/hypothesis	Clearly presented	Open/closed questions	These are presented
Procedure	The procedure is logical and can be followed/replicated	Examples of questions	Example are presented (range of them)
Sample/sampling technique	Sample size and technique are covered	Scoring of questions	One has a rating
Ethics	Confidentiality and privacy are named but not explained	Interpretation of question responses	Some presented in terms of looking for similarities in experiences
Validity	Nothing explicit	Questionnaires only: Paper/pencil, online, postal (technique)	N/A
Reliability	Enough detail for replication presented	Interviews only: Structured, semi-structured, unstructured (format)	Nothing is explicitly mentioned
Data analysis	Explains how the data could be analysed by gender of leader	Interviews only: Face-to-face, telephone (technique)	Hint that it is face-to-face

This would be awarded Level 4 (7 marks). There is a range of both generic and specific features covered but, as can be seen in the table, some are brief. The response covers the Level 4 response criteria as the plan is in some detail.

Activity or revision strategy

Activity: Using the commentary table, create four more – one for case studies, one for observations, one for correlations, and one for longitudinal studies so that you know the general and specific features that you need to cover in a 10-mark plan a study question.

(b) For **one** piece of psychological knowledge on which your plan is based:

(i) Describe this psychological knowledge. (4 marks)

Candidate A:

The study by Cuadrado looked at how male and female leaders are presented and how they are looked at. Female leaders received better ratings than male leaders.

2 marks

The overall response is basic with some understanding and a little elaboration. The candidate needed to describe more of the study by Cuadrado to get into the next level.

Candidate B:
Cuadrado tested whether there were differences in perception of male and female leaders based on whether they displayed stereotypically male or female leadership styles. Participants read stories where the sex of the leader and their leadership style were manipulated. All hypotheses were rejected showing that leadership stereotypes based on gender do not seem to happen.

> **3 marks**
>
> The response covers some relevant details about the study by Cuadrado. The part about hypotheses needs elaboration to be able to be awarded the maximum amount of available marks.

(ii) Explain how you used **two** features of this psychological knowledge to plan your interview study. (4 marks)

Candidate A:
The Cuadrado study used male and female leaders. So did I in my plan.

> **1 mark**
>
> The response is basic but does make a correct statement. The candidate needed to choose two different features from the study by Cuadrado that directly linked to decisions made in their plan before more credit could be awarded.

Candidate B:
One feature of the Cuadrado study was that it used rating scales to get people to judge certain elements of leadership. Therefore, I chose to use a rating scale as part of my plan to get numerical data to directly compare male leaders to female leaders. A second feature was that Cuadrado looked at stereotypical leadership styles that might have an effect on perceptions/experiences. This is why I wanted to see if any answers from my participants could be classified as stereotypical or not.

> **4 marks**
>
> The first feature is correct as both Cuadrado and their own study used a rating scale to measure elements of leadership style, and so on. The second feature is also well explained – the fact that both studies (Cuadrado and their own plan) were having some focus on the role of stereotypical gender leadership styles.

(c) (i) State **two** reasons for your choice of interview format.
(2 marks)

Candidate A:
Structured so allows for replication not test for reliability. An unstructured interview would make comparisons very difficult reducing the validity of the findings.

> **2 marks**
>
> Both of these reasons are a valid argument as to why a structured interview was chosen. This would be awarded 1 mark for each reason.

Candidate B:
Structured makes it easier for the interviewer to follow. It also means that the interview format can be replicated by another interviewer with any set of leaders for reliability.

> **1 mark**
>
> The first reason is not clear so cannot be awarded credit – why is it easier, in comparison to what? These types of reasons need full justification to be awarded credit. The second reason is correct and explained so would be awarded the available mark.

(ii) Explain **one** strength of your choice of interview format. (2 marks)

Candidate A:

Standardisation of questions means ease of replicability if needed.

> **1 mark**
>
> The response identifies a correct strength of using a structured format but there is no application to their own plan.

Candidate B:

The 'set format' of questions in a structured interview means it has high levels of standardisation to help increase replicability and therefore test for reliability. It means that the same questions about leadership style can be used on different samples in different organisations to make meaningful comparisons as it can be 100% replicated.

> **2 marks**
>
> The strength is clearly presented and then linked back to the plan by the candidate.

(iii) Explain **one** reason for your choice of sampling technique. (2 marks)

Candidate A:

As it was random, every leader has a choice to participate.

> **0 marks**
>
> This response is not answering the question as the candidate used an opportunity sample in their plan.

Candidate B:

As there are only going to be a few leaders in every organisation, using opportunity means I should be able to obtain the 5 males and 5 females more conveniently than asking for volunteers. It would allow me to conduct my study in a faster timeframe reducing the potential effects of extraneous variables like an economic recession affecting the findings.

> **2 marks**
>
> This reason is valid and well thought through by the candidate. Whilst it may not be a 'conventional' response, it is easy to follow the logic of the candidate and it is a correct reason/justification.

★ **Exam tip**

Be careful with questions that refer back to a previous response. They must match up!

Specialist Options: Application and Research Methods

Raise your grade examples

↑ Raise your grade

Clinical psychology

1. **(a)** Plan a study using an interview to investigate what the general public think are the most common obsessions and compulsions of people diagnosed with obsessive-compulsive disorder (OCD). Your plan must include details about the following:
   - sampling technique
   - question format. (10 marks)

   I would stand in a shopping mall and ask people who pass by a series of questions. One could be 'what do you think are the most common compulsions for someone who has OCD?'. I would want at least 100 people, and the sampling technique would be opportunity. I would try to get 50 males and 50 females. I would then work out the most common responses by tallying all the choices. I would do the same with obsessions. Therefore, it would have to be face-to-face.

   This would be awarded Level 2 (3 marks). There is only basic information about the sampling and the type of questions that would be asked. Replication would be very difficult. The candidate needed to cover all of the general and specific features from Table 4.1 on p.138 to be awarded a higher level.

   (b) For **one** piece of psychological knowledge on which your plan is based:

   (i) Describe this psychological knowledge. (4 marks)

   ICD lists the diagnostic criteria as being about obsessions (thinking) and compulsions (behaviours). ✔

   Knowledge of ICD and the difference between thinking and behaving would be awarded 1 mark.

   (ii) Explain how you used **two** features of this psychological knowledge to plan your experiment. (4 marks)

   The questionnaire would ask people about both of these.

   This cannot be awarded credit as the question (part a) is about obsessions and compulsions. As the candidate has simply re-worded the question for the plan, they cannot be awarded credit here.

   (c) (i) State **two** reasons for your choice of sampling technique. (2 marks)

   It is convenient and can recruit faster than other techniques. ✔

   This would be awarded both marks for stating two reasons.

   (ii) Explain **one** weakness of your choice of sampling technique. (2 marks)

   The sample may be biased (I might pick all people of similar characteristics) making generalisability difficult. ✔

   This would be awarded 1 mark. To be awarded the second available mark, the candidate needed to apply this to their plan.

   (iii) Explain **one** reason for your choice of question format. (2 marks)

   It does not force them to choose an obsession or compulsion. ✔ It allows them to tell us exactly what *they* think is the most common obsession so validity should be improved. ✔

   This would be awarded both marks.

   This candidate could earn a total of 9 out of 24 marks.

Specialist Options: Application and Research Methods   AL

↑ Raise your grade

Consumer psychology

1. Consumer psychologists believe that sound and noise can affect how we perceive the taste of food.

    (a) Plan an experiment to investigate how sound/noise affects people's perception of taste of desserts. Your plan must include details about:
      - sampling technique
      - a directional or non-directional hypothesis. (10 marks)

    My hypothesis will be 'when food is eaten with loud noise in the background, participants will rate and perceive the taste (e.g. sweetness, saltiness, etc.) as being of a lower rating than when quiet music is played'. I would plan a laboratory experiment for this. The IV would be the type of music (loud = heavy metal music; quiet = a ballad) and the dependent variable would be the ratings of sweetness (0–10; 0 = not at all sweet; 10 = very sweet) and saltiness (0 = not at all salty; 10 = very salty). I would screen participants first to ensure that they can taste sweet and salt (e.g. reject those with a cold whose taste may be limited, or Covid-19). The experimental design will be independent measures as participants will only participate in the loud or quiet condition. I will randomly allocate people to a condition by flipping a coin.

    The participants will be 40 in total; 20 per group. They will be volunteers as I will put up an advertisement in my college cafeteria asking people if they would like to take part in a study about the perception of food. They will be able to sign up underneath the advertisement and this is how I can gain their consent. The following standardised procedure would be followed:

    The food I will be using for the study is popcorn that is mixed so it has sweet and salty popcorn in the same bag. The participant will come to a classroom, and I will get them to listen to 2 minutes of either heavy metal music or a ballad (depending on which group they are in) whilst eating the popcorn. At the end of the song, they will be asked to rate the sweetness and the saltiness using the 0–10 scale outlined above. They will be told that their ratings are confidential and then I will debrief them, telling them which condition they are in and what I am expecting to find. I will then answer any questions they have, and they can take the remaining popcorn with them. I will calculate the median sweetness and saltiness score for both conditions and display them on a bar chart to see if my hypothesis will be accepted or rejected.

    This response covers all general and specific features so would be awarded Level 5 (10 marks).

    (b) For **one** piece of psychological knowledge on which your plan is based:

      (i) Describe this psychological knowledge. (4 marks)

      The study that inspired my plan was by Woods (2010). He looked at the role of sound on our perception not just of sweet and salt, but also crunchiness and if we like the food. ✔ He played different levels of white noise whilst participants ate biscuits, cheese, crisps. ✔ Those in the loud group rated sweetness and saltiness lower than the quiet group. ✔

      This would earn 3 marks. The response needed one more piece of information to be awarded all available marks.

      (ii) Explain how you used **two** features of this psychological knowledge to plan your experiment. (4 marks)

      They used loud and quiet music like I planned. ✔ They also eliminated people with colds. ✔

      The candidate has only outlined two features that helped with their plan, earning 2 marks. These need to be elaborated on (explained) to be awarded the remining available marks.

    (c) (i) State **two** reasons for your choice of sampling technique. (2 marks)

156

Volunteers tend to be more motivated and likely to participate and take the study seriously. ✔ There is no researcher bias like in opportunity sampling as I will not be involved in choosing who should participate. ✔

Two correct reasons are given by the candidate – 2 marks.

(ii) Explain **one** weakness of your choice of sampling technique. (2 marks)

People who volunteer may be qualitatively different to those who could participate but choose not to. ✔ Therefore, there can be issues of generalising findings from my study about sound and food taste perception to a wider audience. ✔

This response identifies a correct weakness then explains it via an example – 2 marks.

(iii) Explain **one** reason for your choice of hypothesis. (2 marks)

I had chosen a directional hypothesis as past research had shown some consistency in the direction of results. For example, Woods had already shown that loud noise decreased perceptions of saltiness and sweetness, so I expect to find the same result. ✔✔

This response identifies one reason and explains it with an example – 2 marks.

This candidate could earn a total of 21 out of 24 marks.

↑ Raise your grade

Health psychology

1. (a) Plan a case study to investigate the misuse of health services. Your plan must include details about:
- techniques used for data collection
- sampling technique. (10 marks)

The aim of the case study would be to investigate why a person is misusing health services. I would approach a local health centre to ask them for a volunteer to participate in my study. I would ask them to find someone who has Munchausen syndrome. I would want someone who is willing to be interviewed and complete some self-reports. The person can be male or female, but I would like them to have been diagnosed for at least three years but has stopped misusing health services. This means that I can ask them more in-depth questions to see if we can look for causes. For the interview, I would make it semi-structured so then I can ask a series of questions directly about causes, but it will also allow me to investigate further if they say something unexpected – I can then ask further questions if necessary. I will ask questions like 'do you know what may have caused your syndrome?' and 'how did you overcome it?'. There will be some self-reports for them to complete – some will have similar questions to the interview. This means that I can compare the interview answers with the questionnaire answers to see if they are giving me the same information. I will analyse transcripts of the interview and then look at the responses from open questions asking the same thing to see if the responses can be interpreted in the same way. The case study will have full confidentiality when I write up the report.

This would be awarded Level 4 (7 marks) as the plan is coherent. However, there are some elements missing. For example more on the sample and what the questionnaire would also have on it. Also, slightly more on ethics would have been good considering the sensitive nature of this case study.

(b) For **one** piece of psychological knowledge on which your plan is based:

(i) Describe this psychological knowledge. (4 marks)

The case study by Aleem and Ajarim of a 22-year-old female with Munchausen was used to help me plan my study. ✔ She had reported quite a few health problems to her doctor like swellings of abdomen. ✔ It was found that she was injecting herself with faecal matter. ✔

Specialist Options: Application and Research Methods

> Three correct pieces of information were given by the candidate – 3 marks.
>
> **(ii)** Explain how you used **two** features of this psychological knowledge to plan your experiment. (4 marks)
>
> The Aleem case study focused on some of the 'health' problems that the lady was showing with a case history of her background before any of this happened. I would also get the pre-Munchausen background from my case study to see if there are similarities. ✔✔
>
> This would earn 2 marks. The candidate has only written about one feature. They needed to choose another feature and explain how that also helped them with their own plan.
>
> **(c) (i)** State **two** reasons for your choice of techniques to collect data. (2 marks)
>
> Would allow me to get in-depth responses about the background of the case study which improves validity in terms of trying to explain the syndrome. ✔ Also, as I am using interview and questionnaire I can compare the responses to similar questions to improve reliability. ✔
>
> Two correct reasons were given by the candidate, so this is awarded full marks.
>
> **(ii)** Explain **one** weakness for one of your choices of techniques to collect data. (2 marks)
>
> With the questionnaire, there is no way of knowing that the information is correct and valid. This is because people can exaggerate (which is a symptom of Munchausen) or show social desirability and want to look 'perfect' to the person conducting the case study. Validity may be compromised. ✔✔
>
> This is a well explained weakness that earns 2 marks.
>
> **(iii)** Explain **one** reason for your choice of sampling technique. (2 marks)
>
> Volunteer sampling tends to recruit people who are motivated to participate. This should mean that the participant recruited is more willing to tell their story about the syndrome improving the validity of findings. ✔✔
>
> This is a well explained weakness and it earns full marks.
>
> **This candidate could earn a total of 18 out of 24 marks.**

↑ Raise your grade

Organisational psychology

1. (a) Plan a study using observation to investigate the most common techniques used to manage conflict in a workplace. Your plan must include details about the following:

- type of observation
- number of observers. (10 marks)

The aim of the study would be to investigate different ways in which people at work manage conflicts in meetings. I would approach five different organisations asking if they would be willing for me to covertly observe at least five meetings. I would ask them if I could record the meetings but as soon as my observation analysis is complete, the recordings would be deleted and I would also tell them that no one person's management of conflict technique would be identifiable. If the organisation is willing to consent to this, then I would choose the first five meetings of over five people to record. I would view each meeting and code each type of management technique used, for example, asking people to remain calm, or simply ignoring it. Once all meetings have been coded, I will get a second observer to look at the video footage and also code the conflict styles seen in them. We can then conduct a reliability analysis to make sure we have recorded the same styles. The participating organisations will get a copy of the findings.

Level 3 (6 marks) as it covers a few general points well like ethics, but other parts are missing (the sample is too brief). It also covers a few specific points including it being covert and it hints at maybe some structured element if a checklist had been used; however, the candidate has not told us this! The plan does have some coherence.

Activity or revision strategy

> **Revision strategy <u>and</u> activity:** For all of the different research methods that can be asked about for the plan a study question, write each of the specific features on one index card each. On the reverse of each index card, write which research method it is a specific feature for. Then shuffle <u>all</u> cards and attempt to sort the specific features into piles, one for each research method. Turn over each index card to see if you have them all in the correct pile.

(b) For **one** piece of psychological knowledge on which your plan is based:

(i) Describe this psychological knowledge. (4 marks)

Thomas-Kilman identified that there are five conflict-handling styles/modes that can be used at work. ✔ *One of these is avoidance which is simply to walk away and withdraw and can be used if the conflict is very heated.* ✔

This would earn 2 marks. Requires descriptions of other styles/modes to be awarded more credit.

(ii) Explain how you used **two** features of this psychological knowledge to plan your experiment. (4 marks)

It will be interesting to see if any of the styles/modes are observed. I think they will be as it looks like the five styles cover virtually all types of conflict that will be seen in meetings.

This is not answering the question as it is not using the features to explain how they helped form the observation plan in question (a) – 0 marks.

(c) (i) State **two** reasons for your choice of type of observation. (2 marks)

Covert so everyone would act naturally as no one knows they are being watched in the meetings. ✔ *Also, structured using the five styles so that we can be sure we are observing each type reliably.* ✔

Two correct reasons were given by the candidate – 2 marks.

(ii) Explain **one** strength of your choice of type of observation. (2 marks)

One strength of using a covert observation is that it should increase the ecological validity of the findings. ✔ *As the people in the meetings do not know they are being observed, they will show true conflict management styles because they are unaware that the meeting is being recorded to be observed later. They will not change their behaviours.* ✔

This is a well-explained strength that would earn full marks.

(iii) Explain **one** reason for your choice of number of observers. (2 marks)

Two different observers were used to increase the reliability of the observations and the checklist of behaviours. ✔ *As we will be looking at the same behaviours independently, we can see if the checklist is a reliable measure for observing conflict management styles in the workplace.* ✔

This response identifies one reason and explains it with an example - 2 marks.

This candidate could earn a total of 14 out of 24 marks.

Index

adherence to medical advice 102–103, 136

advertising
    consumer psychology 91–92, 135
    volunteer sampling 36, 43, 44, 56, 144, 146, 147, 155

aim of a study, definition 10

Andrade's cognitive core study on doodling 4, 11, 16, 19, 24, 31, 36

anxiety and fear-related disorders 80–85, 89, 121–123, 134
    see also phobias

ASMPR (aim, sample, method, procedure, and results) 83, 87, 93, 115

assumptions 14–16, 18
    definition 13
    from different approaches 25–27
    supported by findings 15

background noise, music in restaurants and when eating 95–96, 99, 156–157

background of a study, definition 19

Bandura et al.'s learning core study on aggression 6, 12, 16, 21, 24, 25, 37

Baron-Cohen et al.'s cognitive core study on the eye tests 4, 12, 16, 19–20, 24, 31, 36, 48

biofeedback and imagery 104–105

biological approach 10–11, 15, 18–19, 22–23, 26, 28–31, 36
    see also Dement and Kleitman's study; Hassett et al.'s study; Hölzel et al.'s study

cause and effect, definition 33

CBT see cognitive–behaviour therapy

central tendency measures 44, 51

children
    ethical issues when using in research 20, 23
    health psychology 103, 136
    use in hypothetical study designs 60–61, 103, 136
    see also Bandura et al.'s study; Pozzulo et al.'s study; Saavedra and Silverman's study

classical conditioning 13, 24, 27, 82, 134

clinical psychology 80–89
    applications and research methods 121–124, 134, 139–142, 155

cognitive approach 11–12, 16, 19–20, 23–24, 26–27, 31–32, 36
    see also Andrade's study; Baron-Cohen et al.'s study; Pozzulo et al.'s study

cognitive dissonance 90

cognitive–behaviour therapy (CBT) 83, 134

comparing studies, similarities and differences 27–29, 31, 32, 34, 35

conclusions
    on evaluations within answers 38, 85
    related to hypotheses 14, 35, 153, 156
    versus results 11, 14

conditioning 13, 24, 25, 27, 32, 82, 134

confidentiality 143, 147, 148, 151, 152, 156

conflict at work 112–113, 115

confounding variables, definition 33

consent 20, 21, 23, 34, 58, 140, 144, 147

consumer psychology 89–99
    applications and research methods 125–127, 135, 143–146, 156–157

context, importance in answers 16, 17, 20, 30–31, 35, 37, 38

core studies, approaches, issues and debates 2–39

data collection techniques 45, 48, 51, 53, 60, 63

debates 19, 21, 23, 25, 85, 100
    definition 19
    see also idiographic debate

debriefing 21, 37, 38, 47, 52, 54

deception 21, 38, 47, 52, 58

demand characteristics 20, 34, 35, 49, 95, 136
    deception used to avoid 52, 58
    definition 20

Dement and Kleitman's biological core study on sleep and dreams 2, 11, 15, 18–19, 22, 24, 28, 32

dependent variable (DV), definition 33

describe, meaning of term in questions 43

design, consumer psychology 89–90, 92, 94

detailed evaluation points, importance in answers 38

detail needed in answers
    if question says explain 45
    marks assigned 20, 25, 29, 30, 121, 122

differences and similarities between studies 27–29, 31, 32, 34, 35

dreams
    study design 64–65
    see also Dement and Kleitman's biological core study on sleep and dreams

DV see dependent variable

electroencephalograph (EEG) 32, 135

essay questions 28–35, 37–38, 83–85, 94–96, 103–105, 113–116

ethical guidelines 56, 124

ethical issues
    animal experiments 18, 33–34, 48, 56
    confidentiality 143, 147, 148, 151, 152, 156
    consent 20, 21, 23, 34, 58, 140, 144, 147
    debriefing 21, 37, 38, 47, 52, 54
    deception 21, 38, 47, 52, 58
    definitions 21, 124
    health psychology 136

Index

human studies 20–21, 23, 32, 34, 37, 38, 52, 53, 59–60
    organisational psychology 137
    privacy 137, 151, 152
    real-world applications 12
    right to withdraw 21, 23, 144, 147, 148
    strengths and weaknesses, discussion 18, 19
    using children in research 20, 23
experimental design 16, 37, 44–45, 48, 50–52, 58, 60–67
    definition 37
    planning 138–159
explain, meaning of term in questions 45, 122
extension booklet 43
external reliability, definition 31
extraneous variables, definition 33
eyewitnesses, *see also* Pozzulo *et al.*'s study on line-ups
eyewitness testimony, definition 24

Fagen *et al.*'s learning core study on elephant learning 6, 13, 17, 20, 24, 25, 33–34, 48
fear-related disorders *see* anxiety and fear-related disorders; phobias
findings, definition 15, 126

GAD-7 *see* generalised anxiety disorder questionnaire
generalisability 38, 84–85, 95, 103
generalised anxiety disorder (GAD-7) questionnaire 80, 84–85

Hassett *et al.*'s biological core study on monkey toy preferences 3, 10, 15, 18–19, 23, 24, 29–30, 36
health psychology 99–109
    applications and research methods 128–130, 136, 147–150, 157–158
Hölzel *et al.*'s biological core study on mindfulness and brain scans 3, 10, 15, 23, 24, 28, 36, 44, 45
hormones 26, 36
hypotheses
    conclusion related to 14, 35, 153, 156

    directional/non-directional 15, 49, 157
idiographic debate 93, 100
    definition 116
    versus nomothetic debate 80, 110, 116
impulse control disorders 82, 88, 123–124
independent measures, definition 37
independent variable (IV), definition 33
informed consent 21, 23, 34
internal reliability, definition 31
internal validity, definition 33
inter-rater reliability 60
IV *see* independent variable

JDI *see* Job Descriptive Index
Job Characteristics Theory 137
Job Descriptive Index (JDI) 109–110
job satisfaction 63, 109–110, 112–113, 119

Lauterborn's 4Cs marketing mix model 90, 91
learning approach 12–13, 16–17, 20–21, 25, 27, 32–34, 37
    see also Bandura *et al.*'s study; Fagen *et al.*'s study; Saavedra and Silverman's study
line-ups, Pozzulo *et al.*'s study 5, 11–12, 16, 19, 23, 24, 31, 45

marks, indication of detail required 10, 14, 20, 25, 29, 30, 44, 121, 122
matched pairs, definition 37
matching games, psychologists and studies 88, 98, 108, 118
measures of central tendency 44, 51
Milgram's social core study on obedience 8, 14, 17, 24, 26, 34, 38, 43–44, 47
mind maps, revision strategy 89, 99, 109, 119
moral issues 21, 124
motivation at work 110, 111, 113–115
mundane realism 19, 35, 135
music in restaurants and when eating 95–96, 99, 156–157

nomothetic debates 80, 110, 116
non-adherence to medical advice 102–103, 136

obsessive–compulsive disorder (OCD) 81, 83–84
operant conditioning 13, 24, 25, 27, 32
opportunity sampling 36, 60, 63
organisational psychology 77–79, 99–119
    applications and research methods 130–133, 137, 150–154, 158–159

pain
    assessment 103
    mind map 109
    as negative reinforcement 34
    treatments 100–101
Paper 1, approaches/issues/debates 2–39
Paper 2, research methods 40–67
paper 3, specialist options, approaches/issues/debates 68–119
paper 4, specialist options, applications and research methods 120–159
participants *see* samples/sampling
patient–practitioner relationship 99–100, 106
Perry *et al.*'s social core study on personal space 8, 14, 17, 21, 22, 24, 26, 34–35, 46, 48, 50
personal space
    investigation 62–64
    see also Perry *et al.*'s study
phobias
    anxiety measures 84–85
    causes 134
    misdiagnosis of anxiety disorders 81
    treatment 82, 121–122
    see also Saavedra and Silverman's study
physical environment 98, 99
physical work conditions 118
Piliavin *et al.*'s social core study on subway Samaritans 9, 14, 17, 21, 24, 34, 50
planning experiments 138–159
positive correlation 47

161

positive reinforcement 13, 17
Pozzulo *et al.*'s cognitive core study on line-ups 5, 11–12, 16, 19, 23, 24, 31, 45
privacy 137, 151, 152
psychologists, matching to studies 88, 98, 108, 118

qualitative data, strengths and weaknesses 30, 38, 46
quantitative data
    definition 29
    strengths and weaknesses 30, 33, 34, 38, 48, 84–85
    versus qualitative data 17, 30, 45–46
questionnaires 17, 53, 57, 63, 65, 66–68
    GAD-7 80, 84–85

random sampling, definition 36
real-world applications 11, 12, 33–34
reductionism 102
reinforcement 13, 17, 20
    see also conditioning
relevance
    keeping answers focused on the question 14, 20, 26, 44
    reading the question carefully 10, 11, 13, 45, 64, 89, 99–102, 127
reliability
    clinical psychology 81, 83, 84
    definitions and types 31
    health psychology 104–105
    hypothetical studies 57, 60
    specialist options 126, 139, 140, 144, 148, 152–154, 157, 159

    strength and weaknesses of core studies 31–33, 38
    versus validity 21
repeated measures, definition 37
replicability, definition 25
research methods 40–67
    general and specific features in syllabus 138
    specialist options 120–159
results, versus conclusions 11, 14
right to withdraw 21, 23, 144, 147, 148

Saavedra and Silverman's learning core study on a button phobia 7, 13, 17, 20, 24, 32
samples/sampling
    bias 38
    definitions 10, 36
    describing 10, 14, 32, 34, 134
    methods/techniques 16, 36, 43, 52, 54, 56, 125
    planning experiments 138–159
    sample size 18, 31, 34
    strengths and weaknesses 34, 43–44, 125
    see also ASMPR
satisfaction at work 109–110, 119
schizophrenia 134
secondary positive reinforcement, definition 17
self-reporting methods 46, 49, 56, 64, 142–144, 150–152, 157
situational explanations for behaviour 100
social approach 14, 17, 21–22, 26, 27, 34–35, 38
    see also Milgram's study; Perry *et al.*'s study; Piliavin *et al.*'s study
social hormones 26

socialisation, definition 23
social learning, definition 25
specialist options 68–119
    applications and research methods 120–159
    approaches/issues/debates 68–119
    clinical psychology 69–71, 80–89
    consumer psychology 71–74, 89–99
    health psychology 74–77, 99–109
    organisational psychology 77–79, 99–109
subway Samaritans, Piliavin *et al.*'s study 9, 14, 17, 21, 24, 34, 50
suggest, meaning of term in questions 46, 123
syllabus, features of research methods 138

terminology, importance in answers 33, 35, 60–64
testimony of eyewitness, definition 24
test–retest reliability 59

utility theory/model of consumer decision-making 92–93

validity and reliability 21–22
volunteer sampling 36, 43–44, 54, 62

withdrawal from studies, rights in ethical research 21, 23, 144, 147, 148
work, *see also* organisational psychology